LONELY PLANET UNPACKED AGAIN

Travel Disaster Stories by Tony Wheeler and Other Lonely Planet Writers

With a Foreword by Don George

D1456641

LONELY PLANET PUBLICATIONS
Melbourne • Oakland • London • Paris

Lonely Planet Unpacked Again: Travel disaster stories by Tony Wheeler and other Lonely Planet writers

Published by Lonely Planet Publications

Head Office:	90 Maribyrnong Street, Footscray, Vic 3011, Australia
	Locked Bag 1, Footscray, Vic 3011, Australia
Branches:	150 Linden Street, Oakland, CA 94607, USA
	10a Spring Place, London NW5 3BH, UK
	1 rue Dahomey, 75011, Paris, France

Published 2001

Printed by The Bookmaker International Ltd
Printed in China

Map by Wendy Wright
Designed by Simon Bracken
Edited by Martin Heng

National Library of Australia Cataloguing in Publication entry

Lonely Planet unpacked again: travel disaster stories.

ISBN 1 86450 319 X.

1. Travel – Anecdotes. 2. Humorous stories. I. Wheeler, Tony, 1946– .
II. Title. (Series: Lonely Planet Journeys).

A823.010803

CONTENTS

FOREWORD
BY DON GEORGE

THE TRAVEL ADDICT'S TRUEST FRIEND

Last week I was marooned on a South Pacific Island, almost killed on a brake-less bus in the mountains of northern Peru, kidnapped by a Moroccan in a Mercedes, downed by dengue fever in Sumatra, robbed on an Amazon river boat and arrested by soldiers on Papua New Guinea.

Too many mushrooms on my pizza, perhaps? Or too many hours hunched over my new 'Don George: Traveller at Large' computer game?

No, I've just been reading the book you now hold in your hands, a collection of on-the-road tribulations and travails written by thirty of Lonely Planet's intrepid global writers and workers.

After reading these tales, I've begun to feel like a peripatetic Pollyanna. Oh, I've had my share of diarrhoea days and mosquito nights, of course, my bone-busting bus journeys, my stained-sheet humid hell-hole hotels, my interminable inexplicable interludes at tumbleweed train stations, my heart-stopping hold-ups at obscure border posts.

But I can't remember any times when I felt that my life was truly in danger. I've never had a gun pointed at me – though there was that one day in Athens: I was living there during the volatile reign of the Colonels, and I had decided to pose as a Canadian and infiltrate a demonstration outside the US embassy just to get a close look at all the fuss. When the riot troops began to move in, I decided it was time to move out – and that's when I careened around a corner and ran almost smack into the muzzle of a slowly rolling tank. This taught me that riots, like football games and presidential inaugurations, are usually best viewed on television.

I've never been imprisoned – but there was that one time at the Tel Aviv airport, where I was changing planes in transit from Dar-es-Salaam to Athens. When the customs officials saw that I had been in Cairo a month before, I was ushered out of the immigrations line, interrogated for about twenty minutes in a window-less closet of an office and then driven in a truck to an obscure corner of the airport compound. It was about 10 pm and there, in pitch blackness, I was deposited with my backpack at the end of a long paved track. The truck backed about 150 metres away and I was ordered to take every item out of my pack, slowly, to hold it in the headlights' glare and shake it out thoroughly and then throw it onto the ground. You haven't really lived until you've stood on a cool Israeli tarmac in your boxers in the middle of the night, shaking your pants in the glare of a truck's headlights. This is what your mother was thinking of when she implored you to do your laundry more often. I missed my plane, of course, but I did get to see a side of the Tel Aviv airport – and of the Israeli psyche – that I had never expected to see.

I've never been attacked by wild animals – though there was that ignominious night in the Tanzanian bush: I was on a safari with two local families and one of the last of the great white hunters, and he had concocted the brilliant idea of hanging fresh meat in the trees to attract hungry lions for our viewing plea-sure. After far too many post-dinner gin and tonics, eight of us clambered into a Range Rover and set out in search of the lions. Before long we were bumping over huge boulders and scraping over sharp rocks and then grinding to a halt with a flat tyre. Of course, in our stupor we had left the spare tyre at camp. So we decided that four of us would stay in the vehicle and four would walk across the dark, wild, animal-populated plain toward the pinprick of light that we figured was our site. The great white hunter grandly declared that he would stay in the vehicle to make sure nothing happened to the ones who stayed behind. And to my eternal chagrin, I mumbled some inanity and chose to stay in the vehicle too, waiting for the meat-crazed lions that never came.

Now that I think about it, misadventure is probably the inveterate traveller's most loyal companion. It's the flip side of serendipity, and like serendipity, it brings unexpected gifts.

One gift is the antidote to hubris. If we ever begin to imagine we are immune or immortal, misadventure generously reminds us otherwise.

Another gift is the grace of perspective: misadventure makes us stop and recognise the small miracles - health, home, food, friends – we enjoy every day.

The third gift is a lasting lesson: the heart does not fail. If we have the adventurer's passion for the road, the insatiable curiosity and abiding sense of wonder, whatever dangers and disasters befall us, we pick ourselves up and keep on plodding. This is the mark of the true traveller, the sheer will to keep going over the next hill and round the next bend, the absolute need to keep forging connections, exploring corners, embracing the unknown. So what if we were almost eaten by lions – tomorrow is another day, and more lions await!

And the fourth and final gift is one this book makes amply clear: when the adventures are over and you're finally back, intact, reflecting over beers, they give you one hell of a good story to tantalise your fellow travellers' ears.

NORTH
AMERICA

ATLANTIC
OCEAN

HMOND

PACIFIC OCEAN

● JOHN MOCK

HELEN FAIRBAIRN

OWAN McKINNON

● TONY WHEELER

MARK LIGHTBODY ●

DEANNA SWANEY

SOUTH
AMERICA

● JEAN-BERNARD CARILLET

RANDALL PEFFER

TT FLETCHER

WANTED!

Imogen Young

Forced by her parents to fly regularly from one end of Australia to another as a child, Imogen had her travel bug well and truly developed by the time she was old enough to pay her own airfares. Unfulfilled by studying chemistry and art history (possibly because she was trying to study them both at the same time), Imogen ran away from Melbourne at the age of twenty-two. She managed to live in London for eighteen months without getting arrested and she returned to study in New York city, where her only run-in with the law was a New York cop on a mountain bike asking her out.

A slightly older and wiser Imogen now works in Lonely Planet's Melbourne marketing department.

'HOW WELL DO YOU KNOW YOUR BOYFRIEND?' Connor and Brooke asked as Matt was led away by two Dutch policemen. I stared at their faces and was lost for words. How well did I know him? We'd met three and a half years ago, but in the span of a lifetime – the time it takes to really know someone – was that long enough?

What started out as a routine passport check after we were pulled over for speeding had become increasingly sinister. The police seemed particularly interested in where we'd been and, precisely, when. Now the VW kombi was impounded in the police station car park, we'd missed our afternoon ferry across the bay to Hoek van Holland, we were being held in a police station in a Dutch town whose name none of us knew, and if we were really unlucky we were going to miss our ferry back to the UK the next day too. Not to mention whatever trouble Matt was in, wherever he'd been taken. I wasn't surprised that Connor and Brooke had turned on me.

I felt queasy as I turned their question over in my mind. I felt a flash of fury at Connor for speeding but soon realised the futility of that and returned to pondering how well I knew Matt. How well can one person know another? Did I really know Brooke and Connor? All of us had come together after answering Connor's ad in a London newspaper for travelling companions to join him and his kombi on a jaunt around Europe. I'd shared the same four feet of kombi floor space with them every day for four months and felt like I knew them but if one of them turned out to be a lunatic, would I know?

I contemplated the posters on the wall of the waiting room. They were all in Dutch but there seemed to be a mix of WANTED and MISSING posters. I felt my heart contract as I looked at the grainy snapshots pulled from old albums of people long lost and I shuddered when I imagined what the hard-faced people in the police mug shots had done. I tried to read the Dutch, tried to decipher one or two words to see whether I could work out their crimes but nothing made sense to me. I returned again to the question . . .

How well did I know Matt? That first question was only the beginning. What was he capable of? Did I trust him? Did he behave like a criminal?

What if he were a criminal? What if the rest of us were implicated? I felt guilty about Brooke and Connor – it had been my idea to answer the ad in the paper in the first place. What if I had unwittingly made them travel around Europe for four months with a felon?

And what would I do? Hopefully, the others could have the van back and go home but I couldn't leave without Matt. I had visions of calling my father – ashamed – to ask for help, of endless police bureaucracy. I had a particularly cartoonish vision, set inexplicably in Mexico, of me sitting outside the barred window of a concrete cell for years waiting and hoping to hold my love again . . .

Did he behave like a criminal? I knew he was capable of lying: I had caught him telling complete untruths to me the year before. But then, at an earlier time, I had done exactly the same to him. We'd smoked our share of ganga since we arrived – but the Netherlands was the one place in Europe where that was legal, wasn't it? So surely he couldn't be in trouble for that?

He HAD behaved weirdly on this trip. On our very first day in Vienna he had insisted on spending an afternoon alone. In Brussels he refused to wait for me one morning, though I promised to get ready quickly, and left with apparent relish refusing to meet me later. He'd been cagey about what he'd done on these days, brushing me off with mutterings of art galleries, wandering the streets, soaking up the culture . . . Then there was the time in Germany when I found a postcard with a cryptic message in his daypack. When I confronted him about it he gave me an unusually vague answer that left me uneasy . . .

I began to feel sick and stood up. I walked the length of the four walls of the small room, stopping to look out the window as

I tried to pull my thoughts together. For someone who had dreamed of roaming about Europe like a gipsy, I seemed to be confined in a pretty small space now.

As soon as the cops had asked us to accompany them to the police station – calmly, politely informing us that we would be under armed escort and warning us against trying to escape – I'd begun racking my brain for things I had done wrong. It felt like the primary school principal had summoned me. No, I hadn't wagged class. No I hadn't cheated on a test. No I hadn't tried to beat up whiny Jenny again. No we weren't smuggling illicit drugs. No we hadn't broken any international laws. No we weren't wanted criminals . . . I hoped. What WERE we in trouble for?

Matt knew that it was him they were after. He said he could see them looking at his passport more carefully than the others, but I couldn't tell any difference. During our half-hour drive under armed escort, he kept saying, 'It's me, it's me.' Did he know that he had done something wrong and was about to go down for it?

I continued to pace, scanning the posters, looking out the window, observing the awful eighties decor of the waiting room. Why were we here? What had Matt done? How well DID I know him?

We had lied to each other, cheated on each other, broken each other's hearts, cried rivers of tears across phone lines connecting New York, London, Melbourne and Dublin, Thailand, Spain and Italy. One day as I watched my tears fall onto the ground of the Forum in Rome, I calculated that by the end of my travels I would have cried in public at every monument in Italy.

But I knew instinctively that, deep down, we loved each other absolutely. We would protect each other and fight for each other to the ends of the earth. I didn't care if I'd known him for only three and a half years. I KNEW him. And I knew he wasn't a criminal. He might lie, be selfish, behave badly and act unthinkingly, but he was not a bad person. He was human and sometimes fucked up, but so did I, and I knew he could never intentionally set out to hurt another human being.

And I understood why he ran off sometimes – four months, four people and four feet of van space. It was too intense. Some days he needed space. His way of finding that was rising at dawn, being at the first museum as the doors opened for the day and losing himself for as long as possible in the art, culture and history of our location. I found my space by retreating. I needed days on my own, at base camp, when everyone else was away. Time when I could potter about, lie in the sun, write in my journal, read books and recharge. He wasn't sneaking around being a criminal. He was just cleaning his head.

So why were we here? I toyed with it some more but couldn't figure it out. I was certain of one thing. I sat down, looked at Brooke and Connor and said, 'I don't know why we're here, but I know it's not Matt.' They looked unsure, but seeing my conviction they relaxed a little, nodded and we all sank back into bored silence again.

Just as my circling brain was about to begin on another mental bender, there was movement in the hall. Through the glass doors we watched Matt walk down smiling and laughing with the cops who had looked seriously unamused earlier. He walked into the room, straight up to the WANTED posters and thumped one with his fist. Laughing, he said, 'Blame that bastard for this.' Suddenly ashamed for doubting him, I felt a hot flush and laughed with him, awkwardly and too loud, not understanding why we were staring at a picture of a tattoo on a shoulder.

As he explained, the cops' detailed and persistent questioning of our itinerary made sense. Only a month after Matt arrived in the UK, a man using Matt's name as an alias had killed a person in the North of England, then escaped to the continent. The police possessed only one defining detail of the man's physical appearance – the picture of the tattoo on his left shoulder. I was more grateful than ever that Matt had never got around to getting a tattoo. There had been a night in Bangkok in the company of Sang Thip whisky and Matt's new best friend, an accommodating Thai taxi driver, when it looked as though Matt would be tattooed in the back yard with a rusty nail and India ink before the night was through, but that is another story.

Taking Matt into an interview room, the police had asked him to strip to his waist and, upon observing his bare back with no tattoos, became jovial. They apologised for the inconvenience and offered to accompany us to the nearest ferry so that we could still make it to Hoek van Holland before our camping ground closed for the night.

After setting up camp that evening we celebrated the finale of our adventures with laughter, good cheer, endless beers and ganga so strong it rendered us speechless for an hour. We may have been degenerate, but at least none of us was a criminal.

CAST AWAY

Tony
Wheeler

Tony was born in England but grew up in Pakistan, the Bahamas and the USA. He returned to England to study engineering, worked as an automotive design engineer, completed an MBA then set out with his wife, Maureen, on an Asian overlanding trip that ultimately led to them founding Lonely Planet in Australia in 1973. They have been travelling, writing and publishing ever since.

TOM HANKS SHOWS HOW IT'S DONE IN *CAST AWAY*. Real life isn't anything like that. My Pacific castaway experiences have been much more mundane. Measured in days rather than years and on inhabited, even crowded, islands, I've been a much more comfortable castaway than Mr Hanks. In fact, watching *Cast Away*, I wonder why I'm complaining at all.

'The flight's been cancelled. You can't fly to Wallis today,' the young woman at the airline office, perched above the hardware store in Sigave, announced cheerily.

'What?!' I blurted out. 'It can't be cancelled. I've got a flight from Wallis to Australia tomorrow.'

'Well that flight will be cancelled too,' she responded and then went on to deliver a long explanation in French. One word recurred ominously: '*grève*'.

A year in Paris had imprinted the great French tradition of the *grève* indelibly on my mind. The metro drivers would hold a *grève* and subterranean Paris would grind to a halt. At least once a month, it seemed, newspaper printers would hold a *grève* and there would be no copies of the *Herald Tribune* at my local kiosk. On one occasion truck drivers held a *grève* on the airport freeway, blocking traffic so effectively my wife not only ran up a $200 taxi bill she also missed her flight and had to pay another $500 for her non-refundable airfare. Yes, I knew all about the French propensity for strikes.

The French Overseas Territory of the Wallis and Futuna Islands sits about halfway between France's two other South Pacific colonies – New Caledonia to the west and French Polynesia to the east. Wallis takes its name from a 1767 visit by the English explorer Samuel Wallis, homeward bound from 'discovering' Tahiti. Wallis is a long way from anywhere. Futuna, where I found myself marooned, is even more remote. It lies across 220 kilometres of empty ocean to the south-west, separated by a narrow channel from uninhabited Alofi.

Despite their isolation Wallis and Futuna are really not that hard to get to. Strikes apart, there are a couple of flights a week between Papeete in Tahiti and Noumea in New Caledonia that stop at Wallis en route. It's just that very few people bother to drop in. Not counting French government employees and the like, forty-three seemed to be the total number of visitors during the previous year.

For an unvisited dot – three dots if you count all three islands; twenty-odd if you add in all the *motus* and islets around the Wallis lagoon – the tiny colony has a surprising amount going for it. The main islands of Wallis and Futuna may be bereft of beaches, but the islets of the Wallis lagoon and Alofi have all the sparkling white sand and gin-clear water you could wish for. The dark and ominous waters of Wallis's perfectly circular crater lakes, reminders of its volcanic origins, provide an interesting contrast to its shimmering lagoons. If you could peer beneath the surface of their inky black you might discover the American military equipment which, it is said, was dumped into them at the end of World War II.

The Catholic church's iron grip on the islands' inhabitants is brought home by an amazing collection of imposing churches. The sombre Our Lady of Good Hope Cathedral in Wallis's main town, Matu Utu, may be the island's religious centre but the Church of St Joseph, at its south-east corner, is a positive delight. Every square centimetre of the church's interior has been covered with naive Biblical scenes or versions of the island's trademark 'land and sea' *tapa* designs. If anything, Futuna is even better endowed with churches. There's the ornate and beautiful Leava Church and the church of St Pierre Chanel, dedicated to the Pacific's first saint, whose war-club-to-the-head death may have had as much to do with local politics as distaste for the new religion.

Wallis also has impressive reminders of the island's pre-European history. Repeated invasions from Tonga commenced around AD 1400 and not far from the beautifully painted Church of St Joseph stands Talietumu, a recently excavated archaeological site where the invading Tongans built a fortified village around 1450. It's certainly one of the most remarkable ancient sites I've seen anywhere in the Pacific both for its size and the quality of the restoration work but it's even more amazing for being almost totally unknown. But then so is Wallis . . .

Talietumu isn't the only ancient site on the island, over on the west coast there's Tonga Toto, another fortified settlement. The name translates as 'swamp of blood', perhaps a reminder that the Tongan invasions were marked by such ferocity that memories have survived in the islanders' oral histories right down to the present day.

By the fifth day of what should have been a two-day visit I was ready to turn to religion myself. Beaches, churches and history were interesting to muse about while I kicked my heels on Futuna but I wanted to get back to Wallis and get home to the business meeting which I had promised I absolutely, positively, definitely could not and would not miss, and now clearly would.

'We'd better go to church tomorrow morning,' announced Bernard Riou, the only other guest at the island's one, four-room hotel. He'd flown down from Wallis to fix something at the airport and, like me, was marooned. We were watching the Tour de France, retransmitted by the single television channel available on the island. 'Perhaps praying will help,' he explained.

We strolled the couple of hundred metres from the hotel to the church for the dawn mass. The huge Sausau Church in Sigave, the island's main town, looks for all the world as though it was intended for EuroDisney and somehow got warped to the other side of the world. In fact it was built at record speed by the islanders to replace its predecessor, toppled by a disastrous earthquake in 1993. The women turned up in their Sunday best snow-white dresses, the men in technicoloured shirts, flowers in the hair for everyone. But prayer didn't help.

I wandered off to climb Futuna's 524-metre highest peak, the engagingly named Mount Puke, but as usual in the Pacific the trail eventually faded away after leading me halfway across the island. I tracked down Tui Savaka, a local village chief who carved out gigantic *tanoa* – majestic, multi-legged bowls used for *kava* ceremonies on Futuna. A chainsaw was the delicate instrument used to whack these spa-pool-sized containers into shape. I brushed up my Futunan in the town library. I drove round and round the tiny island in its only rent-a-car, the owner having kindly offered me a free extension of my two-day rental for as long as the strike lasted.

Each morning Bernard phoned his office in Wallis and each morning the message was the same: nothing was happening. I took to sitting at the end of the pier, watching for passing ships, but none appeared.

'We've created a perfect little replica of France, here in the Pacific,' commented Bernard over dinner one night.

'We have fine food,' he went on. We certainly did. Futuna's only restaurant, attached to the island's only hotel, produced fine food in such awesome quantities that it took me the entire day from breakfast until dinner to build up an appetite.

'And fine wine.' He was right there as well: we had shared a bottle of French red wine with dinner each night. Where cans of tinned fish and packets of minute noodles are all you expect to find on the shop shelves in most remote Pacific islands the small supermarket in Sigave had a tiny, but well-stocked, wine department offering four different champagnes, including Moët et Chandon!

'And completely ridiculous strikes,' Bernard concluded.

It was especially hard to disagree with that sentiment. Flights had ceased to operate through Wallis because the island's two weathermen had barricaded themselves in the control tower and were refusing to come out. The Wallisian weathermen were demanding pay equality with their French counterparts. They'd suddenly realised that their French co-workers enjoyed a pay loading, due to the hardship they suffered from being so far from

Paris and having their choice of wine labels uncomfortably restricted. Well, if that was tough for the French workers, it must be equally tough for a Wallisian, the weathermen concluded. After all they were equally distant from the comforts of Paris, weren't they?

Having decided a strike was in order they quickly realised that simply refusing to put out weather reports wasn't going to get them very far. After all, who believes weather reports anyway? No, they'd decided occupying the Wallis airport control tower and locking out the air traffic controllers – not to mention the island's four gendarmes – would be far more effective. They were absolutely correct.

Of course, the strike did end, flights recommenced and I managed to get home for the last days of the conference. Meanwhile, life on Wallis and Futuna is probably going on as usual. It must have been much more romantic, I mused, to be truly cast away or shipwrecked on a Pacific island.

Being cast away on Futuna was frustrating enough, so why was I so foolish as to repeat the experience, only more comprehensively, less than two years later on Nukufetau?

The plan was quite simple: photographer Peter Bennetts and I were to do a quick circuit of the nine islands that make up the Tuvalu group. Peter had already made several earlier visits with a view to a photographic book about a country reaping the benefits of scoring the two letters .tv as its Internet address while under imminent threat of disappearing due to rising sea levels. Nowhere on Tuvalu is the land more than four or five metres above sea level.

We'd made an abortive trip the previous year, which had ground to a halt when bad weather confined our ship to port after just three islands. Now we were setting off on the fishing boat *Manaui* to cover the other six. We sailed north from the main island of Funafuti to Vaitupu with a six-person *National*

Geographic film crew, a team of freezer plant engineers and enough other hangers-on to make deck space a commodity in extremely short supply. The first seven hours of the trip were idyllic: on calm seas I slept soundly under a clear starlit night squeezed between the anchor chains right up at the bow. The second six hours were distinctly less comfortable as we ploughed through a tropical downpour, pitching and rolling over large swells. There was scarcely enough deck space for twenty-odd people when it was dry; there was pitifully little when it was wet. I spent the time crouched under a tarpaulin stretched out in front of the bridge with water dripping down my back.

The *Manaui* dropped us in Vaitupu, took the freezer crew on to Nui and came back for us three days later. Peter and I were dropped at Nukufetau and the ship continued on to Funafuti to drop off the *National Geographic* crew. It would then turn about and pick us up a couple of days later to continue north to the remaining islands.

Except it didn't.

On Day One, we'd phoned our contact in Funafuti and all was well. The *Manaui* had returned safely to Funafuti and would be setting out again the next day.

On Day Three, when we went back to the phone office to find out why the boat hadn't turned up, the phone was down.

'This keeps happening,' the island *kaupule* (secretary) explained. 'Last time it didn't work for two months.' Outside, two men were fiddling despondently with the telephone satellite dish.

The next day, we managed to get a radio connection to Funafuti and discovered the *Manaui* had broken down but was being repaired and would set out later that day. We packed our bags and went to bed, calculating that if it left Funafuti just before sunset it would turn up in the early hours of the morning.

It didn't. The fourth day of our two-day stop dawned.

What's so great about coral atolls anyway? On the first day we had taken a boat across the lagoon to look for the wreckage of a World War II American bomber in the jungle. The scene was something straight out of *Cast Away*: a gleaming white beach separated clear turquoise water from gracefully swaying palm trees. The trouble is, if you stay out in the sun for more than thirty seconds you cook, but when you move into the shade it takes less than thirty seconds for the flies and mosquitoes to find you. Our little bash around the bush looking for aircraft wreckage hadn't helped: the cuts, scratches and nicks on our ankles and legs instantly became infected in the tropical climate and proved even more attractive to those hungry flies and mosquitoes. To top it all, the nearest cold beer – or cold anything else for that matter – was over a hundred kilometres away.

Of course the sun didn't shine all the time; half the time tropical downpours soaked the clothes you'd hung out to dry and swept in through the window across your bed. Still, the water came in useful: since every tap in the guest house leaked profusely, each day the gravity-fed water tank would empty and we'd have to shuttle water from the cistern until it was refilled.

Our little home on Nukufetau was right by the very first primary school in Tuvalu – the Tutasi School – which was the source of considerable island pride as its establishment had been a completely local project and its success prompted the government to open schools on other islands. If Peter and I were at home the children would line up outside the windows and watch what we were doing at every opportunity – before school, between classes, at lunchtime, after school. We were never short of a line of small faces at the window practising their two English phrases: 'Bye, bye' and 'What's your name?'

The school indirectly kept us fed on Days Two and Three. Our visit had coincided with Founding Day, the island's proud celebration of their school's opening in 1947. Activities took place one after another in the island's open meeting hall or *falekaupule*, and all featured meals. We were invariably invited to join in the feasting on fish, breadfruit, *pulaka* (a form of taro) and pork. Pigs are plentiful on every island in Tuvalu, but are usually eaten only at festival time.

Other than that we had to make do with what we could buy from the *fusi*, the village cooperative store. It had to be something the shop had available, which wasn't much, and which didn't require cooking since the gas cylinder for the guest house's cooker was empty. That meant a diet of instant noodles (just add hot water), canned fruit (just wield your Swiss Army knife), cereal (which we added to the canned fruit) and salty crackers. There was no fresh fruit or vegetables and we refused to stoop to that Pacific Island staple, tinned corned beef, or *bullamacow* as it's known locally. We did indulge in an occasional cold can of Coke.

Shopping at the *fusi* was a leisurely affair. When they weren't lounging in the adjacent office the staff stood behind the counter. Some of the goods were arrayed on the shelves; others were concealed under the counter; more were scattered in cardboard boxes all over the floor; yet more were hidden away in a storeroom. There was neither rhyme nor reason in what was on display – a manicure set, a set of Nintendo controls, a huge box of neckties – and what was hidden away – all the tinned peaches, all the instant noodles.

'Two packets of chicken-flavour noodles,' I requested one lunchtime. The assistant dug into the cartons on the floor until he found them, brought them back to the counter, flipped open the ledger labelled 'foodstuffs' and wrote down the purchase and its price. I noticed other books inscribed 'freezer', 'textiles', 'hardware' and 'drinks'. 'A can of peaches,' I continued. He went off to search for canned peaches. By the end of our stay we'd worked through the really rusty cans and were into the really rusty but also battered cans. Shopping did, though, take a reasonable chunk of time from the daily routine.

Soon after dawn a gentle scratching and clinking noise would drift in through the windows. The scratch-scratch-scratch came from brooms as women swept up leaves that had fallen during the night. The assiduous tidiness with which they kept the paths clean contrasted with the untidiness everywhere else – cans, plastic bottles, clothing, broken television sets and tape recorders, bits of wire and glass, and an amazing number of broken kettles were dumped seemingly at random. The clink was of glass bottles as men tapped their toddy trees, whose sap makes a pleasant drink, vaguely reminiscent of lemonade, which can be used in cooking and fermented to produce alcoholic sour toddy.

Soon after these morning wake-up calls, the first school children would appear outside our window. Just behind them, boats were heading out across the lagoon to fish or to bring back coconuts from the other islets. Most of these coconuts went to feed the village's healthy population of pigs.

Savave, the islet with the village, stretches precisely 800 metres from one end to the other and is often only a couple of hundred metres wide. It didn't take long to walk around even stopping to watch the progress of the various building projects – the old church building was being re-roofed and the pastor was getting a new water cistern. Or we could wander around talking to people, snorkel in the lagoon or even walk to another islet. It was easy to wade across the lagoon to Fale, the islet immediately to the west, where villagers have their *pulaka* pits, or east to two more islets, first Temotuloto and then Motumua.

It was at night that the village really came alive and it was *fatele* which provided the life. Electricity had arrived on the island only a few months previously but the small explosion of video recorders which followed clearly had no effect on the popularity of *fatele*, a traditional music, singing and dancing session with the added attraction that it's competitive.

There were *fateles* in the village *falekaupule* both nights of the school founding festival. Tuvaluan villages are conveniently divided into two 'sides' so each side of the village takes up station at one end of the *falekaupule*. In the centre of each group is a wooden platform, about a metre and a half square and twenty centimetres off the ground. Men sit around this 'drum' and thump on it with the palms of their hands to produce the background beat. Another man drums on a metal cabin cracker tin, creating a wonderfully noisy racket. After a spell on a diet of stale cabin crackers, island visitors may conclude that this is a much better use for them.

Around this central group of musicians the singers, male and female, sit cross-legged. All face the centre when they are performing and look towards the other team when it's their turn. The rhythm starts gently and builds, the tempo getting faster and faster, the drumming likewise becoming louder and louder until it peaks in a thumping, crashing crescendo. The singing follows suit, starting gently and harmoniously and building to a full-throated melange of harmonies and counter-harmonies. *'Fatele'* means 'to multiply', hinting at that steadily increasing speed.

To one side of the musicians and singers are the dancers, a group of often substantial dames with flower *fous* wreathing their heads and brown grass skirts that invariably failed to circle their Mother Hubbard–shrouded bulk. Occasionally a male dancer may jump up to do a short warrior-like bent-leg knee-knocking, but it's generally left to the women to sway statuesquely until ending their dance with a graceful twirl whose inference is 'So beat that!'

Which is precisely what the other side tries to do.

Even after the two nights of competition at the *falekaupule*, *fatele* practice sessions continued each night in one house or another. Sessions would sometimes be going on in several locations at once and we would stand outside one for a while, then go on to see how the others were doing. By this time we were a familiar enough sight to be beckoned in to sit amongst the singers and join in with the clapping. I liked *fateles*.

On Day Five we got through to Funafuti on the radio. They were still trying to fix the ship's generator, which was sucking up water or something, but the *Manaui* was set to sail the next day. We would, then, miss our flight out of Funafuti.

Day Six dawned quietly. It was a Saturday so there were no school bells but the kids still turned up to stare through the windows. Saturday also meant the radio office was closed so we couldn't check with Funafuti if our boat had departed. Just before the *fusi* closed at lunchtime we bought enough noodles and tinned fruit to last out the weekend, just in case we weren't rescued.

Despite my earlier experience, here I was again: frustrated on a beautiful tropical atoll. I calculated, for perhaps the fiftieth time, that if the *Manaui* didn't turn up by sunset we would not have enough time to complete our circuit of the islands even by the following week's flight.

We walked around the island, stopping to chat with various people. Our predicament was well known and the 'coconut news' had stories and rumours enough to entertain us. A ship was coming to Vaitupu to bring fuel for the generator; the island passenger and cargo vessel *Nivaga* was due in a few days; no it wasn't, it was delayed. Everybody had a different tale to tell.

An hour before sunset Peter suggested we wade across to Fale islet, Nukufetau's southernmost point, to see if anything was coming our way. Halfway across, looking out over the reef edge I realised I was looking at an islet where an islet shouldn't have been. A ship! It wasn't the *Manaui*, which had never left Funafuti, but we took it anyway. Before long we were headed north.

LEARNING FRENCH THE HARD WAY

Anthony Ham

Anthony worked as a refugee lawyer for three years, spending most of his time doing battle with a mean-spirited Australian government. Tired of banging his head against a brick wall, he set out to see the world and restore his faith in humanity. He has been travelling ever since throughout Asia, Africa and the Middle East, finding previously unimagined uses for his Master's degree in Middle Eastern politics. On his travels for Lonely Planet, Anthony has been held up at knifepoint in Cameroon, arrested in Iran and found himself constantly overwhelmed by the many kindnesses from anything-but-ordinary people. He remains otherwise intact. For Lonely Planet, Anthony has contributed to *Africa on a Shoestring*, *Middle East*, *Iran*, *India*, *North India* and *Libya*.

THE INITIAL RESPONSE TO MY FIRST, TENTATIVE APPROACH TO LONELY PLANET WAS HARDLY ENCOURAGING: 'YEAH, A LOT OF PEOPLE WANT TO WRITE FOR LONELY PLANET.' FAIR ENOUGH.

Almost eighteen months later, I found myself bound for the tourist hotspots of Niger, Chad, Cameroon and Sudan, excited to be heading off on my first assignment for Lonely Planet and wondering why I hadn't asked for Venice.

First stop, Johannesburg, a city with a reputation for muggings – a high proportion of whose victims seemed to have been Lonely Planet authors – that was well known. I survived my thirty-six-hour stopover, no thanks to those travellers with a ghoulish love of recounting in detail the latest alleged attacks. (Upon closer examination I worked out that at least one of these had taken place in Botswana.)

Fighting complacency at having survived one of Africa's most dangerous cities, I steeled myself high over the Atlantic for my imminent arrival in another: Abidjan in the Côte d'Ivoire. I tried not to contemplate the warning in the previous edition of my Lonely Planet guide, which said with disarming simplicity that 'Abidjan can easily induce paranoia'. On the negative side, arriving after midnight was less than ideal. On the positive, at least it wasn't Lagos and Abidjan airport HAD reopened after the coup a few weeks before.

Before launching into the arrivals hall, I ran over my well-honed checklist for confronting potentially dangerous situations: look confident, ignore or dismiss the most aggressive touts and pretend you've been here before. Thus armed, but only vaguely reassured, I set off, head down, through the gate. Satisfied that I had eluded the waiting crowd, I looked up to find myself a few metres away from a dead end, a few hundred away from the exit.

Needless to say, I was soon surrounded by a group of intimidating young men scarcely able to conceal their smirks. Cursing my beginner's mistake, I fought my way through with a little too much aggression to the Air Afrique office, the only place for changing money and the only haven in which I could catch my breath.

When I emerged a few minutes later, the touts had disappeared. Instead of seizing the moment and heading for the nearest taxi, I strolled into the balmy, tropical air, put my bags on the ground and lit up a cigarette. A sitting target. This time, with me the only passenger crazy enough to linger, the group of young men returned, urging upon me a range of promises seemingly backed by threats for which my crash course in French proved hopelessly inadequate. The one English speaker among them assured me I was 'fucking gone, man'. The policeman in attendance screamed at me rather than my assailants.

The taxi driver demanded four times a reasonable price for a hotel he'd never heard of, then, before we could pull away, five of my new-found friends piled into the taxi with just a hint of menace. Fortunately, scuffles among four of them saw the number dwindle without me saying a word. The fifth finally stormed out of the taxi a few hundred metres down the road, welcoming me to his city with a string of parting expletives. My taxi driver stared impassively into the distance as I slumped into the back seat like the victim of a cataclysm.

When, a mere two hours later, we found the hotel I collapsed into the bar. Its lurid yellow lighting and life-sized statues looming out of the shadows made me long for Venice.

Things looked up next morning when I met the owner of the hotel, Tyson, a *nom de guerre* attributable partly to his uncanny resemblance to the boxer of the same name and partly to his current title of undisputed (least of all by me) heavyweight boxing champion of Côte d'Ivoire. A good man to know in Abidjan.

I stuck close to his side, attending his sparring sessions, his drinking sessions and even his visits to the countryside to take presents to his small army of children who were, coincidentally, the same in number to his former girlfriends. On one such expedition, we stopped off mid-morning at a roadside *maquis*, an open-air restaurant under the palm trees. We downed draughts of palm wine with a man who was permanently attached to the still, whose teeth numbered less than two and whose eyes wore that faraway look of any who happen to be drunk by lunch time.

I had come to trust Tyson, for the fact that he looked out for me as much as for his imposing bulk. So much so that I let him order the food. Mine was casserole-like, the taste a little unusual, the texture a little stringy, but certainly more filling than the bones with token fish I had eaten elsewhere. Tyson told me it was *agoute*, a word on which my limited French could shed no light. Tyson was sitting across the table devouring a goat's head with keen-eyed diligence. 'The eyes, they are particularly good.' I took his word for it and assumed I, too, was eating goat.

With my world back in a state of apparent equilibrium, I reluctantly bade farewell to Tyson and flew to Niamey in Niger.

Niamey, the sand-blown, largely mud-brick capital city of one of the world's poorest countries, felt like the end of the earth. My taxi driver was most concerned that I had chosen the Hotel Moustache ('very bad') but took me there nonetheless, resigned to the fact that I would get what I deserved for trusting a foreign guidebook over his expert local opinion.

I checked into my cell, marvelling at how many people seemed to work in this hotel and impressed by how many of them were women. Friendly lot, too. I did a quick run-through of my things to do by sunset: nine hotels, four restaurants and the tourist office. A quick detour to the toilet and I'd be away. I didn't emerge for the next three hours as I proceeded to vomit violently everything I had eaten over the past week, including a few things about which I had no recollection.

Midway through this spectacular start to a new career, I finally gave in to the persistent knocking on my door. I reasoned that the owner of the hotel was concerned for my welfare. The fact that I opened the door just slightly proved no impediment to Chantelle, a brassy, scantily clad beauty who pushed her way in, announcing (and describing) with a complete absence of subtlety how she could fix any problem. In her own special way, she promised (complete with actions which left nothing to the imagination) that she had a foolproof way to take my attention away from my stomach. Bowing to the inevitable, I returned to the bathroom and Chantelle soon gave up, leaving with promises of an imminent return with some of her friends. 'You are special case,' were her parting words. As I locked the door, it occurred to me that that this wasn't quite how I had planned to spend my first night as a Lonely Planet author.

A few weeks later, feeling every bit the veteran, I was travelling with Rob, a Canadian who spoke maddeningly fluent French. We were in a restaurant in the western Niger town of Zinder and we were each trying to outdo the other in pretending we didn't care about the rat which had just disappeared into the kitchen.

It all prompted Rob to say, 'Of course, you should never eat the *agoute*.'

My reply was casual, if a little forced, my curiosity finally winning out over my need to preserve my reputation or any remnants of street-cred. 'Of course not . . . why not?'

'Because it's rat.'

For a fleeting moment, I contemplated ordering the *agoute* in a bid to show that I was as hard-core a traveller as they come. Then I remembered Niamey, the Hotel Moustache and Chantelle. I smiled knowingly, the smile of someone who knows what not to do in strange countries. After all, I was an experienced Lonely Planet author.

AN ANGKOR ODYSSEY

Daniel Robinson

Daniel was raised in the USA (the San Francisco Bay Area and Glen Ellyn, Illinois) and Israel. His passion for shoestring travel was kindled at age seventeen with a trip to Cyprus, and since then he has spent several years on the road exploring some of the more remote parts of Asia, the Middle East and Europe. Over the past twelve years, Daniel's work for Lonely Planet has included the award-winning first editions of *Vietnam*, researched one step ahead of the secret police (the story of his expulsion from Hanoi appeared in *Lonely Planet Unpacked*), and *Cambodia*, at the time still in a state of civil war. He has worked on all four editions of *France*, covering virtually every region of the Hexagone, and was a co-author of the first edition of *Paris*.

Daniel is currently finishing up an MA in Israeli history at Tel Aviv University. He is based in Tel Aviv.

JUST AS BANGKOK HAD EMERGED AS THE GATEWAY TO *PERES-TROIKA*-ERA VIETNAM, IN 1989 HO CHI MINH CITY – though linked to the non-Communist world by just one or two flights a day – was the gateway to Cambodia, to the degree that such a thing existed. The Phnom Penh government was recognised by only a handful of Soviet-aligned countries, so the Cambodian consulate in Saigon was one of the only places on earth where you could try your luck for a visa. Authorisations in hand, you could then board one of the four weekly flights – on ageing Soviet aircraft flown by airlines too poor to purchase spare parts – linking Tan Son Nhut with Pochentong. The only other scheduled flights to Phnom Penh came from Hanoi, Vientiane and occasionally Moscow.

My final destination was the world-renowned temple complex at Angkor, in a remote part of north-western Cambodia surrounded by thick jungles largely controlled by the Khmer Rouge. Land routes from the capital – to the extent that roads of any sort still existed – were blocked by fighting. Other than taking a two-day ferry trip or chartering a military helicopter, the only option was to fly to the airfield at Siem Reap, served twice a week by Antonov An-24 turboprops. The good news was that during most of the forty-minute flight, the Soviet pilots stayed over the vast Tonlé Sap (Great Lake) to avoid Khmer Rouge ground fire. If you arrived on the Saturday flight you had Angkor – one of the most stunning and sublime architectural achievements ever conceived by the human mind – virtually to yourself until the following Wednesday. Less fortuitously, you were stranded in the middle of a war zone, and if you became ill or injured you'd have to make do with the almost nonexistent local medical facilities until the next flight out.

As I boarded the daily bus to Phnom Penh in front of Saigon's ornate, French-built city hall, I was unaware of such logistical details. Indeed, the whole purpose of my trip was to ferret them out. Lonely Planet was finally doing a guide to Indochina, and I had pretty much finished up my research in southern Vietnam. Cambodia – still in a state of civil war – had been tacked onto the project almost as an afterthought; my contract called for twenty pages of whatever information I could come up with. The very idea of tourism to Cambodia – renamed Democratic Kampuchea by the ousted Khmer Rouge regime – sounded like a tasteless joke.

The main advantage of taking the bus, other than saving the US$51 airfare, was that it meant one less white-knuckle flight on Vietnam Airlines. I am generally the sort of traveller who will board any aircraft with both wings visibly intact, but my cavalier attitude changed after an in-flight schmooze about Vietnam Airlines' safety record with the first secretary of the Indian Embassy in Hanoi. I breezily told him about several cases in which aircraft I'd been on had landed only after several aborted approaches, and mentioned the rumours that Soviet technicians refused to fly on the planes they themselves serviced. In equally good humour, he told me that his ambassador had been killed just months earlier when a Tupolev Tu-134 had gone down near Bangkok. As we chatted, a middle-aged cadre – obviously new to flying – tried to open an emergency exit; incredibly, he had wanted to dispose of a cigarette butt. I can still hear the swoosh of the air being sucked out of the cabin of the Tu-134, which was not outfitted with oxygen masks. This could never have happened on a Vietnam Airlines plane I had flown on not long before: its emergency exits had been permanently bolted shut.

My fellow bus passengers included a number of young Vietnamese soldiers heading back to Cambodia after home leave. As we made our way west towards Moc Bai, one of them acciden-tally fired his AK-47 out the window; the loud report caused little more than some laughter and scolding from the other passengers. During the Vietnam War, the towns and villages we passed had made world headlines, and the nearby forests had been defoliated with Agent Orange. Although the road linking the Cambodian frontier with Phnom Penh was the only major highway in the whole country not menaced by the Khmer Rouge, my official hosts were alarmed that I had slipped into the country by land, and later they made very sure that I returned to Vietnam on an airplane.

Despite the torture rooms of Tuol Sleng and the mass graves at Choeung Ek, the most disturbing thing about Phnom Penh was the shell-shocked expression and blank eyes on almost everyone you passed, limbless or not. The city's humid, dusty streets, with their uneven pavements and giant potholes, were populated almost exclusively by rural folk who had moved into the deserted city after Pol Pot was ousted. They lived in apartments vacated by the city's pre-1975 inhabitants, who had been force-marched into the countryside as part of the Khmer Rouge's radical social revolution. Few had lived to return.

Until the late 1960s, Phnom Penh had been one of the most elegant and gracious cities in Asia. I tried to imagine what life here had been like before Cambodia was drawn into the American war in nearby Vietnam and then emptied of its inhabitants when the Khmer Rouge proclaimed Year Zero. As I wandered about, clipboard in hand, it was hard to keep the pre-execution photos on the memorial walls of Tuol Sleng from coming to mind: the spectacles framing terrified eyes or the French once spoken by pursed lips had been reason enough for a summary death sentence. I kept imagining those very faces – except smiling and at ease – in the doorways and windows of graceful colonial buildings or in front of the altars of Buddhist temples whose statues were now smashed and ancient libraries destroyed.

Phnom Penh in the late 1980s was the most visibly traumatised place I had ever visited. Day-to-day life seemed permeated by wartime fear, unbearable memories and the palpable absence of countless loved ones who had perished either during the Khmer Rouge's reign of terror or in the ongoing civil war. There was a railway station, but every train that pulled in or out had an armoured carriage sprouting machine guns and, in front, two flat cars to detonate Khmer Rouge mines before the rest of the carriages rolled over them. Poor peasants coming into the city to sell their produce would ride the flat cars to save the fare, playing Russian roulette for a few riels. During the years that the city had stood virtually empty, the rafters of the glorious National Museum of Khmer Art & Archaeology had been taken over by thousands of bats whose guano now floated down like volcanic ash. As I walked among the ancient stone carvings, taking notes for the Things to Do section, a nauseating, sour taste spread over my tongue each time I inhaled.

The city's hotels – classy joints back in the 1960s – were half-trashed, and the rooms got cheaper as the floors got higher because the lifts weren't working: if you were willing to climb eight flights of stairs you could get a great deal. One incongruous bright spot: if you didn't mind paying US$4.75 a minute, international phone calls were a relatively simple matter thanks to a direct satellite link to a Russian-accented operator in Moscow. The only Westerners in Phnom Penh were a few aid workers.

My gracious guide, Madame Tan Sotho of the General Directorate of Tourism, helped arrange an air ticket to Angkor. I soon discovered that Kampuchean Airlines had a policy of squeezing three passengers into each pair of seats, originally designed for the corpulent bodies of well-fed Soviet cadres. Other than the awkward seat assignment, the flight to Angkor was problem-free, and we enjoyed great views of the Tonlé Sap – an extraordinary inland sea that is filled by the Mekong during the rainy season and drains back into the river during the dry months. Around much of the perimeter of the lake, government forces were largely confined to a few outposts and garrison towns, among them Siem Reap.

At the airfield, Claire (a Phnom Penh–based French aid worker) and I were met by So Hoan of Conservation d'Angkor, who would be our guide; our driver was at the wheel of a black Russian sedan. We were also assigned a police minder, a fellow barely out of his teens who was clearly not one of the country's top intelligence operatives. We were told not to wander around the depopulated town of Siem Reap, but I needed to update my 1920s town map (found in a used book shop in Hanoi) and Claire was curious, so we gave *l'Espion* ('the Spy') the slip. For a couple of hours we were on our own. I had made great progress with the map by the time *l'Espion*, looking hugely relieved, tracked us down. We were spared chastisement because he spoke neither French nor English, but his boyish face begged us, for his sake, to avoid such stunts in the future.

Claire and I were the only guests staying at the 62-room Grand Hôtel d'Angkor, a once-elegant colonial building inaugurated in 1928. Every night, heavily armed government troops took up positions around the building, which – like the rest of town – had electricity only from 6 to 9 pm. A general curfew was in force from 7 pm to 5 am. Day and night, gunfire rang out in the distance, and we never knew if nervous soldiers were just testing their weapons or if fighting were actually taking place.

Siem Reap had been a thriving tourist destination in the 1960s, but the people who had once welcomed visitors from around the world were gone. The lucky ones had become refugees. Many others had found a final resting place in one of the local memorials, usually little more than a few carefully sorted piles of skulls and human bones on a wooden platform. Still more victims had been left in shallow mass graves; fragments of clothing clung to the bones that had worked their way to the muddy surface. These people had been killed no more than fourteen years before, and had Cambodia not gone berserk most of them would still have been alive.

A short drive out of town, away from the deserted buildings and their ghosts, took us into the rainforest and back eight or ten centuries to the height of the Khmer Empire. Contrary to press reports, the many magnificent temples remained virtually undamaged, though some of the sugar palms had holes shot clear through their trunks. At the Bayon, 216 gargantuan faces of Avalokiteshvara smiled icily in every direction. As we wandered around, a dozen or more of the visages could be seen at any given time – full face or in profile, almost at eye level or peering down from on high – in an ever-changing phantasmagoria. Bas-reliefs depicted everyday life in the late twelfth century: market women selling fish, a pig about to be dropped into a cauldron, people picking lice out of each other's hair, a woman giving birth. And, of course, there were vivid scenes of war in which the Khmers (with slicked-back hair) did battle against the Chams (wearing headdresses). The Bayon was especially enchanting right after dawn, when the rainforest was shrouded in mist and the air was filled with the songs of invisible birds and the sound of giant dew drops bursting on the vegetation of the jungle floor. The only other people around were a few monks in light yellow robes – survivors of Pol Pot's concerted effort to exterminate the Buddhist clergy – and groups of young government soldiers, wearing bits of uniforms and cotton *kramas* (chequered scarves) and armed with AK-47s or loaded RPGs (rocket-propelled grenades). Somewhere nearby, unseen in the thick jungle, lurked the shadowy Khmer Rouge.

The French archaeologists who, starting in the 1860s, did so much to study and preserve the Angkor complex intentionally left one temple exactly as they found it. Ta Prohm – its friezes enmeshed in tendrilous nets, its stones slowly being pried asunder by the roots of centuries-old fig trees rising from its galleries and towers – stood as a monument to the awesome fecundity and power of the rainforest. Doorways were blocked by delicately carved stones dislodged by the roots of long-decayed trees; window frames were carpeted by a dozen different kinds of mosses, lichens and creeping plants. Bats flew in and out of the vaulted stone galleries, their nests hidden among the ancient eaves. Surrounded by so much pulsating, creeping life, I wondered if perhaps the jungle might somehow try to reach out and grab me, twisting its vines around my neck just as it had done to the dancing stone *apsaras* lying corpse-like nearby.

One humid day, while driving past Ta Prohm, I noticed some unusual military activity: scores of soldiers were arrayed around the temple's perimeter in a classic infantry deployment. 'What's going on?' I asked the guide, who explained that the troops were there to protect a Japanese film crew that had flown in for the day by chartered helicopter. I thought to myself: here we are, the five of us driving around the jungle unaccompanied, while the fat cats from the news media are provided with proper security. Trying to sound firm, I suggested that perhaps we, too, should have at least a modest military escort.

I need not have worried. The local army brass had convinced the Japanese that Ta Prohm was so risky that even in broad daylight nothing less than an entire company of heavily armed infantrymen could ensure their safety. The television men – lacking any information to the contrary and obviously keen on seeing their loved ones again – gratefully accepted the officers' recommendations. Of course, top-flight security doesn't come cheap, but that's what company expense accounts are for. The entrepreneurial commander and his pals pocketed the cash, and the troops probably also saw some small benefit. Capitalist enterprise of the first order!

Our guide was very excited when he informed us that the local authorities, both civilian and military, had authorised a tour of the late twelfth-century Preah Khan temple, which neither he nor any outsiders had visited since a *National Geographic* team had passed through seven years before. At one time cleared of the all-devouring jungle by archaeologists, it had not been subject to any significant upkeep since 1972 and was now overgrown by vines and young trees. However, the four concentric walls and the many galleries were said to be in an excellent state of repair.

We entered through a stone gate decorated with carved scenes of gods and devils churning the Sea of Milk in order to extract the elixir of immortality. Entranced by the beauty and mystery of the temple, we began to explore the long, dank corridors. Above us, the holes in the stone roofs were covered with a thin layer of back-lit foliage. Suddenly, two breathless young soldiers, Kalashnikovs slung across their bare shoulders, appeared out of nowhere and ran up to our guide. A family man with a dozen children waiting at home, he was horrified by what they told him: government troops laid mines in Preah Khan each night to keep out the Khmer Rouge, and on this particular day soldiers had removed a number of filament mines only an hour before. In the past year alone, right around Preah Khan, mines had killed three people and maimed five others; five water buffalo had also been blown up. It wasn't clear whether these antipersonnel devices had been planted by government forces or the Khmer Rouge or both, but from our point of view it hardly mattered. The soldiers ordered us to evacuate the temple. Familiar with the maze of pathways through the undergrowth, they would escort us out.

As we took one last look around the central section of the temple, swarms of bats fluttering erratically in the galleries' darker recesses, we spotted a bright green Hanuman snake, whose fatal poison has no antidote, slithering through the undergrowth. One of the soldiers killed it with a stick. Nearby, along the side of a stone stupa, red ants devoured a dead bat. As I followed the soldiers out of the complex, I scanned the undergrowth for the telltale sparkle of nylon trip wires, and – familiar with infantry tactics from another life – I kept ten metres between myself and the others in case one of us was unlucky. The grass and brush yielded no signs of mines, but I did spot a palm-sized black tarantula searching for something to eat among the decaying leaves.

The distance to the paved road became shorter and shorter and, finally, the black sedan came into view. No explosion had interrupted the usual sounds of crickets, birds, rustling leaves and distant automatic weapons fire, and for the moment we were all safe again. For a few terrifying minutes, I had been a candidate for random and meaningless death, as vulnerable – and as dependent on good luck – as the local villagers. Of course, I would soon board a flight from Siem Reap to Phnom Penh, and from there progressively larger aircraft would take me to Ho Chi Minh City and then Bangkok and then San Francisco. Angkor and its people would carry on, darkened by horrific memories and menaced by the daily threat of random mayhem.

THE CRUISE

John Weldon

John is half English, half Australian and half Irish. Do the maths and you'll easily be able to work out which half is dominant. John saw Kiss on television at the age of twelve and decided that rock-'n'roll was the life for him. Twenty years and a lot of fun (but little in the way of financial reward) later he decided it was time to get a real job and so he threw everything in and became a writer. So far he has made a surprisingly respectable living out of writing football, food, comedy, bad cheques, travel and Op/Ed for various organisations, including Lonely Planet. When he grows up he wants to play fullback for the only football team in the world – the Western Bulldogs – until then he will just have to be patient.

EACH MORNING THE VERY FRENCH CAPITAINE CLAUDE, HENRI AND I WOULD GO SPEAR FISHING; OR RATHER THEY WOULD GO SPEAR FISHING AND I WOULD TAG ALONG.

Henri had a remarkable eye for the inedible and always returned laden with fish that even other fish would struggle to eat. The Capitaine, for his part, had an uncanny knack of attracting barracuda. I had no aptitude for anything related to spear fishing, but I imagined I looked rather James Bondish snorkelling along, spear gun in hand.

On the final day of our trip, as the *Isabelle* sat at anchor off desert island number four, somewhere in the Andaman Sea, the Capitaine, perhaps sensing my disappointment at not being able to catch anything, took me lobstering. Henri and our respective partners opted to sunbake on the beach.

We anchored the dinghy at the bottom of a cliff, which dropped straight down into about five metres of clear blue water that teemed with lobsters. Even I could see their antennae poking out from under the coral. Soon we had half a dozen and were ready to return to the boat. However, the Capitaine felt compelled to spear a huge golden trevally, really too beautiful to kill, which dragged the gun from his hand and headed out to sea in a cloud of blood. We had no choice but to follow.

The trevally, desperate to be rid of this spear, thrashed and threw itself about spasmodically. We were now a hundred metres or so offshore and I could no longer see the bottom. This was serious ocean; not the piddly reef water I was used to and I didn't like it. The Capitaine reeled in the dying fish, but not before the usual fleet of toothy barracuda hove into view.

Their presence brought home to me just how much of a non-seafaring city boy I was. These barracuda had arrived in seconds. What other fish were even now homing in on this scent?

There were tiger sharks in this area, the Capitaine himself had told me that. What the hell was he doing shooting fish in a place like this? My fear was quickly joined by anger, directed at the Capitaine, but I tried to let it go as I suddenly remembered that sharks can smell fear and are attracted to it – or was that dogs?

Whatever, when the Capitaine signalled that we return to the dinghy I couldn't have been happier, although I fully expected to be chomped on the way. We scampered aboard, he now covered in blood, and I asked him if he were worried that there might be sharks. He gave me his best Gallic shrug and answered nonchalantly, 'But of course.' I would have hit him, but I didn't know how to start the outboard.

Minutes later we arrived back at the boat to find the women frantic about Henri. Apparently, he had decided to go off spear fishing on his own just after we'd left and had not returned. The Capitaine set off at once in the dinghy to look for him.

I remembered the barracuda and I pictured Henri, his belt full of bleeding fish. Maybe he was gone for good.

An hour and a half later the Capitaine returned with a very sheepish Henri, whom he'd found sitting on an isolated strip of beach too scared to go back in the water after having been menaced by a couple of sharks. Apparently, he'd been successful for once and had a few decent fish in his belt. The sharks had sashayed in and begun to circle him. In an effort to distract them, he'd unclipped the fish from his belt and let them float away. Immediately the sharks had bolted in and picked the fish off one by one. Henri took his chance and swam to shore as fast as his adrenaline could carry him and there he stayed.

The lure of Capitaine Claude's 'four-day desert island cruise' (as promised on the poster taped to a lamppost back at Ao Nang beach) had obliterated all sense of precaution. We realised that none of us knew how to sail, where the safety gear was, how to fire a flare or even how to use the radio – let alone where we were, other than somewhere off the coast of Thailand. What's more, a quick survey revealed that none of us had told our families or indeed anybody at all where we were going. If something went wrong who would know to look for us – or indeed where to look for us?

All thoughts of disaster were quickly banished, however, as the Capitaine – very annoyed at Henri for delaying our departure and, for some reason, in a desperate hurry to get going – urged us to pack up quickly and make ready to leave, which we did.

Soon after setting sail, the wind began to pick up a little. Henri and I rode the bow of the boat, enjoying the spray and the rise and fall of the *Isabelle* as she cut through the swell.

The morning's perils had well and truly slaked my thirst for adventure and I longed to be back on dry land. I pined in particular for the tourist beaches of Phuket and the chance to sink my teeth back into the latest Kinky Friedman novel. Not for me the wild and dangerous briny.

Still we thrilled to the grace and power the *Isabelle* displayed under full sail. For days the sea had been glass calm, often meaning that we motored rather than sailed along, so our gloom was quickly forgotten as we enjoyed the breeze and the cool ocean spray on our faces.

Gradually the air became much cooler and the breeze stronger. The *Isabelle* now began to rip through the water and, for the first time in weeks, I began to feel uncomfortable in wet clothes so I went below to change.

I returned on deck to find the Capitaine securing hatches and stowing gear. I joined in, enjoying the exercise and the chance to do something useful: to actually crew the boat, instead of merely lounge around on it. So involved was I that I did not notice the sky darken or the sea turn from pale green to leaden grey. Only when the wind started to gust and I again started to feel uncomfortably cold did I realise that all was perhaps not well.

The Capitaine, as usual, stood stoic and stone-faced and made no comment. I trained my eyes on him, looking for a sign: was this a storm? Should I be worried? After a little prompting he explained, while casting a withering look in poor Henri's direction, that our delay had meant that we were now riding the front of a storm which we should have been well ahead of.

'Will we be okay?' I asked.

'It's nothing,' he shrugged. I didn't believe him.

Minutes later a stronger gust sent spray skittering across the deck and caused the *Isabelle* to lurch sickeningly. The Capitaine shook his head and yelled something at Henri.

'He says we have to take the jib down; too much wind in the sails or something,' Henri translated. 'He wants to know if we want the safety harnesses.'

The Capitaine indicated a box of tangled straps and buckles at his feet. The boat slewed sideways again. There didn't seem time enough to untangle the harnesses so we elected not to put them on . . .

We inched our way along the deck to the bow, finding handholds wherever we could as the bow rose and fell heavily. With one arm and one leg each wrapped around the rail we began to haul in the sail.

The boat ploughed right into a wave and for a moment I was totally submerged. I came up spluttering for air. Henri, too, was soaked, and although we said nothing I could tell he was as scared as I. If we had let go we'd now be overboard. This was serious. We quickly secured the sail and headed back to the safety of the cockpit.

Eve, Henri's wife, met us there. She had seen us both go under and was very upset. She made Henri promise he would not go forward again without a harness, and she shouted angrily at the Capitaine in French, something I too would have done had I been able to speak French – and if I had had the guts.

With the jib down the boat was much more responsive, despite the continued rise of the sea, but the wind still threw us around at every possible opportunity.

I felt both scared and stupid. Embarking on such a trip without telling anybody was so unlike me. I guess I'd become so bored and my mind so sun-addled by endless days on the beach that the promise of any excitement at all had caused a complete brain

bypass. I pictured myself reading about four brainless tourists sign-
ing up for a crazy trip with a mad Frenchman to the middle of
nowhere without even checking if the boat had life jackets. 'They
deserved everything they got; serves them right,' I would have said.

I was jerked from my mental self-flagellation by a sound that
almost made me vomit. Above the howling of the wind there was
a loud crack followed by a vicious tearing sound. The boat
seemed to stop and I looked along the deck for a sign that the hull
had split.

A loud *'Merde!'* from the Capitaine brought me back to Earth.
I followed his gaze to the mast where the mainsail, torn in two by
the wind, flapped uselessly.

Without thinking, Henri and I ran to secure what was left of the
sail. Eve popped her head out of the cockpit but Henri shouted
something to her before she could protest about his going out on
deck again.

The Capitaine struggled to control the now powerless boat,
while Henri and I wrestled with the sail. Once done, we ran back
to the cockpit, where the Capitaine thrust the wheel into Henri's
hands while he frantically tried to start the engine. The boat was
all over the place as Henri fought the wind and his own inexperi-
ence at the helm. Thankfully, the engine started first time and a
grateful Henri handed the wheel back to the Capitaine.

We now ran on a small triangle of sail and a motor; barely
enough power to keep us going in a straight line. We had no hope
of outrunning the storm.

I so wanted to go below to Anna, my partner, but I knew that
I could do nothing other than make her feel worse. Later she
would tell me that she had lain in our cabin, clutching our passports as water dripped onto her through the deck, convinced
that I'd been washed overboard. Why else hadn't I been to see
her?

I waited for the moment when we would fail to crest the next
wave, and instead slide back down into the maw of the one behind
and from there . . . I felt powerless, defenceless and yet disbe-
lieving; this would be far too exotic a death for the likes of me.

For four hours we rode that storm, sitting silent in the cockpit, the Capitaine at the wheel and Henri and I waiting for the next disaster. Finally, having long given up hope of making the mainland, we found safe harbour in the lee of an island.

After tearful reunions between the men and womenfolk, we all gathered in the galley where we sat silently listening to the radio. Two other boats had been damaged in the storm and one had gone down; luckily they had found safe anchorage first.

We were drained and too tired to talk. Perhaps none of us really knew how close we had come to disaster except for the grumpy Capitaine and, as usual, he was saying nothing. He sat by himself, looking small and suddenly very pale.

'How bad was it really?' I asked.

'I've seen worse,' he said and lapsed back into silence. The only sounds were the radio and the rattle of a bottle against glasses as, with suddenly very shaky hands, the Capitaine attempted, none too successfully, to pour us all very strong whiskies.

SPOKE NIPPLES

Sally Dillon

Sally wandered the world for a few years, seeking adventure and trying her hand at journalism, public relations, and teaching university students before joining the Lonely Planet staff as an editor. She was given parole from the office for a short stint of research in France, where she cycled 3000 km with way-too-heavy panniers as a co-author of *Cycling France*, mastered the French for 'Yes I am married, but I'm travelling alone – it's for WORK' and dabbled in nude bike maintenance.

IT WAS MIDNIGHT. I WAS NAKED. AND I WAS FIXING MY BIKE IN A HOTEL ROOM, IN FRANCE.

I didn't have much choice. Although I'd managed the near-impossible feat of reserving a place on an early tour of the Font de Gaume's cave art the next day, my rear wheel had two broken spokes, with more threatening to pop. The bike shop was 'a few kilometres' out of town (which could mean anything up to ten) and wasn't likely to open before the tour. And the tour was sure to end just as the mechanic began his long lunch, giving me no chance to get my bike back in time to cycle the sixty kilometres to the next town. I certainly couldn't afford a day out of my research schedule, so I would have to change my own spokes . . . or miss my flight home.

I'd seen it done before; I had the tools. The naked part I hadn't figured on.

I'd cycled into town, wheel wobbling, at 9 pm, after a day of roadside repairs – broken gear cables, a puncture – and hills. I had managed to find Les Eyzies' last affordable hotel room and was insistent about checking it had a well-lit place to fix my bike. ('Yes, of course, out the back', the manager waved, looking vaguely puzzled.)

'*Vous êtes toute seule?*'

'Yes, I'm travelling alone.'

Raised eyebrows. '*En vélo?*'

'Yes, by bike; I'm travelling for two months.'

'*Ahh, vous cherchez un mari.*'

'No, I don't need to look. I'm already married.'

Confusion. '*Mais, où est votre mari?*'

'He's at home, in Australia.'

Horrified look. *'Mais, ce n'est pas l'habitude, non? De permettre sa femme voyager toute seule!'*

'Well, he had to let me travel alone. I'm working.'

'En vélo?'

'Oui. En velo.' Emphatically. Two months in France, and this whole why-are-you-travelling-alone thing is one of my most fluent conversation pieces. But I wasn't about to explain 'I'm researching a cycling guide', especially as it was his hotel I was testing, but mostly because my rumbling stomach was starting to drown both of us out.

Comprehension and a knowing wink. *'Ahhhh! Voilà! C'est une ruse.'*

He mistook my pained look for one of hunger and accommodatingly pointed me towards the restaurant most likely to be frequented by Les Eyzies' eligible men.

Loaded with pasta and an encouraging glass of wine, I wheeled my bike around the back of the hotel. Above a small patch of muddied concrete, bugs fought for space on the dim light. The warm glow the wine had given me cooled a little as I considered my options. It was 11 pm and the low light, chilly evening and concrete work area were conspiring to make a tiny, carpeted hotel room look like an excellent place to fix a bike. Sure it was on the fifth floor, but the manager was probably asleep or else propping up the front bar nudging his friends about this strange woman cycling *toute seule* for a few months.

I opened the door and tiptoed along the corridor, opening a set of heavy doors to the stairs, which wound tightly past the manager's room (*'Privée!'*) on the first floor. Hmmm . . . manageable. I propped the outside door open with a shoulder and wheeled the bike into the corridor. With foot wedging one of the next doors open, I arched over the bike, using outstretched fingertips to open the other door and then push the bike through in front of me, holding it upright with one knee while I eased the latch quietly into place. At the stairs I hoisted the frame under one arm and tried not to clack my cleated shoes against the stairs' metal edges or whack the handlebars into the walls. The bike had to go up on one wheel to manoeuvre around the corners, and then be retucked under the arm for the stumble to the landing. I slipped quickly past the glass door to the bar, praying everyone would be too deep in their brandy to notice me, and softly bumped my way to the top floor.

Inside my room, I turned the bike upside down, and stood back to admire my work, already feeling like a real mechanic. I'd lugged that piece of steel up five flights of stairs, without being seen; the light was great; the room warm; and I had just enough space between the bed, the wall and the basin to work in. This was going to work!

I rummaged for my nifty Hypercracker – a palm-sized gadget for removing a bike's rear cogs in just such an emergency, a trick usually requiring two very long spanners and lots of twisting, grunting and coordination. I went to lay the tool over the cogs. Oops – upside down wasn't going to work. It looked like a professional start, but it was obvious I'd have to lie the bike on its side for this to work.

Yes! Everything made the right kind of twisting noise. It all felt loose. I pulled the wheel out from the frame and the sprockets exploded across the room, shaking off their load of ground-up grease and grime in a kind of inverse Milky Way across the cream carpet.

I collected all eight cogs, transferring a fair bit of their grime onto my hands in the process. I tried to pick a blob from my only 'off-bike' shirt and managed to turn it from a fleck into a smear. Eeagh: should have removed the white shirt first. (Don't *all* travel writers wear white?) My sweaty riding clothes, already decomposing in one corner of the room, needed a wash anyway and would do as mechanic's garb.

I went to the basin to wash the grease from my hands, swiping a trail of black on the porcelain as I reached for the . . . hmmm, no soap. I put only a few dirty fingertips on the shower recess as

I checked for a cake of soap there. Grimy culprits held in the air, I circled the room searching for one of those little packs of soap (*savon, jabún, sabun, sapone*), a pack just like the ones I'd thrown out in a weight-saving frenzy that morning. This left me in a hotel with no stars . . . and no soap.

I sacrificed my travel loofah to the cause and at least changed the black to grey, then chewed and elbowed my way out of my shirt and levered my pants down with finger knuckles and toes. I kicked my clothes out of the grease zone, doing a little jig: 'I AM capable. Nothing can stop me!' I grabbed my bike clothes and . . . whoa . . . it had been a hot day, hadn't it? Smelly, sticky clothes, bike grease and no soap. Naked it was going to have to be.

So, nude, calm and collected, I started back on the bike. Just deflate the tyre and whip the spoke out. Well it was almost that easy; it took a bit of twisting to loosen the spoke nipple – the hollow screw that held the spoke into the rim – but it wasn't long before I had extracted the broken spokes from the warped wheel.

I'd bought some spares a few days before, after the last batch had snapped and I'd had to wait a day and a half for a bike shop to repair them. They were cheap and thick but they'd do the job, even if threading them was going to be a pain. I poked and twisted and passed spokes over and under one another, managing to avoid bending any beyond straightening.

A few twists of the spoke nipples and the spokes would be in place. I'd just have to true the wheel and sneak the bike down the stairs. Mission accomplished.

I started visualising clean sheets and a comfy pillow as I twisted the spoke nipple over the spoke. And twisted. And twisted. I wobbled the spoke, but it still didn't seem to want to settle into the thread. I peered into the nipple. What kind of stupid, stingy manufacturing practice was it to cut the thread only halfway down? Made by a bloke who only ever fixed bikes in a workshop full of vices and wrenches, no doubt.

I tried jamming the spoke up to the thread and holding it in place while I turned the spoke key. But the bloody thing still wobbled. Staying very calm, I crossed my legs and wedged the wheel between my knees, wrapping one arm around the back to pull the spoke towards the rim and turning the spoke key with the other hand. The spoke still wobbled. Knowing that getting frustrated wasn't going to help, I lay the wheel on the carpet, knelt on one edge, leant my head against the bed and heaved forward on the spoke as I turned. The spoke still wobbled. Swearing softly, I gave the wheel a few more heaves, banging the headboard against the wall, at least giving the manager some satisfaction that he was right about my '*ruse*'.

Patience. Stay cool, calm. Rocking back on my heels, I tried to look on the bright side. At least it was midnight; I didn't have to worry about a cleaner swinging open the door to find a nude woman straddling a bicycle and grunting and sweating.

It was midnight. I was naked. And I wasn't fixing my bike. And I was in a hotel room, in France, where everyone who knew anything about bikes was safely in bed. What to do now? . . . Of course! All of France may have been asleep, but in Australia most people were awake, and hopefully one of them would be able to impart a simple trick to get my bike on the road.

I loofahed off some grease and started looking for the phone. A sense of *déjà vu* swept over me as I amended my hotel description: no stars, no soap . . . and no phone. I had seen one, though, on the street corner outside the front door. I'd have to risk the grease all over my clothes if I was to get to that cave in the morning. Nude bike maintenance was one thing; prancing nude to the phone was another.

With my darkest, most grease-coloured cycling gear on, I crept downstairs, blackened hands hidden in case the manager wondered what I was doing wandering the corridors at midnight.

I dialled home. Peter, my husband, was getting used to this after all my earlier calls about the broken gear cables, the heat, the tiredness, the stupid bitch who wouldn't let me stay *toute seule* in the camp site because 'It's not normal!' No answer. Shit. Shit. Shit. I remembered Peter was out of town for the weekend. Okay. Stay calm. Who else can I ask about bike maintenance? It's 11 am on a Saturday. I know; call Simon at the bike shop. Now, what's his number? Damn; I don't have it. The directories number should be on the wall here somewhere. But then I remembered the awful recorded voice that speaks impossibly fast and costs about a dollar a minute; and always keeps you on hold for about three minutes. I decided it would cost me the same to call home and I wouldn't have to struggle with an operator not understanding my accent.

'Hi, oh Ian, you're visiting for the weekend. Hi, yes, I'm calling from France. I just – ah, Mum or Dad home?'

'Sorry love, they've just ducked out to the shops.'

Hmm. Parents might understand these things, but Uncle Ian? . . . I'll give it a go. 'Look, Ian. I wonder if you could just look up a number in the phone book for me? . . . Yep, sure – ah, I think they keep them in the corner, on the floor . . . Yep, that's it. I've got a little problem with my bike and Peter's not home so I need to ring my bike shop.'

'Hang on, I don't have my glasses. I'll get Dot. Lo-ove, phone. It's Sally: she needs you to look up a phone number.'

'Isn't she in France?'

'Yeah. Some problem with her bike.'

Grrr. Come on guys. Speed!!

'Oh. G'day Sally. How's it going? Enjoying the riding?'

'Mmm. Sort of. I'm getting pretty tired and I've had a few hassles with the bike lately. Actually, just wondering if you could quickly [subtly] look up a number of a bike shop for me? It's Ridgway's Cycles, in um . . . some suburb near Stafford.'

'Ridgway's, you say. Yep. Okay. Q . . . R. Rennie . . . Rhodes . . . Richard . . . Getting there. Ridgway. There's a lot of them. This looks like it. Ridgway's Cycles. That it?'

'Yes. Ta.'

'Okay. Well, here's the number.'

'Thanks Dorothy. Look, I'd love to talk, but it's after midnight and I have to fix my bike. Tell Mum and Dad I'll call them back another day . . . What? . . . Oh yes, I'm fine . . . No, really . . . Yes, I'm sure. Only a few little hassles. Actually, there's no soap, and I'm getting a bit dirty, so I've been fixing my bike in the nude.'

Oh dear. Shouldn't have said that. Wind it up, Sally.

'Look, Dorothy. Gotta go. Bye to Ian. See you.'

Okay. Bike shop. Here goes.

'Hi Simon. Glad you're open. It's Sally Dillon.'

'G'day Sally. What can I do for you?'

'Actually, I'm calling from France.'

Stunned silence. I remembered meeting Simon's wife and feeling in awe of the woman who had obviously managed to get a word in edgewise with Simon, even if it was just to say 'I do'. I took this unaccustomed opportunity to forge ahead. 'Ah. It's a bit complicated. I'm having trouble changing a few spokes, and I can't get onto Peter, so I was hoping you could help with some advice.'

'Sure, what's the problem?' said Simon at his most succinct. I imagined him standing in mild bewilderment in his shoebox shop, surrounded by tyres hanging from the ceiling and shelves cluttered with every spare anyone had needed since the days his grandfather had managed the shop.

So I told him about the spokes, leaving out the hotel room details, but explaining the need for urgent repairs.

'Yeah, look, spokes can be a bit tricky to get into the nipples at times but if you've tried all that and they still won't go in I reckon you might have the wrong size.'

'But I bought them from a bike shop! The mechanic said they were the right size.'

'Well, sometimes they look the right size, but it only has to be a millimetre or so out. Yeah, they can be tricky. It sounds like you've tried a few things to get them tensioned. Why don't you just pull them out and true the wheel; you should be able to ride 60 kays on the wheel like that.'

'Oh. Okay. Thanks Simon. I hadn't thought of that – I didn't think the wheel would take it. I'll give it a go.'

'Yeah – that should work. I wouldn't go jumping off any gutters though.'

Fair enough. I wasn't about to jump gutters anyway, laden with laptop, ten kilos of camera gear and a pannier full of tourist brochures and business cards. From here on, it all seemed pretty straightforward. If I could get to the next town I could leave the bike for repair while I checked out the restaurants and hotels. I just had to whip those spokes out and put the wheel back together.

Clothes off and newly laced spokes removed, I piled the cogs back onto the hub, slipped on the Hypercracker, fitted the wheel into the frame and turned the pedals. Whoa! Eight circles of steel with sharpened teeth exploded around the room. Must have done something wrong there. Let's just try again.

The cogs didn't fly quite as far the second time, and most of the excess grease had already been flung. What was I doing wrong?

It was time for the getting-dressed-using-teeth-and-toes wriggle again, so I could make my way I made my way downstairs to the phone.

'Simon. Hi. It's Sally again. Ah, I'm just wondering if I'm doing something wrong. I can't put the cogs together with the Hypercracker . . . Oh. Okay,' I said, interrupting his reply. Simon was obviously getting used to the concept of an international phone call for bike maintenance advice. 'So I just screw in that top nut and then put the Hypercracker on. Yep, I know the one. Okay. That should be easy . . . Actually, Simon, while I've got you on the phone, could you just refresh me on which spokes I'll have to tighten to straighten the wheel?'

And he was off. You could do it this way. If that didn't work, you could try doing it another way. I imagined a queue of people snaking out the door of his shop as he patiently explained all the variations, giving out little nods as each new person joined the queue. Buy a bicycle bell and you'd get the same attention to detail; you had to be prepared to spend an hour or so in the shop, but you'd get exactly what you needed. Then, having given me all the options, he told me the sure-fire way to do it.

'Okay. Thanks S–'

'Yeah . . . ah, you should be able to ride a few hundred on the wheel like that, but if you do happen to break another spoke . . . though if you true it right, you really shouldn't . . . but if you do, you just need to re-true the wheel. Yeah, well, just loosen . . .'

I listened to the explanation, hoping Simon couldn't hear my foot tapping. 'Okay. Thanks, I hope I don't need that adv–'

'You'd better get them all changed though once you get to a shop.' Before he could launch into a detailed explanation as to why, I cut in: 'Thanks Simon. That's great. Look it's one in the morning and I'd really better go. Thanks for your help. You're a life-saver.'

Up to the room, off with the clothes, and on with the Hypercracker. Easy when you know how. I trued the wheel and, bike intact again, I hoisted it under my arm for the trip downstairs, taking extra care not to leave black fingerprints over the wall. Upstairs I put the loofah to work – on me, the sink, the shower, then on removing the trail of tell-tale black smudges from around the room. I picked the biggest flecks of grease off the carpet between two folds of toilet paper and scrunched another few sheets to give the basin a final scour. I hoped the doormat, moved discreetly, would cover the worst of the grease spots by the door. Finally, I rolled into bed, still-grubby palms pointed at the ceiling, away from the starched white sheets.

Only a few hours later, I nodded goodbye to the grinning manager and rode gingerly to Font de Gaume. There they assured me the bike shop was only 500 metres up the road, so I left my panniers behind and rode in the direction indicated to me. Past the restaurant, the *foie gras* shop, the open fields and . . . the mower and motorcycle shop? With bicycles as a small sideline, I supposed. And I needed a wheel rebuilt? Ah well, I had to try my luck . . .

Inside the high wire fence an Alsatian snarled at me and I wondered whether whacking him with my bike pump would hinder my bike repair prospects. I settled on looking menacing and managed to get past. The mechanic didn't look too fazed by someone wheeling a bike onto the shop floor, so there was some hope. I explained the problem with the wheel, mentioning I'd need all the spokes changed. I showed him the replacement spokes I had, telling him, 'I think these are too short.'

He measured my brandished spares and the spokes in my wheel. *'Oui. Ils sont trop courts,'* he agreed.

'You have the right ones?'

He disappeared into a room hung with bike wheels and tyres in every size. My prospects were suddenly looking up.

'Oui.'

'Is it possible to fix the bike before lunch?' I could have kissed him when he nodded

'Mais certainment', and promised to readjust the gears and brakes as well.

Back at the Font de Gaume the ticket seller took pity on me hanging around outside and asked if I wanted to join the earlier, English-language tour. The best original cave art still open to the public; only 400 people a day allowed to visit; and somehow I was managing to get an earlier place. Fantastic. There is a god looking after travel writers. I'd finish my research, pick up my bike and make the plane home and back to work. Work – I wondered what they'd say back in the office if I told them about the time I fixed my bike, naked, at midnight, in a hotel room in France.

TURNING VEGETARIAN

Mason Florence

A native New Yorker, Mason migrated west to the Rocky Mountains to pursue his childhood dream of becoming a cowboy. After barely graduating from the University of Colorado, he gave up a budding career on the rodeo circuit, traded in his boots and spurs for a Nikon and a laptop, and relocated to Asia. Now a Kyoto-based photo-journalist and correspondent for the *Japan Times*, he spends around half the year on the road in South-East Asia, and free moments restoring a 300-year-old thatched-roof farmhouse in rural Shikoku. Mason has worked on Lonely Planet's *Hiking in Japan*, the *Kyoto*, *Ho Chi Minh City* and *Hanoi* city guides, and the *Japan*, *Vietnam* and *South-East Asia on a Shoestring* guidebooks. His articles and photographs appear frequently in newspapers and magazines worldwide.

**SOME OF MY MOST PROFOUND LESSONS FROM ASIA WERE
LEARNED ON THE TOILET.**

My education started in Japan. Bowing to the country's obses-
sion with the absurdly high-tech, even the lowly toilet has become
subject to space-age options about which even astronauts could
only dream. Japan's ubiquitous, computer-operated toilets are
armed with so many secret functions that undercover CIA operatives longing to decipher their codes liken these bathroom fixtures
to sitting on the Pentagon.

At the touch of a button on a fully armoured Japanese toilet,
the shameful sound of flatulence is drowned in the simulated
whoosh of a waterfall or trickles of water prompt the nervous to
overcome their stage fright, while an electronically heated seat
cosily warms your behind. Push another button and, reminiscent
of a scene from *Star Wars*, a metallic probe surfaces like a
periscope to deliver an upward burst of water that would shame
any European bidet.

However impressive these high-tech machines are, during my
first, wide-eyed year in Japan I vowed to 'go native' by adopting
the time-honoured posture of squatting. The Western-style seat
was a luxury I could happily live without. Along with the
hygienic considerations, I found squatting to be a more natural
position for purging the bowels, toning the thighs and toughening
up the knees. Before long I found myself at parties arguing the
merits of straddling ceramic holes in the East over the failings of
perching on porcelain thrones in the West. Friends were stunned
to see me proudly march for the 'Japanese-style' stall when an
upmarket hotel or restaurant offered the option to sit or squat.

Since my arrival in Kyoto, the Japanese had showered me with
plentiful bogus praise for my shoddy command of their language,
as well as my clumsy chopsticks skills. If only they had known

that this foreigner had actually mastered one of their most funda-
mental customs. A year in Japan had brought my proficiency in
proper heels-down squatting to a level – to the best of my knowledge – unrivalled among my fellow *gaijin*. If only Japan had followed the historical lead of China, where unfettered communal
crapping is the law of the land, my technique would have certainly received the praise it so richly deserved. I had the poise, the
aim and the confidence that, should there have ever been a con-
test, I would have no doubt triumphed, and maybe, just maybe,
the feat might actually lead to some sincere praise – right up there
with those who master Japanese arts such as karate, calligraphy
and the tea ceremony. In such a perverse competition, I might
have been crowned king of the pan-Asian art of squatting.

Finally freed from the shameful tedium of my English-teach-
ing job, I gathered my hard-earned yen and ventured out of Japan
for my first tramp through South-East Asia. Of course, already
steeped in the mysterious ways of Asian defecation, I was primed
to confront the toilets of the territory. Culture shock was not a part
of my vocabulary.

First stop, the Philippines. After a short stopover in Manila, I
boarded a cliff-hanging, rattletrap bus that groaned its way up to
the high mountain reaches of Northern Luzon. Two endless days,
two sleepless nights, countless breakdowns and dozens of fare-
paying farm animals later, I found myself in the middle of
nowhere. From here, I was to hike to the middle of the middle of
nowhere: the striking 2000-year-old rice terraces of Banaue.

A distant straw shack eventually resolved itself into my humble lodgings for the night. Across the bamboo threshold, I was
greeted by an ear-splitting pack of young Israeli travellers,
recently discharged from their compulsory military service and
arguing their way around the region, at that moment ecstatically
singing folk songs from the Holy Land with the ten-year-old
daughter of the proprietors. The only thing more astounding to
me than hearing this young mountain-bound girl who had
learned to speak Hebrew – and sing it beautifully – was the
havoc my dinner had started wreaking on my stomach. I'd

ingested two hearty helpings of spicy *adobo* – a stew in this case featuring the not-so-delicate meat of the Philippine fruit bat – washed down with several bottles of warm San Miguel beer. It was the red flag that my bowels had awaited: my first chance to take my squatting skills to the 'real Asia' was rushing toward me like a speeding train.

Exhilarated at the challenge that lay before me – my fated rendezvous with a bona fide hinterland toilet – I gave the guest-house owner that hopeless look which could only mean 'I gotta go!'. His response: a rusty old torch and a finger pointing out into the night. Buzzed and bubbling up inside, I stumbled out onto a narrow dirt path winding its way through the rice fields to an unlit rural outhouse. The eerie creek of the opening door gave me pause – perhaps I could survive until morning, even with the Israeli choir. But no, I would not back down from this challenge simply because of some silly Western aversion to rickety, slippery steps and a darkness that promised nothing but doom. I slowly entered the structure, gingerly, careful not to end up with a face full of cobwebs or a shoe sole covered in faeces. Closing the door behind me, I slid the simple lock into place. There was no turning back. The torch's anaemic beam revealed a daunting sight – my feet, two wooden boards, and between them, a seemingly bottomless pit.

Positioning myself was no easy task, but my year in Japan had empowered me with the fortitude I needed. I gritted my teeth, dropped my drawers and settled into a perfect squat. Now in my element, I switched off the torch and allowed my eyes to adjust to the darkness of the hut. I began to meditate on the stillness of my pastoral surroundings: the soothing song of cicadas, the gentle pitch of the wind coursing through the rice fields. As I spied the moon through a crack in the outhouse wall, I muttered to myself with pride 'If they could only see me now . . .'

But in the midst of this self-congratulatory trance, my reverie was shattered by a most unexpected sound and an even more unnerving sensation. No sooner had I begun to part ways with my dinner than warning bells shot from butt cheeks to brain stem. I couldn't fathom how, but a warm, steady breeze had just caressed my buttocks. Through my panic, I made out the deliberate sound of shuffling beneath the floorboards. Caught between fear and bewilderment, I scrambled for the torch, teetering on the planks as I fought the urge to stand at that most inconvenient of moments. I snapped on the torch, quickly directed the beam down between my legs into pit below and came face to face with the source.

Not a poisonous snake, not some undiscovered cannibal, but Sally, beloved sow of the village, and a particular favourite of the local children. Her whiskered snout deftly positioned just centimetres from my pasty white bottom, her open mouth jawing in expectation, it was immediately apparent that this clever beast had found a way to dine in style – her dinner would never touch the ground.

Having contributed to Sally's culinary experience for that evening, I beat a hasty retreat, shaken but secure in the knowledge that even a lazy, shit-eating pig couldn't dislodge me from my finely honed squat. I had been equal to the challenge. I also recognised this to be a most opportune time to start going veggie.

SPOOKED IN BRAZIL

Randall Peffer

As a boy Randy hopped a freight train out of Pittsburgh, Pennsylvania, his home town, in search of the King of the Hoboes. His mother claims he's still looking. A widely published feature writer, Randy has contributed to *National Geographic*, *Smithsonian*, *Islands*, *Travel Holiday*, *Sail* and *Reader's Digest*. He is the author of Lonely Planet's *Puerto Rico* and *Virgin Islands* as well as the coordinating author of *Virginia & the Capital Region* and a contributor to the first *Lonely Planet Unpacked* collection. He has also written National Geographic's driving guide to New York, New Jersey and Pennsylvania and two nautical memoirs, *Watermen* and *Logs of the Dead Pirates Society*. In addition to writing, Randy captains a research schooner and teaches literature and writing at Phillips Academy in Andover, Massachusetts.

THERE ARE MANY STRANGE WAYS TO FACE THE DARK ON THE ROAD. BUT IT'S THE MEMORY OF EVENTS BEGINNING ONE NIGHT ON THE COAST OF BRAZIL THAT STILL MAKES MOTHS FLUTTER IN MY MOUTH.

I had come here to research a magazine feature on Brazil's islands. After a day of trekking over the island of Ilha Grande south of Rio de Janeiro and listening to islanders spin their tales of local lore, I sat in the glow of a dying fire on the beach. As my new friends Adriana and José-Negro strummed their guitars and sang Caetano Veloso ballads, I felt something rising in my chest. The truth is that we had drunk way too much *cachaça*. Now, I felt at sea in cane liquor. My mind seemed to be drowning in the weird stories I had heard on Ilha Grande. Thoughts of ship-wrecked mariners rescued by Iemanjá, goddess of the sea, swirled through my mind. Images of the ghosts of an island pirate, Juan Lorenço, and his daughter/lover taunted my imagination. Then there was the story of a talking rock and a seven-note song a fisherman named 'My Saint' whistled to cast a spell on crabs that made them swim right up to his boat.

'Como vai?' asked José-Negro. 'What's the matter with you?'

'Do you really believe in all this mysticism?' I blurted.

'Of course, this is Brazil.'

I shook my head as if coming up for air. Adriana laughed softly.

'Don't worry, Americano, spirits are the music of Brazil; just give in to the rhythm.'

'And how to I do that?' I asked.

'Maybe it is time for you to talk with a *pai-de-santo* – a "father of saints" – a Candomblé priest,' said José-Negro.

'When?' I asked.

'I think the sooner the better,' said Adriana. Then she kissed me suddenly on the lips and disappeared into the tropical night.

Try sleeping after that exit.

░░░

I never saw Adriana again. But two weeks, and 1000 miles further north along the Brazilian coast, the taste of that kiss and Adriana's prophecy came back to me when I met TiTiTi. The black man's name is Brazilian slang for 'gossip'. He was a chef at the restaurant where I was eating on the island of Comandatuba. His shrimp *moqueca* was heavenly, and when he appeared at my dinner table to ask me how I liked the meal, I tried to compliment him by using the first Portuguese words that popped into my head. But when I pronounced his dish *magia dos santos, um presente de Iemanjá* (magic of the saints, a gift of Iemanjá), he gave me a withering look with piercing green eyes and mumbled something in the lilting Portuguese of Bahia.

'Como?' I asked because his words had sailed right over my head.

The baby-faced black man locked me in his stare.

'You think my religion is some kind of amusement,' he said more slowly, 'but you will see.'

Clearly, we were having some kind of misunderstanding.

'What's his religion got to do with this?' I asked the Brazilian friend who had brought me here.

'You spoke of magic, the saints and Iemanjá,' she said. 'He is a *pai-de-santo*, and he doesn't take such references lightly.'

TiTiTi had already turned his back on me and had begun to walk back to his kitchen when I called my apology in his wake. Could he forgive a stupid American?

He spun around to face me.

'You have a problem with the ancestors,' he said. Then he told me to meet him by the river at sunset the next day. We would talk to the saints.

░░░

I don't know what I had expected from my first encounter with one of Brazil's Candomblé priests, but this was not it. Before this moment when the *pai-de-santo*'s words flew in my face, my only association with Candomblé had been that strange night back on Ilha Grande and Adriana's romantic tomfoolery. Sure, I had done enough reading to know that Candomblé – like Haitian Voodoo and Cuban Santería – was a collection of Yoruba beliefs surrounding ancestral worship imported from West Africa with the blacks who had been slaves in Brazil until 1888. I knew that on New Year's Eve tens of thousands of Brazilians gather on Rio de Janeiro's Copacabana and Ipanema beaches. They launch offerings of combs, flowers, lipstick and even money into the sea to gain the good graces of their beloved Iemanjá, mother of waters. I had even heard people say that Candomblé was the unofficial national religion of Brazil, having well over 100 million believers.

But when it comes to the spirit world, I have always been a sceptic. Candomblé seemed little more than a collection of pretty stories. And in my experience self-proclaimed mystics were capable of telling you vague and fanciful things about your life . . . only before relieving you of a considerable number of dollars and sending you off to deal with your crumbling romance and a bad hair day on your own.

Still, as the sun dropped into the jungle the next day, I found myself heading to my appointed meeting with TiTiTi, feeling a bit unsettled and unable to shake Adriana's cryptic warning. When I found TiTiTi in the jungle bordering the river he wore a white turban and flowing white robes. He sat chanting at a table covered with a richly coloured cloth. Burning candles, joss sticks and monkey dung scented the mist already beginning to fume from the river. Mosquitoes cremated themselves in the flames with sharp hissing sounds. The scene reeked of Indiana Jones claptrap.

'This is going to cost me a bundle,' I thought, before the *pai-de-santo* commanded me to sit in a chair facing him.

He used a collection of cowrie shells called *búzios* for divination, casting his handful of shells on the table as if he were rolling dice. As his green eyes shuttled back and forth between the cast and recast *búzios* and my face, he quickly told me a number of things about myself.

'Xangô, the god of justice and thunder, rules your life. You are a man who believes only in free will. You earn a lot of money; you spend a lot of money. For you life is a road.'

These ambiguous remarks seemed like the prophecies of a third-rate carnival fortune-teller. And behind the earnest mask I had fixed on my face, I began to laugh at myself for having been anxious about my meeting with TiTiTi.

'What is my problem with the ancestors?' I asked in my fractured Portuguese. Then I waited for the *pai-de-santo* to dream up a tawdry fantasy while darkness rose out of the surrounding jungle.

'Your problem is that you don't believe in spirits, and one has been trying to contact you. It spoke to me yesterday. It is stronger than any spirit I have felt for many years, and it said that I must read you whether I want to or not.'

TiTiTi caught my eyes and continued.

'You can be sure I am not here as a favour to you,' he said. 'You are white, you speak Portuguese like an Argentinian, you are a journalist and you think this is all a big joke. I have a hundred things I would rather do than be here with you right now, but the spirit calls to us.'

I shrugged.

'It is a woman, and we must try to make contact.'

Terrific. I could hardly wait to hear what TiTiTi would dream up next. A powerful female spirit? I thought Adriana or a mermaid would be nice.

The *pai-de-santo* cast the *búzios* on the table with a clatter. His eyes darted among the shells, surveying their pattern and counting the number that were face up or face down.

'Did you know a black woman well when you were young?'

My answer was 'yes'. My mother had continued teaching during the first five years of my life. My caregiver throughout those years had been a childless African American woman.

TiTiTi threw the shells again. It was almost dark now and tree frogs were trilling all around us.

'Is she dead?' he asked.

I nodded.

The father-of-saints swept up the *búzios* and shook the handful of shells next to each of his cheeks. His eyes closed and he whispered words that sounded African. After a long time he cupped his hands open and let the shells fall in a broad pattern across the table. Seconds after TiTiTi had cast the shells, he still sat with his hands extended palms up in the act of releasing the *búzios*. More time passed, and I noticed that the black man's hands had begun to shake in the glow of the candles.

'Her name is Gertrude,' he said at last.

The breath in my lungs escaped with a piercing sigh. Tears welled in my eyes, and the hair on my arms rose to attention.

'Gertrude is the spirit watching over you,' said the *pai-de-santo*. 'She has brought you here to learn that she is always with you, protecting you.'

As he spoke, TiTiTi began to weep along with me. Both of us wiped our eyes and stared at the shells on the table as if at any moment the face of Gertrude Gaston might show itself in the shadows of the *búzios*.

At last the father-of-saints gathered the shells and cast them several more times. The *búzios* told us several more things about my life with great clarity and specificity. Truths that still catch in my throat when I think of Brazil. But throughout all that TiTiTi said, I only half listened.

In my mind I kept asking, 'How? How? How did this man 7000 miles from my childhood come up with Getrude's name?'

'Do you want to know your future or put a curse on somebody?' he asked after a while.

I shook my head. I said I'd had enough surprises for one day.

TiTiTi looked at me as if I had just set fire to a thousand-dollar bill.

The next day I found the *pai-de-santo* waiting for me at the boat landing as I prepared to leave his island.

'I have something for you,' he said.

He handed me a long necklace made of clear beads that gave off a white glow.

'What is this?' I asked.

'Wear this *aleke* for Iemanjá and she will protect you.'

I pulled out $50 to pay him. He had not taken any money from me yet; I was betting now was the moment when I was expected to cough it up.

'Keep your money,' he smiled slyly. 'You're going to need it.'

So how are my finances these days? Trust me, you don't want to know.

RIOTOUS TIMES

Virginia Maxwell

Virginia is the veteran of many travel disasters across several continents. Her wayward adventures have occurred in Europe, Asia, the Middle East and Central America. When she is not avoiding overly amorous camel drivers in the middle of a Rajasthani desert or attempting to prevent a (totally imaginary) theft of Rembrandt's *Night Watch* by a Canadian tourist, she looks after the production of Lonely Planet guidebooks to Africa, the Middle East, central Asia and the Indian subcontinent – and tries to prevent her son Max from following in her footsteps.

I SPENT A FAIR PROPORTION OF 1986 IN HEAVEN. The celestially named London nightclub, that is. An enormous, cacophonous, totally wonderful pleasure palace where many a poor traveller's – let alone poor Londoner's – budget was blown to smithereens, Heaven was the place in which to dance, ingest illegal substances and generally party hard at that time. It and I were the proverbial marriage made.

Getting to Heaven entailed sacrifice, of course, and my predilection for its delights meant I was forced temporarily to postpone my much-anticipated trip through Europe and get a job. A friend found me work behind the bar at the National Film Theatre, which, though menial, had a whiff of glamour – I once served Julie Andrews a G&T and Oliver Reed seven straight scotches. I was, however, homeless and sleeping on the floor of an eccentric friend. I managed to romantically ensnare a committee member of the local squatters association, who was concerned enough for my welfare that he insisted on breaking into and changing the locks of a council flat in Brixton for me. He was keen on bumping me up the national waiting list and getting me a place in salubrious Westminster but I liked the notion of living where the action was, so I chose Brixton.

The flat was in the infamous Moorlands Estate, scene of the early 1980s race riots, and I was one of the very few white people living there. My friend Isobel and I set up house and soon settled right in, smoking lots of ganja, becoming reggae aficionados and eating practically every evening meal at the local cockroach-infested Indian restaurant, The Star of India. Life was going swimmingly when I received a letter from my younger (and considerably more innocent) sister. She and a school friend were coming to London – could they stay with me? This was accompanied by a note from my mother, who laid down the law in no uncertain terms: If anything happened to Elizabeth and Jane she would blame 1. Colonel Gaddafi (Libya had just been bombed by the US and was threatening reprisals) and 2. Me.

I resolved to be on my best behaviour when the girls visited. Isobel and I cleaned the flat, got rid of all drugs and shopped for vegetables. I told Frank and Remy, our Rastafarian friends who lived on the next floor up, that we would not answer the door past 1 am and that they would be looking for us in vain at the Atlantic over the next week. (The Atlantic was our local, a rough and filthy place that harboured criminals of every variety. The first time I drank there I was so terrified of the clientele that for most of the evening I sheltered under the table, far too close to the verminous floor for either comfort or good health. After our first few months in Brixton, though, Isobel and I started to feel quite at home there.)

The day to pick Elizabeth and Jane up from Gatwick Airport arrived. I caught the train out in plenty of time. The plane was late but eventually they came through customs and I escorted them home. Clearly jetlagged, they looked to me like they needed a quick bite at the Star of India and an early night. This they agreed to.

We went back to the flat, where they showered and unpacked. After this, a vindaloo beckoned and we made our way towards our dinner destination. Almost as soon as closing the door behind us, I had a feeling that something was up and I soon worked out the source of my unease: there was no-one on the street. Now, in Brixton, there is ALWAYS someone on the street, whatever time of the night or day. I had just started to ponder this strange fact when we reached the junction of Atlantic Road and Coldharbour Lane, only to see at one end of Atlantic Road a large group of people yelling and gesturing in an aggressive manner. A demonstration, I thought, but I was wrong. For at the other end of the road was some type of armoured vehicle and a bevy of policemen in full riot gear, with shields and nasty-looking truncheons. It was an OK Corral situation and we were slap bang in the middle of it. In fact, it was a riot.

To this day I don't know how we managed to circumvent the local roadblocks that had been set up as soon as the riot began. I guess that due to its history, the police had been wary of cordoning off the estate and inciting further violence. Their strategy (of assuming that streetwise locals not involved in the riot would stay out of the way) would have worked if it hadn't been for me. The strange truth of the matter was during my months of living in Brixton. I had developed a perverse lack of regard for personal safety. I was totally oblivious to what was going on around me for most of the time. It was inevitable that if a riot were going to happen, I would get stuck in the middle of it. Elizabeth and Jane, quite oblivious to what was happening, were asking me about shopping destinations in Kensington as I froze, too terrified to do anything. One thing and one thing only was in my mind: what on earth was Mum going to say?

As the police moved slowly toward the rioters, who were getting louder and louder, I grabbed Elizabeth and Jane and looked around for a means of escape. The next thing to happen was quite spectacular. Two burly policemen in riot gear rushed towards us and pulled us into the nearest shop, which just happened to be the Star of India. The ensuing conversation went something like this:

POLICEMAN 1: Where the fuck were you three going?
ME: We were coming here, actually. What's going on?
POLICEMAN 1: There's a fucking riot happening. Brixton's been cordoned off, the station's closed.
ME: Oh.
POLICEMAN 2: Are you an Aussie?
ME: Yes.
POLICEMAN 2: Typical.

It turned out that the riot had started around the corner, when police had staged a drug bust at a squat and one of the black residents had been hurt. There had been another incident, too, on the High Street (though no-one in the Star of India seemed to know what this one was about) and the two had merged into an out-of-control situation. The policemen told us to stay in the restaurant until it was safe to go home and so we sat down and ordered – nothing, let alone a simple riot, could stop the Star serving up its noxious but strangely alluring curries. Eventually, Policeman 1 came back, ate a piece of our *naan* bread, and told us that we should scarper. The action had moved to another part of Brixton and we should be able to get home. 'Lock yourselves in and watch it,' was his valedictory comment.

And scarper we did. Isobel wasn't there – the fact that buses and trains to Brixton had been cancelled meant that she was forced to stay at a friend's place for the night – and Elizabeth and Jane, by this stage reeling with jetlag, fell asleep immediately. I sat in the kitchen, planning escape options if the estate were to be torched during the night.

Then came a knock on the door. A rather frenzied type of knock. Voice quavering, I asked who it was. 'It's Frank, man, let me in!' cried my Rastafarian friend from upstairs. I opened the door and asked what was happening outside. This was a bad mistake. 'They're after me, man! They've got machetes!' was his frantic retort. And indeed, the sounds of screams and machetes against wooden doors could vaguely be heard from upstairs.

By this stage, I was feeling quite frantic myself. 'Why?' I asked.

It would have been better not to know, of course. For it turned out that the secondary riot of the day had been triggered by Frank, who had abused a woman behind the counter at the local social security office for the fact that his dole hadn't been paid. (In fact, it wasn't due to be paid until the following day.) Unfortunately, this woman was the mother of the two leaders of the Moorlands Estate's most feared gang. They, quite understandably, had taken exception to the fact that Frank had called her something unspeakable (I never found out what this was) and decided that it was time to get rid of all Rastafarians from the estate. They had chosen to do this with machetes.

Frank flatly refused to leave our flat, and I can't say I blamed him. He assured me that no-one had seen him make his way to my place and that the violence hadn't turned on whites – yet. If he hadn't used the word 'yet' I might have felt reassured. As it was, I resolved to take the only action I could think of: I would single-handedly drink a flagon of Valpolicella and try to ignore the entire situation. Isobel and I had stockpiled these flagons when they were sold for a song following the infamous 'antifreeze in Italian wines' scare of late February. The threat of blindness or death certainly wasn't enough to deter us when it came to cheap booze. Frank elected to join me in my undertaking and so the two of us stacked the few pieces of furniture in the flat against the front door and sat in the kitchen doing our best to block out reality.

Our strategy worked. The next morning the two of us stirred from our Valpolicella-induced stupor to a quiet day and to the sounds of Isobel trying to open the front door and get through our makeshift barrier of a bookcase, a coffee table, a futon and a pyramid of Valpolicella bottles, at least two of which were empty. Elizabeth and Jane also woke, full of plans to descend on Harvey Nichols and see Trafalgar Square. Life, as always in Brixton, went on . . .

ROUGH RIDE TO ETERNITY

Mark Lightbody

Mark has travelled in about fifty countries. He has left all his money and documents on café table tops and under mattresses, been robbed more than once or twice, been eaten alive by bugs, suffered dysentery and diarrhoea (even publicly), been hassled by border officials and state police, and been called a woman by an extremely irate market vendor. He remains innocent but realises many travellers and untold numbers of citizens have scores more and far worse tales to tell than his.

Mark is currently working on *Canada*, *USA* and *Great Lakes* guidebooks for Lonely Planet. He has worked on previous editions of *Australia*, *Malaysia, Singapore & Brunei* and *Papua New Guinea*. He lives in Toronto with his wife, Colleen, and two kids, Trevor and Ava. Buses remain a favourite means of travel.

I REACHED ACROSS THE TABLE WITH BOTH HANDS. ONE GRASPED THE JUG OF COFFEE CONCENTRATE, THE OTHER THE JUG OF WARM MILK. SLOWLY, I POURED AN EARLY MORNING, EYE-OPENING BLEND.

Four of us were sitting at a small wooden table in a hole-in-the-wall café in a now-forgotten town in the central sierra of Ecuador, waiting for the dawn to break and the market to begin. Across the table the well-travelled young woman from somewhere or other was the only one talking. Amid countless fleeting conversations and chance meetings on the road, this never-again-seen stranger's words have remained with me. 'In Asia,' she said, 'everybody talks about how sick they've been. In South America everybody talks about their bus trips.'

Perhaps a year later, Carrie and I were in the middle of a writhing scrum, clambering aboard a repainted, battered, converted school bus. It was heading into the rugged Cajamarca region of the Cordillera Occidental of northern Peru. The bus would leave arid, sun-baked Trujillo, with its curb-side rows of preserved classic taxis, the moment it was loaded with all and sundry. Unless, that is, the driver then decided, characteristically, that he needed a little more breakfast.

It was December, the beginning of the rainy season up in the highlands, and there would be few visitors. Also, if luck were with us, the roads would still be passable and not merely recognisable.

Jostling with the crowd and their bundles of all things inanimate and otherwise, clucking poultry included, we slowly wormed our way in the direction of the door and ultimately wedged ourselves and gear through the opening. We muscled our way past rosy-cheeked, smoke-scented Indians beneath their omnipresent bowler-like hats, careful not to jolt their wrapped infants, a babble of Quechua and Spanish all around us. From our seat we were able, through the window, to do a little last-minute grocery shopping and were handed up a few bananas and a couple of buns.

The assistant satisfied himself that we had all paid our fares while the driver satisfied his stomach. Are these seemingly just-remembered meals viewed as potential last suppers and therefore obligatory? I wondered. Eventually, the bus pulled out and before long we were leaving the coast and the surrounding desert. The bus turned eastward and began to climb. The first several hours were uneventful. We were the only foreigners on the bus and, as had become expected (and not altogether unappreciated) in the rural, Indian areas, we were treated with indifference.

The air cooled and the road narrowed. We serpentined up and over the first set of ridges, many of the peaks at 3000 metres. But the bus rose further as it chugged into the fabulous *puna* or barren heights. Summits in the distance reached 4000 metres and higher. The bone-jarring pits and caverns in the road were periodically sufficient to send someone perilously close to the ceiling as well as random enough to free the odd potato from the bulging confines of one of the bags lining the aisle. From then on the spud would vanish and reappear, tumbling and rolling like a *campesino* full of intoxicating *pisco* in a town's main square on a Saturday night.

About this time I began to have intermittent concerns about the road. Its twists and turns had become increasingly tortuous, in perfect proportion to the ever more vertiginous slopes. Still, many of the other passengers demonstrated the altogether remarkable Andean capacity of being able to sleep profoundly while having their heads bounce uncontrollably and repeatedly off a rattling window.

The first signs of real trouble were agitated voices and a flurry of activity emanating from the front of the bus. Outside, the austere highland landscape presented an endless and grand panorama. While gazing at it with a sort of mesmerised stoicism, the developing drama took several moments to reach me and make itself known. The driver was surrounded by a heated debate. Almost simultaneously, words became linked to sudden, purposeful actions. They, in turn, were joined by the unmistakable grinding of gears. Within minutes all on board were focusing their attention on the rapidly intensifying proceedings. Very soon it became abundantly clear that we were in what bureaucracies refer to as a situation: the bus was heading down the mountain without the benefit of brakes. As it picked up momentum, fear and pandemonium engulfed us all.

My life did not pass before my eyes, but images from past travelling did. There was the carcass of a bus that had tumbled over the precipice and was resting awkwardly at the distant bottom of a vertical-sided valley somewhere south of Oaxaca in the Sierra Madre del Sur in southern Mexico. There were the bleached remains of a once multihued people-carrying cattle truck lying who knows how many hundreds of metres beneath the edge of a mountain track in barely mapped north-eastern Ecuador. There were the one-paragraph news stories skimmed over in countless restaurants while waiting for long-ago ordered *comidas* to appear, the terse, fatality-laden headlines flipping by like the device used in '40s Hollywood movies to indicate the passage of time.

I turned to Carrie and, for the first time in my life, could not speak. My jaws and lips moved but the words wouldn't come. I swallowed, or rather made the attempt, as the dryness in my mouth made that impossible. Trying again I managed to gasp, 'We should get to the back of the bus.' She nodded, her face ashen. Oddly, there were a few empty seats, a very rare occurrence throughout South America. We got up and struggled along with a few others who had had the same idea, stepping on or over the detritus and rubble collecting on the floor. What we were thinking as we staggered uphill to the back of the bus? That a hundred kilometres below on the valley floor we would be on the top of the pile and that this would make a difference? That there would at least be something recognisable to ship back home? You do what you can; it seemed better than passively waiting for the messy end to arrive.

Within the hurtling steel frame the echoes of the shrill, joyous laughter of its former school-kid passengers were now obliterated. The ceaseless Andean music played on, the pan pipes, the strumming guitars and plaintive vocals creating a cultural backbeat to doom. From every direction there came the shrieks of women: *'¡Dios mio!' '¡Dios ayúdame!' '¡Santa Maria!'* and various other panic-stricken utterances without intelligible meaning. The men shouted suggestions, recommendations, advice, admonitions and absurdities. 'Crash into the wall!' 'Roll the bus!' 'Try the brakes!'

The driver and his assistant were oblivious. They could have bailed out – the door was just a stride away – but they worked feverishly. The driver spun the steering wheel in one direction, then the other, all the while madly pumping both the brake and the clutch. He and his assistant worked together attempting repeatedly to jam the gearstick into a lower gear. At each attempt, the long stem protruding from the floor would bounce back after having made an horrendous crunching, rasping growl. The bus swerved and meandered back and forth across the road as they tried desperately to slow its speed or, at least, its rate of acceleration. Amid the din and chaos, another plan was hatched. The bus suddenly veered to the left side of the road, rushing towards any possible oncoming traffic and edged along the mountainside bordering the asphalt. The driver was going to skim the rock face to slow the bus, no doubt peeling back the side of the vehicle like a can of cheap luncheon meat. Several passes and near misses were made but the speed was too high and the precision required to navigate along the rough, pitted, rock-strewn side of the road far too great.

Next we careened back to our own side, the interior din having reached yet another crescendo and yet another grating tune having launched on the tape player. The implorations and exclamations of the passengers rose another notch. Whether one of these notions reached the driver or whether it was part of the master plan all along is neither here nor there, but despite the now terrifying speed of the bus and the lurching around hairpin turns, the outer two sets of wheels were manoeuvred off the semi-sealed road onto the altogether loose gravel of the shoulder. The lip of the cliff was no more than a metre away. The rough, pebbly surface provided some increase in friction.

At the same time, fortuitously, the road inexplicably flattened momentarily. The bus actually slowed slightly. The dust and stones were flying but, through the murky confusion and adrenaline haze, I'm sure I saw the rear passenger-side tyre actually hang over the edge on a couple of occasions. Nonetheless, the vehicle continued to slow marginally, degree by degree. Together the driver and loyal assistant somehow crammed the gearstick into third. We pitched forward, the engine screaming in complaint, but the hell on wheels blessedly began to decrease in velocity. From there a quick series of downshifts followed and we came skidding towards a halt.

When the bus finally taxied to a full stop we could clearly see from our vantage point, looking through the length of the still-intact passenger compartment, that the passengers themselves had fared somewhat less fortunately. There were several groaning bodies strewn along the aisle and numerous others who couldn't be described as standing, sitting or lying. Rather there were limbs and torsos tangled askew in clothes, luggage straps, bags and the various other flotsam and jetsam typically scattered throughout an Andean bus. A few of the bodies were not conscious. It was to those that the attentions of the still coherent and readily mobile were quickly turned. Several elderly women were gently picked up at each end and delicately carried over the debris to the open door. A couple of chicken feathers wafted through the air. Crying babies were passed from arm to arm and the limping or feeble were aided through the bus and down the steps.

Stepping down gingerly and squinting into the late-afternoon light I had a quick glance around. The landscape was a mix of scattered, brilliant, near-vertical gradients set amid angular chunks of virtual blackness formed by the long, irregular shadows cast by the surrounding mountains. There was little vegetation, just a dry, parched, rocky starkness. Dust was still swirling around the bus as it sat cooling on the pebbly shoulder adjacent to the road, no more than a couple of rotations of the wheel from a precipice of some several hundred metres. Across the road the passengers were collecting on a hillside softened with patches of stubby grass and graced with a thread-like but swiftly flowing stream. The water was only centimetres deep but it bubbled and splashed, foamed and soothed. It was alongside here that the faint, the dizzy and the visibly distraught were carried and eased down.

Bandanas were dipped in the cold water and dabbed on foreheads. With these and the cool air, the woozy were brought back to this world. The creek gurgled, but little was said. There was banging from the bus and glancing over I could see the driver and his assistant by the front bumper, their shirtsleeves rolled up. The driver was on his back, half under the bus fidgeting with something up in the wheel well. The assistant, meanwhile, was half on his knees, bent over the tyre and he too seemed to have a hammer in his hand. No sooner had the last collapsed passenger been revived (although there may still have been one or two imagining themselves at heaven's door) when the hush was broken by a confident bellow from the direction of the bus. '*Ya está reparado! Suban al bus!*'

The silence deepened. Everyone on the hillside looked up in a blend of astonishment, incredulity and dread. 'Come on let's go.' There was no mistaking the meaning of what we had heard or the no-nonsense urgency with which it was uttered. It said, 'We're wasting time, my time, and I am not going to put up with it. This is my gig and I'm running the show. Move it.' We slowly pulled our eyes away from the two men who were now standing in front of the wheel, casually wiping their brows with their naked forearms. Stunned, we glanced at one another, without speaking. For an instant nobody moved.

I looked around. The immense hillsides and steep canyons and gorges looked to be completely bereft of life more complex than something scruffy, green and herbaceous – the last representing the only visible characteristic differentiating the alpine growth from the alarmed passengers. I knew we were miles from any town. The stillness seemed almost to be daring us to defy the driver. And so, reluctantly dragging our feet and our misgivings with us, we all began shuffling toward the bus and its seemingly smirking door.

Once again fully loaded we recommenced the trip, with a little more stop in the heart-stopping turns and bends. Nobody spoke; there was barely any movement at all. The bus climbed and descended; we inhaled and exhaled. Time passed – whether minutes or hours was indiscernible – and eventually, down in the distant valley but still at about 2750 metres, a sizeable collection of rooftops could be seen glinting in the sunlight. Once in a while an open, slat-sided cattle truck laden with goods and people would pass by.

We drifted downward into town almost peacefully. The bus wound its way through the narrow streets of town amid the usual parting of pedestrians and a resigned burro or two. It seemed, though, that we were greeted with somewhat less nonchalance than was typical. It felt as though people were looking at us, as if we were part of a disbanding parade. We eased into the depot, nobody on board moving, as if it were a plane nudging up to the terminal and we had all been told not to budge. The instant the wheels finally stopped, the bus exploded into a cacophony of hoots, giddy laughter, smiles, pats on the back, hugs and handshakes. The passengers were all on their feet applauding. The driver had sprung from his seat and, turning to the passengers, stood beaming and basking in adulation as though he had performed a miracle. The assistant stood beside him equally proud. It wouldn't have been out of place had they bowed like actors on a stage. Never had such folly appeared so beautiful.

Regardless of the road travelled there is not much sweeter than death cheated, even if it be for just twelve hours and the rise and fall over the journey's next pass.

A DINGO'S GOT MY BREAKFAST

Matt Fletcher

Matt first began staggering around hotel corridors in the early hours of the morning when just eighteen months old. His most formative travel experiences were family holidays taken in small, rain-soaked English beach resorts (usually in the off-season), but despite many a lame Sunday afternoon stuck in the car park of some God-forsaken coastal pub with an irritable younger sister and a bottle of pop for company, his love of travel remained untainted. Trips to the wonderful northern coast of Spain in a VW van and an Inter Rail tour of Europe (which was really more of a test of endurance than a holiday) cemented an incurable wander-lust, and Matt has been travelling pretty solidly ever since leaving Art College with a strange rash and a 'Sportsman's Degree' in ceramics. Matt has updated a number of guides, contributed to the first *Lonely Planet Unpacked* collection and co-authored *Walking in Australia*, which forms the backdrop to his sorry tale.

THE DINGO, *CANIS LUPUS DINGO*, IS AUSTRALIA'S NATIVE WILD DOG. A natural scavenger, opportunist and candidate for my own personal 'World's Most Sneaky Wild Animal' competition, few other Australian species can claim to be the subject of so many campfire tales. Stories of their cunning, ingenuity, baby snatching and callous disregard for personal possessions are common. They may have been in Australia for a mere 4000 years, possibly as domestic canine escapees from South-East Asia, but they have more of than enough wild Australian in them to cause problems for the humble British trekker.

When we set off to Fraser Island, the fantastic sand island and World Heritage Site just off the east coast of Australia, we thought we had the dingo situation taped down. Dingoes are wild animals and those found on Fraser are a unique strain. They may be a delight to watch from a distance, but precautions must be taken. There should be no interaction whatsoever between people and dingoes as this breaks down natural barriers and leads to problems later.

What this means is that, like luggage in an airport, one should never leave food out in the open (or alone in your tent) for a moment. The skinny little bleeders will steal your sausages off the barbecue in the time it takes you to rummage around in the car for the ketchup. Put a bag of crisps down on the left of your deck chair to pick up a drink on the right and you might easily find that the crisps have disappeared.

Never leave your shoes unattended. Just like that cunning old bitch, Imelda Marcos, dingoes have a thing about shoes and collect them in similarly large quantities. Even the crusty trainers belonging to Bando, an old friend of mine – footwear that has been known to set off smoke alarms – became the object of dingo desire while he camped near Uluru. In fact, when in dingo country treat shoes like your food and keep them locked up, because to a dingo (which will, when push comes to shove, eat the tyres off a pick-up) they're pretty close to food. And if they don't fancy a nibble at the time they may just take them to save for later. Stories abound of shoe graveyards close to popular camp sites with large dingo populations nearby. One found on Fraser Island was apparently 'a weird and eerie place' (especially for the half-shod), with footwear of all shapes and sizes lying forlorn in a small, dry stream bed. Everything from half-chewed flip-flops to smart Italian walking boots could be seen, though not, alas, in matching pairs. Dingoes don't discriminate when it comes to footwear. Like a kleptomaniac in Woolworths, they'll nick any-thing.

The problem can be overcome by placing all shoes and food in the car or in one of the food cages now common in Australian camp sites with a dingo problem. We knew all this, but then Australia isn't bear country is it? And some Aboriginal cultures domesticated them didn't they, so they couldn't be that danger-ous? Sadly for us, sleeping in our cosy tent after a trek through the bush, we thought little of the dingoes other than that they were interesting wild dogs.

It was work on Lonely Planet's *Walking in Australia* that had led us to Fraser Island and our dingo-inflicted travel disaster. Typically, despite long-standing and frequent affirmations to my partner Clare that this trip would be leisurely and relaxed, my schedule required us walk a loop across the world's largest sand island in just under four and a half days. Six days to stroll across it would have been a joy, as an excellent network of trails links eight lakes – perched above the water table in the heart of the island – and there is much to enjoy. It is one of the finest walks in Queensland, rich in geographical wonders and wildlife, some wilder than others, but there you go.

We left Hervey Bay, cultural mudflat of south-east Queensland, with camping supplies for four days. We had a hard day's walk ahead of us – which really should be done over one and a half days – so on alighting from the ferry we paid no heed to the cold beers and wonderful setting of the Kingfisher Bay Resort (though the temptation to loiter was great) and trudged determinedly across deep sand, in the thirty-plus heat of mid-morning, towards Lake McKenzie. Truly one of the highlights of the island, the lake is stunning, and looked particularly warm, clear and inviting when we arrived in the heat of late afternoon. Waves of backpackers relaxed on its shore and overweight four-wheel-drive owners enjoyed what they clearly believed to be well-earned late-afternoon dips, but we had far to go and ambled past, sweating like packhorses.

Thirty minutes later we dropped down to Basin Lake. The well-fed turtles inhabiting this beautiful pool, cartoon-like in the still water, mistook us for tourists with food to throw away and rose to say hello. A little later we were serenaded by cicadas insects whose chirping vibrated across the forest in waves as thousands of these tiny creatures, hoping to mate, competed against their nearest neighbours in the fading light. Finally, as dusk fell and the forest darkened, we reached Central Station, our camp for the night.

Tall kauri pines, their trunks adorned with bird's-nest and elkhorn ferns towered over an excellent camp site equipped with hot showers (if you had the requisite twenty-cent pieces), gas bar-becues and free fire wood. We camped on an area of soft grass and cooked a sumptuous banquet of steak and sausages that had been defrosting in our packs all day. We ate heartily, devouring all our fresh food. What remained was a motley collection of dehydrated essentials: couscous (in two delightful flavours), a risotto, two-minute noodles (in depressingly large quantities), apricots, trail mix, nuts, crisps, chocolate and a kilogram of muesli, which I swore would get us going in the morning. 'Yes, going to the toilet,' Clare had said, but I'd chosen to ignore her.

It had been a hard day and we were beat. Perhaps that's why we didn't wash the pans properly. Perhaps we just got slack. Either way, sleep certainly came easy in the cool night, despite bedtime talk of dingoes, babies and shoe graveyards. Facing a dismal diet of desiccated rations – foodstuffs well known for bringing on bouts of mid-trek depression and wild restaurant fantasies – for the next few days, the last thoughts I had before drifting off into a deep sleep were of food, specifically, breakfast. Around midnight an uneasy feeling that something wasn't quite right permeated through a rather pleasant dream about Italian restaurants and Land Cruisers. At first, I got the sensation of a cool, pleasant breeze on my head and wet grass beneath my fingers. But I was in a tent, so what was going on? A sharp elbow in the ribs from Clare brought me round. This was followed by a bout of profound and aggressive swearing as she shook me and directed my half-closed eyes towards a gaping hole in the tent, close to where our food bag and cooking pans, not to mention my head, had once been. Clare was now out of the tent, hopping around as she pulled on items of clothing and swore with increasing volume. Another look at the hole and the penny belatedly dropped with a dull clang in my sleep-numbed brain: dingo.

I leapt out of the tent, subjecting my fellow campers to more profanity and a rare glimpse of a man sporting pair of cotton boxer shorts adorned with pictures of Santa's reindeer. By this time Clare had sighted the beast (who I know only as Damien) at the very edge of the camp site, silhouetted in the glare of toilet lights. Our food bag, that is, our food supplies for the entire trip, swung in Damien's mouth as he danced and skipped to avoid the rocks, sticks and walking boots (something of an error in retrospect) that Clare was hurling at him with considerable venom. I picked up a hefty rock and together we ran at him. Damien trotted away like a playful puppy, staying just out of accurate throwing range. We tried a pincer movement, but Damien had obviously played this game before and avoided us with ease, whilst sneering over his shoulder. If I'd had a gun I'm afraid I would have shot him.

Dingoes can run for miles and often will once they have grabbed food from a table, tent or car. They'll disappear in a flash with your dinner and the chance of your retrieving it (should you want to) is precisely nil. There is a story about a water-sports-loving dingo taking off down Seventy-Five Mile Beach (which runs almost the entire length of the eastern side of Fraser Island) with an inflatable mattress, which it dragged around for hours before giving up on it. Perhaps there wasn't a decent-looking surf break. Our Damien must have been full of ill-gotten gains already as he danced happily around the camp site and I got the uneasy feeling that he was taking the piss.

He didn't think much of our dehydrated rations (and who could blame him), but he did seem partial to a bit of muesli, which he clung to as everything else slowly poured from the shredded food bag. Every now and then, usually whilst Clare and I picked up further ammunition, he would pause to sample the joys of our tropical-fruit Alpen, our breakfast. It was a farce not lost on other campers who tried, half-heartedly, to contain their amusement. Some shouted encouragement, though whether this were for the dingo or us I'm still not sure. What I am sure about is that the sight of me running around a camp site in ridiculous boxer shorts shouting, 'that fucking dingo's got my breakfast' must have been pretty damn funny.

Eventually Damien got tired of making sport of us and after a particularly vicious onslaught from Clare calmly dropped the muesli, gave us a nonchalant wag of his tail and scampered off into the night. You had to give him credit for style.

Wrappers, part-eaten packets of tasteless dehydrated food-stuffs, our cooking pans and four walking boots lay strewn around the camp site. Our four-legged friend had demolished a packet of crisps, one of biscuits, some fruit and plenty of muesli, leaving the rest covered in canine saliva. We collected the usable remains, put them in a bag in one of the food cages, so thoughtfully provided and thoughtlessly ignored, and went to bed.

In the morning we tallied up the toll from the raid. There was the gaping hole down the left side of the tent which, as our bodies were testament to, provided Fraser's mosquito population with a happy hunting ground. Worse, judging by the dark, foreboding sky, it would rain at some time during the next three days. (When it did, my taped repairs didn't cut it so we got wet.) Ignoring the odd dingo-bitten packet here and there we now had left six meals, some biscuits and an apple for the remainder of the trek. And no breakfast since Damien had taken such a fancy to it, so every morning we awoke with tight stomachs and looks of deep depression as we shared another meal of 'Special Thai' couscous or 'Authentic Italian Tomato Risotto', both of which tasted so bland they would make Egon Ronay weep.

Two days later we met a ranger out on patrol and related the incident. He said it was uncommon, but as more people flock to the island the problem gets worse. Despite an information campaign to educate visitors dingoes have become accustomed to being fed by tourists who see the animals as not dissimilar from boisterous domestic dogs. Competition for these handouts is fierce and once an animal cottons on to the gravy train and loses its fear of people the trouble begins. In 1998 an eighteen-month-old baby was dragged from a tent on the island, though she was saved by her parents. Problem dingoes are shot.

I suggested that every tourist visiting the island should be given a sling shot specifically for the purposes of keeping dingoes wary of humans. After all, I explained, a friend of mine had admirably demonstrated the importance of establishing people as 'top dog' in a similar situation in Indonesia, though by using a big stick and running towards a pack of wild dogs screaming like a banshee. The ranger was less than impressed with my suggestion of arming tourists and my friend's tall tale, but said he'd report the dingo incident. I got the impression he thought we were yet another pair of dumb tourists who'd learnt a little bush craft the hard way, which is fair enough really.

UKRAINE UNDONE

Debra Herrmann

Debra left behind an existence that lacked meaning in Melbourne, Australia, for the journey of a lifetime, taking years to travel through more than thirty countries, stopping occasionally to photograph, sketch and earn some pounds sterling. In late 1998 she returned to the Ukraine wielding a pre-issued visa and, despite a failed paragliding attempt, a bomb scare evacuation and more visa problems brought on by a Black Sea blizzard, managed to leave, return to Australia and take up a role in print production at Lonely Planet's Melbourne office. She is now committed to a quiet life and legal travel.

IT WAS A RACE AGAINST TIME FROM NAKHIMOVSKY PROSPEKT. I HAD to catch that train. I had the correct platform number; I could even confirm the destination as Kyiv. Arriving a few minutes late might have done it. Burdened beneath twenty-two kilos, I had burst into the compartment with all the grace of Frankenstein's monster. On being shown my ticket, the women sipping tea had advised all was well, nodding emphatically in tandem over railway issue *chay* glasses.

Only when the *provodnitsa* rolled back the door did I fear there'd be trouble. As she waited in the corridor, the woman beside me gave me a clear warning – a hand from an imaginary pocket, rubbing thumb over four fingers, a shake of the head. I could have accepted their offer to disguise myself as a guard and sleep in the provodnitsal quarters where customs wouldn't check, but it might have been a trap. Even if they were true to their promise that I could sleep to Kyiv I wouldn't know what trouble lay ahead in trying to leave Ukraine without a visa.

I was convinced I'd done my research. Warsaw's Ukrainian consulate, my guidebook and Intourtrans, a subsidiary of Russia's largest travel agency all concurred: I COULD get a visa at the border. Although it was a risk I'd sooner not take, my options were few. To comply with Russian visa requirements I had bought a one-way ticket out of Russia into Ukraine. This was back home, where I couldn't know the Ukrainian consulate in Moscow would refuse me a Ukrainian visa. No visa would be issued without a ticket out of Ukraine to match my ticket in. Yet a ticket to leave Ukraine couldn't be purchased unless already in the country and I couldn't even enter Ukraine without a visa – unless I found one at the border. I was confident; the *provodnitsas* were not: 'No visa, not at border. *Nyet.*' But they were train conductors, not customs officers, and to them I was a walking bank.

I felt the bundle of low-denomination US dollars still nestled in my right sock, stashed last night after I'd fled from the bargaining table. On hearing their furious knocking at the toilet door it was, in hindsight, a comic reaction to being placed on alert by the backpacker's sixth sense (I call it extortionary perception). The *provodnitsas'* deal might at least have brought some rest, I mused beneath sleep-denied eyes.

The guard waltzes along the platform towards me taking steady, measured steps. His upturned hat reveals a selection of cigarettes, which my eyes follow, left . . . right. With a flourish of the wrist, it sweeps to a stop just below my chin. He takes a bow. Laughter breaks through the entertainer's smile, the stench of stale spirits riding with it. I hadn't expected Ukrainian nights to end at dawn. It is true that here both your days and your lifetime can be short. I smile nervously hoping such hospitality might wave me on with a visa.

I had arrived at the Ukrainian border. A quick survey of the station confirms I am the only passenger to leave the train, albeit not entirely by choice. My gaze fixes on the entourage of uniformed men who had parted me from my pack and passport, now disappearing into the station. Behind my right ear I hear the train shudder as it slides off in the direction of Kyiv. The mist shrouding the tracks fades with the rising sun, revealing a single, ghostlike figure. The elderly woman ambles on down the line, a thin scarf covering her head, her lips moving in conversation with herself. Her left hand had tried to sell a bottle of vodka; her right, three dried fish.

'*Afstraleeski.* Kangaroo,' I hear, feeling suddenly harmless. My passport must be close. Maybe a visa too? Patiently I wait for the procedure to begin. It should be straightforward. The floor is mopped carefully before me. Within minutes it is mopped again. Swirling movements of the broom lure me into a state of near hypnosis. The guards usher me behind the wooden docks. Have I been arrested? I scan the room for a telephone or my vodka-breathing friend. I learn there'll be no visa issued here.

Is this deportation? I'm being sent back to Moscow! I wave at my passport, still firmly in the hands of a guard already on board the train. Desperately I splutter *'Ya . . . nyet viza! Nyet Rhooski viza'*, one hand flapping at my passport. The guard stands resolute, with the look of someone charged with the care of a performing seal while having no fondness for seals. A second guard places my pack beside him. Without a new Russian visa, I'd be illegal. My previous visa was gone, surrendered as the train left Moscow. This journey would make an illegal alien out of me.

'Ochin bloha!!' I use the few negative statements at my disposal. I launch another plea: *'Mozhna viza.'* I demand to call my consulate and watch my options drain away as the station slips behind me. The guard positions himself outside the compartment, determined to oversee my journey. Did he really believe a wayward backpacker in a peeling vinyl jacket could be a threat to his nation's security? As if to show he's slightly overestimated me, I plug in my headphones and resolve to slide into alienhood with a St Petersburg dubbing of Depeche Mode while searching my guidebook for disclaimers.

When my Russian visa was taken, I ceased to be of Russian concern. Nor was I about to concern Ukraine. Inhaling deeply, I reason against fear. These are independent nations, since the Soviet superglue that held them together had crumbled and collapsed. Rules must be in place for travel across the new frontiers. There must be some mercy shown to those who fall between the cracks. The amount of misinformation around would certainly warrant it. . . . It is a meek rehearsal of my own defence.

The journey lasts less than an hour. Flags on guards' uniforms reveal I'm still in Ukraine. Another small village on the border. I ask for a telephone and get my own guard: tall, blond and not yet twenty, with freckles that deride the severity of his uniform brimming beneath the broad visor of his military-style cap. I follow him through the village as he asks for the way to the telephone exchange from curious locals. It's clear I've disturbed the peace.

My trembling fingers catch in the rotary dial. I gamble on correct area codes. A recorded message plays. In moments the line falls dead. Dialling again I reach the official, his broad accent surreal from where I stand. 'I think I'm having a deportion . . . deportment . . . deportation . . .' Where am I? I fumble for a map. 'A small country border town . . . must be near . . .' CLICK. In dire rage I try the next booth, where of course there's no dialling tone as it isn't my booth. I try again in the first booth: no line. I would have to clamber back to the counter and pay for another. Frustration compels me to throw down the phone and kick the door, creating a scene of passing interest for those standing by. The guard ushers me away.

Hours seem to pass. I study the guards going about their duties while I take solace in a chocolate bar. My first trip overseas and now this. It was the antithesis of the independent travel towards which I had aspired. I had little money, no real language skills, no Russian connections and no yearning for souvenirs. Was it too much to expect to see and meet people, to get some opinions from over the Cold War fence? I wanted to put to rest the paranoia I'd been programmed with in my youth. Cold War kids had to be curious. You can't grow up threatened with nuclear annihilation and let it all pass without trying to understand why.

Ukraine held a different appeal. Beyond the Black Sea, Odesa's Potemkin Steps, the Crimean palaces of the khans and the sacred *lavra* catacombs beckoned. The capital, Kyiv, was the mother of mother Russia, its ancient, spiritual source. The city that had given rise to a superpower had been consumed by it. Territorial clashes throughout history had carved new boundaries and left scars, entrenched alcoholism and hunger, long before Chornobyl. Yet now after centuries of oppression, the resurgence of Ukrainian culture was under way. Kyiv had emerged again, its glittering gold and silver domes and Byzantine mosaics beckoned like a traveller's buried treasure.

However naive or noble my intentions, I have to concede my travel plans were slowly coming undone. Testing security I venture outside. Seconds later the young guard appears and promptly seats himself beside me. I smile at the arrival of company, albeit uninvited. Moments pass, feeling as awkward as on a blind date. He smiles, shaking his head, seeming to share disbelief in my circumstances . . . or perhaps at the living proof beside him that Westerners are *stranny*.

We watch dogs run along the tracks and birds dive-bomb empty freight carriages from trees. I offer bread and conversation. The bread is politely refused but I learn that he's eighteen and went to St Petersburg, too, when he was four fingers old. We speak new words and talk about music. Viktor Tchoi died before my new friend could see him perform. I offer my Walkman. He produces a dictionary perhaps twice his age. Eagerly he looks up a sentence in Cyrillic, the English translation to which reads, 'What mountain is this?' My laugh reflex aches on revival.

I'm instructed to buy a ticket by the guards who still hold my pack and passport. I can now wait with local travellers and soon I realise I'm being discussed by those around me, among them a young Asian Ukrainian girl and her partner from Vietnam, who is illegal too. She answers the questions of the three elderly babushkas seated together opposite, their curiosity as bold as their presence.

The late afternoon train arrives. My bags and I are placed aboard, my passport returned. I ask for some documentation, a certificate or letter to announce my sudden, uninvited return, but I receive nothing. The guards wave me on and the train soon departs. In eight hours I'm back in Kievsky Vokzal. It's midnight. No visa equates to no hotel. Fortunately, the station seems to be the respite of choice for the homeless and travellers alike. I fall asleep on a plastic chair, too tired to keep the mandatory one eye open.

Sunlight streaming through a grimy window wakes me. I stow my pack and buy enough *zhetony* to cover the day's metro travel, starting with a trip to the Australian consulate. I'd called before leaving Moscow, hoping their advice could direct me towards the better of two bad options. Should I stay illegally in Russia or leave with a chance of getting a visa at the border to avoid illegality in Ukraine? Now I'd created a third option: being illegal in both Russia and Ukraine.

I'm greeted by the official whom I had called earlier and explain how I came to gatecrash two nations in the space of sixteen hours. I had to leave Moscow: I had a ticket, my train was departing and my Russian visa was due to expire at midnight. I'd sooner go than wait out the weekend with no visa for Russia or Ukraine. I had no 'official' accommodation, insufficient funds for an Intourist hotel (without a valid visa they may refuse me anyway) and I could expect problems changing money. The border visa had been my best, indeed my only, option. I just hadn't taken the right border crossing.

The consulate advises that I should report to OVIR (the Department of Visas and Registrations). Extortion bells ring again. I've heard how OVIR charges dearly for late extensions of visas or mysterious insurance. OVIR would open later that morning so I venture back to the Ukrainian consulate hoping again to procure an emergency visa and then a ticket to argue my desire to leave. It's no surprise that I have no chance of getting a Ukrainian visa unless I first have one for Russia.

OVIR had opened minutes ago. The overheated room is already crowded with immigrants and Russian would-be travellers. African, Middle Eastern, Central Asian – the mix of peoples is an exotic contrast to the pale, city-weary Slavs on the streets outside. I take my place among this cast of extras. A woman seated in a congested corner records names on a sheet of ruled paper. I watch mine encoded in Cyrillic at the end of the second column. No-one has left the room in twenty minutes; with a list this long it would be my turn on Thursday. Desperation negates patience. Distress is the cure for shyness. In emphatic English I impress the importance of my case on the list-maker, which has the surprise outcome of instant service.

Within moments I find myself in a room with two interrogators. I produce a dishevelled photocopy as proof I once had a Russian visa. I'm told it is not a visa . . . or perhaps that it won't work as a visa. I reply that I have left my visa at the border. They ask how I'd arrived in Moscow. I try to explain but communication breaks down. I'm then asked the whereabouts of my husband.

As no husband transpires, the call goes out for an English speaker and a volunteer steps forward: an elegant man in his mid-thirties, who might have been born in the trench coat he was wearing, so well did it suit him. 'They won't give you a new visa,' he conveys. 'No, you can't leave'. I should take my problems to Sputnik, the headquarters of the former USSR's official youth travel agency, where I might contact a representative of my travel agent based here in Moscow. OVIR argues that I am my travel agency's problem, my predicament their fault. I should not have been sold a one-way ticket to Ukraine. Despondently I leave OVIR. I am just a tourist needing a visa. Why involve so many people? The trench-coated mathematician offers to escort me. He is running early now that his English skills have fast-tracked him at OVIR and Sputnik is near the academy where he is based.

Riding the metro seems second nature now. Moscow's underground train network is efficient and user-friendly, provided you plan your route ahead, interpret the signs correctly and surface at the correct exit – quite an analogy for a safe Russian holiday. Some stations resemble galleries, with bronze sculptures, heroic mosaics and chandeliers adorning marble halls; the underground journeys of Muscovites were ennobled by art. A grand setting for each traveller's internalised drama or comedy, each face hints at its wearer's own story. I keep my own hidden, resting my forehead to contemplate on a carriage support bar. A burning sensation takes hold of my forehead as my thoughts deviate towards despair.

We surface and pass a line of women selling pens, lighters, breads and hand-knits. It seems anything can be bought or sold on a footpath now. Gone are the queues of buyers, replaced by clusters around Western luxury goods or prospects for dinner. 'It's Gagarin,' the mathematician says, directing my eyes skyward towards a monument to the first cosmonaut. My fear is disarmed, converted to awe at its grandeur. Gagarin had been frozen, magnified, chiselled . . . and was now poised to eject into space. I fantasise about an 'eject now' button and thoughts of latching onto the statue's ankles to make good my escape. Reality and the maze of overhead electric bus wires deter my imagination.

We arrive at Sputnik and enter a small office with a handful of industrious staff. We are directed towards a tall, robust woman conversing on her phone in German. She promptly advises that she cannot help; I should return tomorrow and ask for Alexeivitch. With slight compassion she suggests that I book myself into a hotel and presents me with glossy brochure detailing tariffs that would challenge my credit limit. I raise the prospect of a charge towards the border. 'No. You can't leave.' She tells me strongly that I have no right to be here and, without a visa, I have no legal right to leave. I slump into the chair while she makes a reservation.

The hotel receptionist searches my passport. She notes the absence of a visa, regards me with suspicion and reads the letter supplied by the agent. After a phone call she checks me in. The overpriced room is sparsely furnished, a small bunker with high concrete walls and ceilings.

With the first light of morning, I return to Sputnik and am directed to Alexeivitch, a young man clad in a black leather jacket. Presenting me with a bilingual business card, he introduces himself as Alex. His dynamic charisma reminds me of an off-duty game show host. He speaks flawless, very British English. On learning my nationality, he says he enjoyed my city and loved the penguins on Phillip Island. I confess I haven't been to Phillip Island.

Alex ushers me into a road-weary Lada with custom-built driver, a man in his late forties wearing a faded blue beret, with stubby yellow fingers implicated in the demise of many cigarettes. He silently awaits direction from Alex. As we swerve off the curb into traffic my optimism revives: I might just have caught the getaway car.

The Australian consular officials were perplexed. Border issues between Russia and other former members of the USSR were new; they had not seen a problem like mine before, nor did they wield the influence to have me released. 'You'd better call your parents,' is the final advice, ' . . . and ask that they be prepared to pay a lot of money.' I contemplate the humiliation of coverage in local papers as my father reaches into his life savings to pay the rising costs of livestock, farm machinery and the freedom of a daughter.

Next we visit the Department of Foreign Affairs. We are out of there in minutes. I have neither the inclination nor the curiosity to ask what had transpired. Still with no exit visa, it wouldn't be good news.

We resolve to head for the airport. I return to Intourtrans, the travel agency for international ticket sales. I'll take the first flight out, where being less a factor than when or how soon. I have a Romanian visa, Hungarian visa, Czech visa; my Polish has expired; I no longer need a visa for Slovenia or Estonia; as of six weeks ago I was exempted from a Lithuanian visa. Alex's charm and language skills unlock a wealth of advice from the girl behind the desk (whom I had seen previously with no success). Like the consulate in Warsaw and my guidebook, Intourtrans' advice was that I could get a visa for Ukraine at the border. Alex requests that she check again and the same information results. I commit to Aeroflot and Alex awards the consultant a fluffy clip-on koala which is received with delight.

En route to Sheremetevo-2 airport, Alex briefs me on how to behave over the groan of the Lada engine. 'I'm not going to ask you to cry but . . . act like you are upset.' My eyes glaze over at the mention of an emotional outburst, all inspiration for which has long since passed. My mental function has reverted to an almost mechanical set of reactions, responding to nothing outside of the immediate. Had I not acted upset enough before now? This last piece of advice seemed to me to amount to an admission that I was in serious trouble.

At Sheremetevo-2 we reach the customs office. The voice behind an archaic speaker is barely audible, the exchange of words brief. 'No. They say you cannot leave,' Alex translates.

With my pack beside me and ticket in hand, I would still go nowhere without an exit visa. In the fading light, the Lada heads back towards central Moscow. I sense Alex's regret in taking me on.

We arrive in a concreted car park. The building before me – one of Stalin's 'Seven Sisters' – inspires awe. Social Realist architecture – with its hierarchical construction, pointed spires and floodlights – could seem more Gothic than Gotham City. Stalin-era urban planning had streets radiate from each Sister situated at strategic points in Moscow, assuring maximum visibility for all former Soviet government departmental buildings. Nowadays, people like Alex had offices here, on the higher levels. I could stay here overnight. Before leaving Alex advises me against answering the telephone until his call in the morning.

The office had all manner of conveniences, including a microwave oven and a shower with hot water. Luck had tapped me gently on the shoulder. The view from my window is magnificent. I watch the early evening light fade while green and orange floodlights take hold, eerily illuminating the building just beneath the glass. I've been stationed in an almighty watchtower. Looking down onto streets below, I see Moscow's evening unfold, people at street level unaware of my presence let alone my problem. As my consulate had pointed out, with no visa, legally I did not exist.

Barely an hour after phoning the next morning, Alex reappears with a plastic bag. The sandwiches were made by his mother. 'She wishes you luck,' he said, as I gratefully take the heavy slices of rye bread and cheese carefully prepared by the hands of someone I'd never meet.

Again we arrive at the consulate. The now familiar consular official equates my predicament with that of the boat people, those caught illegally entering Australia from the north. That I am not a refugee from my country, just a tourist in a spot of trouble, seemed irrelevant. I am hit with the sudden realisation that if

Russia had adopted the policies of my own country, I'd be interred, potentially for years.

The consulate had devised a solution. Her name was Oksana and she had a reputation for working miracles. All references to her conjured an image of a woman of indomitable strength – like Catherine the Great, she might bend horseshoes in her bare hands – in reality Oksana was a diminutive blonde in a brown tweed suit wearing heavy blue eyeliner. Too smart for fashion, sassy in a Slavic sense, her sharpness of wit inspires hope that she can cut through the most binding red tape.

Full diplomatic assistance ensues with a luxury sedan bearing special registration plates. The back gates swing open and security wave us on as we speed off to OVIR. We bypass the waiting room crowd and following directions procured from a staff member we climb the stairs to management. Oksana's influence can not only open doors, it also allows us to climb stairs.

We are ushered to a room behind double doors. A big man sits at a large wooden desk – his heavy jowls the portal to bad health. All the symbols of influence are around him: mountains of files, subservient staff, valuable paperweights and the high-backed chair of chiefdom. OVIR's chief was the archetypal chief, a frightening almost comic figure holding a phone in each hand – one red, one beige. Behind him stretches a magnificent tapestry of the double-headed eagle.

A barrage of Russian dialogue begins. Oksana. Alex. Oksana. Alex. The Chief returns fire with angry questions and the thumping of a heavy hand. Oksana presents the photocopy of my Russian visa then my passport. The Chief looks at it, then at me, with irritation and disdain. I try not to look back. My pack is on my knees and I lean slightly forward onto it while words pass like weapons over my head. I feign exhaustion, letting hair fall into my eyes while starting to rock a little back and forth. It's a genuine sign of mental distress, which I hope will succeed where tears might fail. Soon Alex falls despondently silent. I sense a concession.

Oksana continues to argue, in a gentle but sure manner. She gestures towards my passport, the visa held by the Chief. His expression remains unmoved, unrelenting. A few minutes later, we leave.

Outside the double doors, Alex and Oksana turn to me, their faces flushed with relief. 'You are free to go now,' Oksana says with a wry smile, 'but you must leave immediately.' I wonder who she really is or what her business card might read. Alex directs me to the window where I can find my exit visa. I already have the required photo. I'm told the US$20 it will cost is incredibly low.

Oksana explains that I am being released because I am young and Australian. If I had hailed from one of the newly independent Baltic countries the situation would be grim. She knows of people kept in Moscow for years. Under the USSR the Baltic countries were regarded as troublesome republics; their citizens, if found here, were prevented from returning to their homes, families or jobs. Caught in the wrong place at the wrong point in history they have their own special punishment.

Alex attributes our success to Oksana. It was the combination of her arguments and her style that had persuaded the Chief. His burly exterior and cast-iron resolve were known to be permeable to the charms of a lady. He also assures me that I'm free to return to Russia in the future. We return to the consulate in the diplomatic car past the Bolshoi theatre. I yearn for my camera, for that photocopied visa left at OVIR. Now that I can leave I crave souvenirs.

En route to the airport Alex concludes, 'At least now you can understand. The history of the Russian people is a history of people fighting against a government.' In just a few days I've experienced a new level of frustration, a futile waste of energy that must be an integral part of life for everyone around me, perpetuated by those whose job it was to help.

I sweep through customs and check my bags. A euphoric sense of independence returns as my feet leave the tarmac. I reflect on my few hours in Ukraine, a preview I never should have had. A brief chance encounter with Ukrainian life along the newest of borders. Ironically appropriate, given that 'Ukraine' translates to 'borderland'. My only souvenir is a *hryvnia* note. The new currency was, I'd learn later, introduced that month. The face of Khmelnytsky, Cossack invader, rebel and national hero stares out defiantly, daring me to return. Sure, but only once I am prepared for Ukraine and Ukraine is prepared for me.

TOOTH

David McClymont

David grew up in a small fishing village on the west coast of Scotland. In 1989, after studying graphic design in Glasgow, playing pop star in London and working as a vegetarian chef in Paris, he accidentally boarded an Air India flight to Sydney. He has lived in Australia ever since. David contributed to Lonely Planet's *Out to Eat Melbourne* and *Australia* guides and is the author of the *Melbourne* city guide. His fiction and journalism have appeared in various publications. David lives in Melbourne with his wife and two grey cats.

THE RAIN PELTED DOWN ON THE GLASGOW RUNWAY. Through departure-lounge windows we spotted our sodden bags marooned on the tarmac as they waited to be loaded onto our aircraft bound for Paris. For some reason we were inordinately proud of those bags, chosen after many hours perusing various luggage shops, and here they were dumped in the pouring rain on a miserably wet Scottish morning. We averted our gaze and sipped our drinks, focusing instead on what lay ahead: a long-weekend escape to Paris before our work updating a guide to Italy began.

My wife Janet's well-developed fear of flying was kept under control only by a medicinal gin and tonic and a packet of salted peanuts. The other reason for this early morning drink was that, as well as being April Fools' Day, the first was Janet's birthday. It was a cruel trick the gods had played on her, but it never dampened her excitement, and arriving in Paris for the weekend was a difficult birthday present to beat.

The take-off was as smooth as could be, and as we left the British rain clouds behind and headed into brilliant sunshine we decided to celebrate a little more with some champagne to accompany the airline's rather odd choice of Indian samosas as the mid-morning snack. We toasted to a wonderful holiday in Paris and a successful updating job in Italy. As segments of spicy potato and pea were washed down with bubbles and froth, an ominous dull crack resounded in the roof of my mouth. I knew immediately that the small, plastic dental plate held in place with metal clips had cracked or, even worse, broken altogether. I emptied the contents of my mouth into a paper napkin and turned to my wife, who was oblivious as she enjoyed her snack.

'I think I just broke my plate.'

Janet looked at me suspiciously. 'This is an April Fools' joke, isn't it?'

I reluctantly held out my napkin for inspection and there amongst the masticated potato and pea were four pieces of broken plastic; a ceramic front tooth floated in a small sea of mashed potato. As I stared mutely at the contents of the paper napkin my dental history came flooding back, all the pain and torture that had led to this pathetic piece of plastic flashing before my eyes. It was the culmination of a damaged tooth, root canal work, death of tooth, loss of tooth, pin in bone, bone infection, removal of pin, scraping of bone, removal of more bone – and all the dental experts could offer me was a plastic plate. There was of course the option of bone grafting and a titanium implant, but at a hefty price and a chance of failure that made it hardly an option at all.

I don't offer these details as a plea for sympathy; rather, as an indication of the ridiculously anxious state I suddenly found myself in. Perhaps jetlag from our flight from Australia had taken its toll. Maybe the apprehension of spending six weeks updating in Italy was also weighing on my mind. Whatever, I was over-whelmed by a neurotic anxiety that would have given Woody Allen a run for his money.

I cleaned the jigsaw of plastic and ceramic, folded it into a clean napkin and ran my tongue over what felt like a gap of about twenty feet before launching into a vitriolic attack on the British health system. It was all thanks to those National Health dentists that the inside of my mouth resembled a construction site. I remembered an Australian dentist saying to me not long after I'd migrated to Australia, 'Ah, the Brits have been here, and as usual they've made a right old mess!'

I sank back into my seat, physically and emotionally exhausted by the ferocity of my tirade, spluttered forth with a newly acquired and almost incomprehensible Scottish lisp. My wife responded with a cautious giggle.

'What's so funny then?'

'It's just that without your front tooth you look like such a country bumpkin.'

'That's it! I'll never be taken seriously in Italy without a front tooth. I'll be laughed out of hotels when I ask them in my lithping Italian, *"Quantha cothhhta una camera per thoooooey?"'*

'I'm sorry, dear, don't worry. Manuelle will sort everything out when we get to Paris.'

And in a rare moment of clarity and bravery I proclaimed: 'I'm not going to let this ruin your birthday or our time in Paris.'

Our friends, Manuelle and Bruno, lived in a tiny apartment on the fifth floor of a lift-less block near Père Lachaise. For nine months Manuelle had carried her pregnancy up and down the five precariously steep floors of highly polished stairs that had us stopped halfway with exhaustion. We reached the top out of breath and with legs like jelly. Manuelle opened the door holding Yoji, who at eight months old was already the size of a small sumo wrestler. I smiled and blurted out a few token French greetings. Manuelle looked at me with amazement.

'Oh sheeeet! What's zeees? You have been in zee fight?'

'No, no,' I tried to explain. 'I've broken my plate.'

Manuelle shrugged her shoulders characteristically. '*Je ne comprends pas.* What is zees plate?'

Before I could launch into a lengthy explanation, she pushed Yoji into my arms and led us into the flat. Yoji grinned a toothless grin which I returned in full.

'Why does Yoji look so cute without teeth while I look like a country bumpkin?'

Manuelle gave me an impish smile. 'I don't zink it looks so bad.'

'I'm afraid it's going to be your job to find me a specialist to repair it.'

'Zis is not a good time,' said Manuelle ominously. 'It's the holiday weekend. Nothing will be open till next Tuesday.'

'But we leave for Milan on Tuesday morning,' I protested. 'I HAVE to see someone before then. I'll never be in one place long enough to have it fixed in Italy.'

Manuelle shrugged her shoulders once again. 'Maybe we find someone on Monday.'

I temporarily forgot my predicament when Bruno arrived and suggested that we visit Place des Vosges for an afternoon stroll and some lunch. We squeezed into Bruno's Alfa Romeo, which he drove like a frustrated rally driver.

'So David, what is zis plate, anyway?'

I tried to explain that it was a denture and not a tooth, and that it was attached to a small plate. Since I spoke abominable French I finally resorted to a drawing. Bruno almost crashed the car while trying to have a look but he finally got the picture and exchanged a few words excitedly with Manuelle.

'Ah, ze plate. Now I see what you mean.'

It seems that no matter where you go in central Paris, someone of note has stayed there previously. Place des Vosges is no exception, with Victor Hugo just one of its illustrious former inhabitants. We strolled through its central garden, packed with Parisian families enjoying perfect spring weather, before disappearing into the narrow streets of the Marais to browse in antique shops and explore the Jewish quarter. The earlier events of the day seemed like a bad dream or distant memory, and although everyone seemed to grin at me with gleaming sets of perfect white teeth, I was happy as long as I kept my mouth shut and was sure to mind the gap.

Back in the apartment, after a few glasses of red wine and a couple of particularly strong-smelling cheeses, I had all but accepted that nothing could be done until Monday morning. With this resignation, I had even stopped covering my mouth with my hand every time I laughed. Bruno had planned a special birthday dinner for Janet but had forgotten she was vegetarian, and that the whole fish he was about to bake wouldn't be very palatable for her.

'But it is good, why don't you eat it?'

'Because I don't eat meat or fish,' Janet replied.

'But you must try it,' continued Bruno.

Manuelle reiterated to Bruno in French that Janet didn't eat meat. Bruno shrugged his shoulders and said, 'But you'll eat the vegetables?' as he went to place the vegetables in the same baking tray as the fish.

'Not if they're cooked with the fish,' Janet explained.

'But it tastes good,' Bruno insisted, totally at a loss to understand the finer points of vegetarianism.

We ate and drank the night away in honour of Janet's birthday, and I fell drunk and toothless into bed, where dark dreams of dissolving teeth and collapsing buildings awaited me.

After another day spent as a toothless traveller, judgement day arrived. Manuelle phoned around dental surgeries, but with no luck – sure enough, everyone seemed to be on holiday. Just as I was about to give up hope, and was resigning myself to spending six weeks in Italy looking like the village idiot and speaking my already bad Italian with a lisp, Manuelle announced that she had found a dental technician only a few blocks away. He was prepared to see me on this holiday weekend solely because he had visited Australia as part of a dental training seminar and had had a great time.

The dental technician was a solid, sturdy little man with a friendly smile and a vice-like handshake. Manuelle immediately involved herself in a protracted conversation that I assumed was about my predicament, but it transpired that they were chatting away about the food of regional France.

Finally, the dentist looked at me and smiled. I handed him the broken pieces of plastic and ceramic, which he examined closely before sending me off alone into an adjoining room. I sat in a chair surrounded by framed colour photographs of gory dental procedures while Manuelle and the dentist chatted to each other. One particular picture caught my attention. It was a close-up of gum sliced through and spread back to reveal infected bone. In an instant, I was transported back five years to a dentist's chair in a London dental hospital.

It was around Christmas, and I could hear celebrations and the clinking of glasses issuing from an adjoining room. A green-masked surgeon stuck his gloved fingers into my mouth, pulled back my gum and jabbed an endlessly long syringe into the roof of my mouth. When he'd injected half of the medication, he yanked out the needle and stuck it into the gum above my front tooth. After repeating this procedure a couple of times he said, 'I'll be back in ten,' and headed back to the party.

When he returned, he was wearing a Santa hat and had an assistant in tow. I'd been led to believe that what I was about to experience was nothing more than a standard procedure, but when the assistant covered my face with green fabric, leaving only a hole for my mouth and eyes, I knew I was in for more than the usual filling or standard polish. As the party in the next room livened up and Christmas carols began to be sung, the first incision was made. Each instument that flashed in front of my eyes was followed by an even more terrifying device. There was no pain as such, but the drilling, hammering and cutting of bone just below my nose reverberated around my head. I gripped the arms of my chair as tears ran down my cheeks. After a few more minutes of hacking and slicing, the dentist made another quick visit to the party room while the assistant stayed behind to suck up the blood trickling down the back of my throat with a suction tube.

I passed out and came to alone in a recovery room. My face was numb and covered with an ice pack. I felt sick. After a few minutes a nurse came in and gave me a prescription for painkillers. 'The surgeon will see you in a week,' she said before showing me the door. I stumbled my way home, blood and saliva dribbling down my chin. That night I awoke in unbearable pain, with a tight feeling around my eyes. I stumbled over to the mirror. An unrecognisably swollen balloon of a face with two puffy black eyes stared back at me. I ran to the phone in terror and rang the local hospital.

'Something's gone wrong,' I screeched in a panic. 'My face has swollen so much I think it's going to burst.' A stern voice on the end of the line urged me to calm down and informed me that the swelling was standard for this particular procedure.

I was pulled back to reality by Manuelle's laughter. In a panic, I ran out of the room and grabbed Janet. 'We're getting out of here,' I yelped hysterically. 'I'll manage all right.'

Janet told me to calm down. 'Everything's fine. The dentist can fix the plate and it should last the trip to Italy.'

'So what was all the laughter and discussion about?' I asked neurotically.

'He's prepared to waive the fee if I write a fax for him in English. He needs to change some accommodation details he's booked in Amsterdam.'

This seemed an unlikely proposition considering that only moments ago I'd had memories of a mad dentist in a party hat hacking half my face off. I gave a pleading look to Manuelle and asked if this was indeed what the dentist had in mind. Manuelle shrugged her shoulders and nodded in the affirmative.

So Janet went to work on the fax, the dentist went to work on the plate and I sat counting my blessings, trying to ignore the assorted dental paraphernalia littered on the table in front of me. After what seemed like an eternity, the dentist returned, shaking the water from a perfectly intact plate. I slipped the chemical-tasting piece of plastic into my mouth, clipping it into place. It felt uncomfortable, but then it always did. After being instructed to nibble on a piece of paper to check my bite, the visit was over.

The following day we said our farewells to Paris, and I smiled the biggest smile I could muster. Yoji clapped his hands and pulled an all-too-familiar toothless grin, sending a shiver down my spine. I pushed the previous days' events into the darkest recesses and filed them under forget, but I knew that with my lack of dental luck this was likely to be little more than a temporary reprieve.

HOTEL AL-CALIFORNIA

Scott McNeely

Scott was born and raised in Los Angeles, California, and he actually likes the place. Scott was once lost for twenty-four hours on a city beach, despite the best efforts of family and friends (and the Los Angeles police) to find him. After that incident Scott was never supposed to travel anywhere, ever again.

Undaunted, Scott spent part of his college years at Trinity College, Dublin, getting into all sorts of trouble (see *Lonely Planet Unpacked*). Before returning home he took a trip to Europe and North Africa with two friends. Their identities have been withheld in this publication to protect them from their mothers.

Scott's very first travel assignment was to Romania in the summer of 1991. He nearly starved to death. He has since written for the Berkeley Guides (RIP), Fodor's, AA Publications, Lonely Planet and various magazines.

Scott is currently a full-time worker bee at Lonely Planet's Oakland office, following stints as an editor and executive editor in San Francisco and New York. Scott has never been arrested.

THERE IS NO SHORTAGE OF STORIES ILLUSTRATING MY ABILITY TO MAKE POOR DECISIONS – just ask my friends – yet bad decisions are rarely made in a vacuum. And, in this case, my friends have the story all wrong. Contrary to what they might tell you, it was not completely my fault. Really and truly I was NOT totally to blame. Thus, when the realisation hit that I and my two lifelong friends had been kidnapped in Morocco and were speeding away from the police in the backseat of a Mercedes, the finger of blame pointed a long way back.

All the way back to a kitchen table cluttered with travel books and wall-size maps, the kind Napoleon no doubt used to plan his inglorious Russian campaign. I remember the three of us pondering a persistent rainfall on a dreary February afternoon, hopped up on tea and dreaming of the sunny Mediterranean.

'So boys, where we going this summer?'

'London,' somebody mumbled. Too easy.

'How about Paris?' Too romantic.

'Israel?' Too dangerous.

'Prague?' Now you're talking.

'Spain. No, wait, how about Morocco?' Bingo. Morocco. An exotic name conjuring visions of spice markets, mosques and desert nomads. Ahhh, Morocco. Book three tickets, boys, we're going.

So went our one and only planning session. Details never did trouble us, three fresh-faced American boys, twenty years of age and hungry for desert adventure. If my mom had been present, the trip would have been cancelled right then and there.

Have you ever sat in 3rd class on a rickety Moroccan train, in the middle of the desert, at a dead stop, in 120 Fahrenheit? If you answered yes to that question, try another: have you ever been so thirsty that you wanted to die? No? Have you ever been so thirsty that you'd accept a friend's sweaty T-shirt and gratefully suck it dry?

We had been in Morocco for three days now and I had made every mistake there is to make. I had fallen for the 'I'm a starving student; let me be your guide' scam – twice. I had been lured into a carpet shop and had come away with a US$250 woven memory (actual retail value: US$50 on a good day). And I had convinced my two travelling companions to board a ten-hour train to Fès, 3rd class, during daylight hours (average midday temperature on a Moroccan train, in kelvin: 610). Even worse, I had managed to forget the water. That's right – I forgot to bring the spare bottles of water. It was my responsibility and I had messed up. I was failing miserably as a traveller and friend. My two lifelong friends had begun to hate me. I was looking for any escape I could find.

Moustafah was a close-shaved, decent-looking guy who spoke good English and smiled a lot. I don't remember him sitting down on our 3rd-class bench, but at some point during our painfully waterless afternoon he sat down opposite us and flipped open a *Time* magazine.

After a few minutes he looked up and smiled. 'You're from America? Congratulations on winning the Cold War,' he said. 'I have always admired the American army.'

We were in no mood for politics. Water was the only thing on my mind. Moustafah quickly discerned our need. He fetched a small bag from beneath his seat and produced two glistening bottles of water.

'Would you like some water? I have extra bottles just here.'

I was sold. Moustafah was my new best friend.

He smiled again. 'I am travelling to Fès to see my wife and children. I am learning English to be a teacher. Would you like me to write your names down in Arabic? Look I will show you how.'

Over the next hour Moustafah charmed the pants off me and my friends. He gave us water and food; he taught us Arabic; he talked about politics, Moroccan music and the meaning of life. He told us about his family, his parents, his ambitions. He informed us about 'good' Moroccans and 'bad' Moroccans and how to tell them apart. By late afternoon Moustafah had us wrapped around his finger.

'So where are you three going?' he asked.

'To Fès,' I offered without the slightest hesitation.

His face grew dark. 'Fès? You're going to Fès on this train?'

'Yeah, Fès. It's in the guidebook. Sounds like a great place.'

'Let me tell you something,' he said with a lowered voice and a cautious look. 'It's no good arriving in Fès after sundown. It's a dangerous city, filled with many bad Moroccans. They will cheat you and steal from you. You cannot trust anybody in Fès.'

This was sobering news from our new best friend. 'What should we do?'

'Do you know anybody there?'

'No.'

'Do you have a hotel reservation?'

'No.'

'That's not good. In fact that's very bad.'

'What should we do, Moustafah?'

After falling into deep thought, Moustafah brightened and beamed with hope. 'I know just the thing. You must leave the train at Larache. It's a small town on the ocean. Very peaceful and safe. You must spend the night there and then continue to Fès in the morning.'

What was not to like about his suggestion? Seriously, if this were you, could you have said 'No, thanks, we prefer to arrive after dark in an unfamiliar, dangerous city. Thanks for your sound advice but we'd rather take our chances in Fès.'

Not a chance. You would have done exactly as I did. You would have agreed to leave the train at Larache. You would have trusted Moustafah completely. And he would have had you – just like he had me and my friends – hook, line and sinker.

The train creaked to a stop at something that, in America's Old West, would be generously called a one-horse town. I remember glancing out the cracked window as I grabbed my backpack, surprised that 'peaceful Larache' comprised nothing more than a few ramshackle buildings. There were tumbleweeds of trash blowing in the late-afternoon wind. The ocean was nowhere in sight. The place was deserted except for a small knot of jellaba-clad men smoking cigarettes and a lone taxi that clearly had seen better days.

'This is Larache?' I asked, incredulously.

'Yes, yes, please hurry. Get off the train quickly.' Moustafah seemed a bit nervous, but it didn't register at the time. He was helping us with our packs, which seemed awfully nice of him. Yet he said nothing each time we turned to say thank you and goodbye. He was acting like an usher, shepherding us down the aisle and off the train. I wanted to say goodbye, but Moustafah didn't look like somebody ready to let go.

Instead he jumped off the train and, to our collective surprise, started barking orders for us to hurry up. Did an alarm bell sound at this point? You bet. Did I listen? Of course not.

'Hey Moustafah, the train's leaving. You better get back on the train or you'll miss it.'

He ignored me completely. He looked right through us like an animal tracking something in the distance. He had no patience for us. The friendliness had evaporated.

'I'm not taking that train,' he said. 'I'm going with you to Larache.'

'That's crazy,' I said. 'What about your wife and children in Fès? We don't need any help. We can find Larache just fine.'

'Shut up,' he said. Off went another alarm bell.

From nowhere a shiny Mercedes sedan pulls up in a whirl of dust and screeching brakes. The driver steps out of the car and the only thing I can remember thinking is, *Oh no! This guy is tall, he's got a moustache and he's wearing mirrored sunglasses. Not good.*

A few hundred metres down the road I spot an official-looking van racing towards us. I'm trying to make sense of its flashing blue light and the blaring siren. I think one of my friends shouted, 'It's the police!' in my ear, which made no sense at all. Are the cops chasing us or the Mercedes? Is Moustafah on the run? Is somebody going to shoot us?

Next I notice that Moustafah and the driver are shoving us, literally shoving us, into the back of the Mercedes. It's no simple thing to toss three young men with packs into the back of a Mercedes. But toss they do, and like a game of Twister my friends and I find ourselves tangled up in the back of the car.

Somebody reaches for the door but – damn those childproof locks – it's sealed tight. In a rare brave moment I consider throttling the driver from behind but – damn those Plexiglas partitions. Pounding on the glass only makes my fists throb with pain. As we tear out of the parking lot Moustafah and the driver are busy dealing with the police van, hot on our tail, barely a dozen metres behind.

'What's happening?' my friend asked.

'I think we're in trouble. Serious trouble.'

'Of course we're in serious trouble,' I screamed. 'We're locked in the back of a Mercedes that's being chased by HEAVILY ARMED Moroccan police.'

'Why? We haven't done anything. Why are the cops chasing us?'

My friend has an obvious and clearly deep distrust for the police.

'They're chasing us because we've just been kidnapped!'

There, I said it. I spoke aloud what had been on all our minds. We three young, ignorant Americans had been kidnapped. From a train. In Morocco.

'Kidnapped? What the hell do you mean?'

'I mean KIDNAPPED! You know, forced against our will into the back . . .'

'Are we political prisoners? Is this a *jihad* thing?'

'Yeah, Moustafah was deeply interested in that *Time* magazine.'

'Maybe they'll ransom us.'

'Ransom? Shit, I've only got a few hundred dollars.'

'Maybe they'll shoot us.' I was more worried about getting shot than about maxing my credit card trying to pay our ransom.

'Shoot us? For what?'

My friend's face darkened and he said, under his breath, 'Maybe they're terrorists. Maybe they'll exchange us with the Israelis for some PLO prisoners.'

'Come on, we're so totally not that important.' I of course meant this in a hostage-ransom context, not as a personal indictment.

'Maybe they'll pretend to exchange us, and then shoot us in the back as we cross the border.'

'What border? We're thousands of miles from Israel.'

'Libya. Tunisia. Whatever. If they shoot it doesn't matter which border we're at.'

'Just pretend we're Canadian, right? Nobody shoots Canadians.'

'But we've got American passports,' I screamed. 'We're so totally not Canadian.'

'Are we going to die? Hey, listen to me! Are we going to die? In the backseat of a Mercedes?'

'Maybe the cops will catch up with us . . .'

'And start a shoot out?'

'No, maybe they'll arrest Moustafah and the driver and we'll be heroes.'

'I wouldn't worry about the cops,' I said. 'Look behind us.'

Bonnie and Clyde, Butch and Sundance – I usually root for the bad guys. Yet the police van was falling behind, first by a few hundred metres or so then by a kilometre or two. Moustafah saw it, too, and yelled at the driver to pick up the pace. He was going to lose them once and for all, even if that meant roaring down a dirt road at something like 180 km/h.

As we made the Moroccan jump to light speed I came to an awful realisation: We were on our own. There was no chance a battered Hyundai van over-stuffed with cops was going to catch us. There was no way the Moroccan police would intervene and save us. This time the bad guys were getting away.

The first ten minutes in the Mercedes were the worst. We kept asking each other impossible questions: where are we going? Are they going to kill us? Should we fight or try to escape? What the hell are we going to tell our parents? The next ten minutes were the 'sinking in' period. We were silent, each alone with our thoughts. I spent most of the time staring vacantly at the back of Moustafah's head, recounting all the steps that had gotten us from a Fès-bound train to a hell-bound Mercedes sedan. The 'sinking in' period was followed by ten minutes of serenity. We calmed down, got comfortable, stared out the window, admired the view. Even Moustafah seemed more relaxed. Apparently there's nothing like a good police chase to soothe the nerves.

As the sun started to set, we emerged from the empty desert into a valley littered with farms and half-built concrete houses. A few people waved as we sped by and, being friendly Americans, we waved back. It felt like we were simply three foreigners out for a drive in a hired taxi. It was easy to forget we had just been kidnapped.

I was nearly enjoying myself, despite my status as a recent kidnappee. My rationale went something like this: if they had wanted to, they could easily have shot us already. Or stabbed us. Or left us standing naked in the blistering hot desert. But they hadn't done any of these things.

No, Moustafah and his accomplice had something else in mind. As long as 'something else' didn't involve torture or black-market slavery, I was content. Angry at Moustafah, yes; angry at being kidnapped, yes; but content that we were still alive and seeing a bit of the countryside. Mentally I upgraded our chances of survival from 10–90 to 50–50. Things were looking up.

Not much later we drove into a town of sorts, with paved roads and a handful of shops and cafés. We slowed to a stop outside an apartment block and the Mercedes' doors unlocked themselves. Our first reaction was to run for it, shouting and screaming for the police. Moustafah was one step ahead of us. He put on his best smile and said, friendliness oozing from every pore, 'Welcome my friends! Welcome to my home! I'm sorry about the police back there, but sometimes it's better not to be caught with unregistered foreigners.'

'What are you talking about, Moustafah? You've kidnapped us. Do you realise that you have kidnapped three American tourists? In our country that's a serious crime.'

'Kidnap? What kidnap?' Moustafah looked flabbergasted. 'No my friends. You have NOT been kidnapped. You are my guests here. Welcome.'

'Not kidnapped? Moustafah you're crazy. You grabbed us off the train and threw us in the back of your Mercedes. You drove like a maniac across the desert and evaded the police, and now you're telling us that we have NOT been kidnapped?' Clearly, Moustafah and I were not on the same page.

'Kidnap? That's ridiculous. I am not a kidnapper. You are welcome to my home.'

'That's not the point, Moustafah. We didn't ask to come here. We didn't ask to be involved in a police chase . . .'

'I already apologised about the police,' Moustafah complained, his feelings clearly hurt. 'The police only wanted to make trouble. They do not respect the businessman.'

'Okay Moustafah, tell me this – can we go back to the train station? Will you take us to the nearest train station RIGHT NOW?'

'No, it's getting dark. And there are no more trains tonight. Did you not listen on the train? Fès is a dangerous place. You cannot trust people there. You are safe here. Anyway, now you are my guests. Welcome. Now please come upstairs.'

At the top of the stairs we met a portly old woman carrying a tray of couscous. Moustafah introduced us to his mother. She was beaming. You have to admire the guy: he's just kidnapped three Americans and his mother couldn't be prouder.

Moustafah disappeared up another flight of stairs and his mom showed us to a room with three beds. 'I am good hotel,' she said, as if we had just been debating the point. Still, the beds were all neatly made with clean sheets and fluffy pillows. Not wanting to appear rude, we dropped our bags and regrouped.

As we unpacked and settled in, my friend asked the question that was racing through all our minds: 'What's going on here? Have we been kidnapped or not?'

'Yes we've been kidnapped. Moustafah may be friendly again and smiling, but there's no getting around the fact that he kidnapped us from a train and brought us here against our wills.'

'But it's not like we're in jail or anything. It's his mom's house after all. And this bed looks REAL comfortable.'

'The softness of the pillow is not the point.' I hated to be a nit-picker, but the gravity of the situation was seemingly lost on them. 'Are you really saying that you don't mind being kidnapped? That you're okay sleeping in the house of the man who abducted us from the train?'

'I don't know. I think we've exaggerated this whole "kidnapping" thing. I mean, Moustafah was totally cool on the train. Maybe the police were the real problem. Maybe he was going to help us out, but then the cops showed up and wanted to throw us in jail. I don't know. Maybe Moustafah is the real hero in this story.'

'And maybe,' I huffed, 'you're a total idiot who doesn't even realise he's been kidnapped by a Moroccan version of Norman Bates.'

'What about his mother?'

'What about her?'

'She seems nice.'

'Nice? NICE? What's nice got to do with it?'

'That food looked good.'

'Your point being?'

'Well, stop being such a pessimist. This place isn't half bad. I think you're being too hard on Moustafah. Anyway, I'm hungry and tired. I don't want to take a train to Fès tonight. Let's just stay here.'

Recognising that I was fighting a losing battle, we agreed to disagree. At the very least we would stay for dinner, maybe a shower, and then we would figure out what to do. As much as it bothered me, the beds did look comfortable. And the food did look good. Maybe I was being a little hard on the guy.

We climbed up another flight of stairs into a dining area stocked with oversized cushions and thick carpets. A few caged birds chirped away, their song mingling with the gentle gurgle of a small fountain in the centre of the room.

Much to my surprise, there were two young blonde girls lounging on a cushion, busily writing postcards. For an instant I thought they were fellow kidnappees, but they looked too damn content. There was no panic in their eyes, no plea for help.

None of us was quite sure where to start. Two blonde girls were the last thing we expected to find in the middle of this Moroccan nowhere.

'Um. Hello,' I ventured.

In unison they responded with an all-American 'Howdy!'

'Is everything okay? I mean, are you alright? How long have you been here?'

'I guess we've been here for about a week,' one of the girls said. 'You'll love it here. It's a great place.'

'What do you mean?' I asked. 'You've been here a full week?'

'Yup. We met Moustafah a week ago. We've been here ever since.'

'So he kidnapped you, too?'

'Kidnapped? Well, no. Sort of. He didn't really kidnap us. At least not in a bad way.'

'Don't worry about it,' her friend added, trying her best to be helpful and upbeat. 'We've met some great people here.'

'Have you tried to leave?'

'Oh yeah, a bunch of times. But the nearest station is thirty kilometres away and none of the taxis will take us.'

'What do you mean? You've been stuck here for a week and you can't leave? Doesn't that piss you off? Think about it – we've all been kidnapped and now we're stuck here!'

'It's not as bad as it sounds. Moustafah promised to drive us to Fès in a few days. And the food here is real good. Plus his mom is only charging us US$8 a day. It's a bargain when you think about it.'

My friends nodded in agreement. I was too tired to argue with her logic so I caved and we stayed. For four days. And we loved it.

A few months later Moustafah received a postcard of Alcatraz Island with the following note: 'Dear Moustafah: We had a great time at your mom's house. Thanks for kidnapping us.'

SUNRISE OVER THE PYRAMIDS

Mark Honan

After a university degree in philosophy opened up a glittering career as an office clerk, Mark decided 'the meaning of life' lay elsewhere and set off on a two-year trip around the world. As a freelance travel writer, he then went campervanning around Europe to write a series of articles for a London magazine. When the magazine went bust Mark joined a travel agency, from where he was rescued by Lonely Planet. Mark wrote Lonely Planet's *Vienna* city guide, the Austria, Liechtenstein and Switzerland chapters for *Western Europe* and *Central Europe*, and coordinated and contributed to *Central America on a Shoestring*. An account of his experiences when working on the *India* guidebook appears in *Lonely Planet Unpacked*.

THE POLICEMAN PULLED OPEN THE BACKPACK ANTON HAD BEEN WEARING. Two apples, bruised and crushed, fell out and wobbled across the table. I could see their skins gaping open and revealing a bone-coloured mush within. Out back, Anton's body was surely in much the same state.

⁂

Initially, it had seemed such a great idea. Ironically, the idea came from Anton himself.

'Lots of backpackers do it,' he said one morning by the pool-side in Cairo. 'They climb the pyramids at dusk – maybe pay the guards a bit of baksheesh first – and then sleep at the top until sunrise. The view of the sun rising over the desert is supposed to be spectacular. We'll see the pyramids bathed in a red glow. It'll be unforgettable, the sight of a lifetime.'

'Is there enough room at the top?' I asked. 'Aren't they, well, pointed?'

'Not really,' he said. 'That's just a trick of scale and perspective. There's plenty of room for three people to lie down up there. We'll take up some food and wine. It'll be great.'

Wayne and I nodded our heads. We were in!

Even though Anton was the youngest, a mere seventeen years old, it seemed natural that he should take the lead. He was Swiss, but his parents had moved to Egypt years ago. He could speak the language fluently and he knew the local customs. Wayne and I, on the other hand, were just travellers passing through. We didn't even know each other until Anton gathered us up and made us his companions for the duration.

The arrangements were quickly made. A few provisions, a few blankets to cushion the stones and to protect against the cold desert air, and permission from his parents for Anton to stay out all night. (Well, he was only seventeen.) That's all it took. A bus ride later and we were walking towards the Sphinx and the three pyramids.

'Camel ride into the desert?' offered an over-optimistic camel owner. 'Very good price.' With less than an hour of daylight left, he must have realised that his pitch was hopeless. The tourist crowds were thinning and a few souvenir vendors were already beginning to pack away their wares. We started walking around the largest pyramid. It looked a long way to the top! Those little indentations down the sides are actually made up of huge blocks, some seventy or eighty centimetres in height. We came across a couple of guards, with guns hanging carelessly from their belts. Anton approached them to negotiate and returned with bad news.

'They'll let us climb up, but they want ten Egyptian pounds from each of us. I've heard the price should be much less than that.' We shook our heads, agreeing that the price was too high. We resolved to climb up without permission and offer a lower price when we came down in the morning. We sauntered on, casual in an exaggerated manner, until we had rounded the next corner.

'Now!'

We bounded up the huge blocks as fast as we could. A pair of different guards spotted us and shouted for us to get down.

'Ignore them,' I yelled, confident that they wouldn't shoot on us for such a minor transgression. I vaulted another stone then looked round to see that Anton was already descending. Wayne and I had no option but to follow suit. After a brief ticking off from the guards, we withdrew to reconsider our plan. We noticed that the smallest of the three pyramids, the Pyramid of Mycerinus, wasn't patrolled by guards. 'That'll do,' we decided. In fact it might be even more spectacular, as we'd see the sun framed by the larger, more impressive pyramids. Accordingly we advanced on our new objective.

An Egyptian approached. 'You're climbing the pyramids? I will guide you.'

'No thanks.'

'You will need a guide. I will show you the way.'

Wayne pointed. 'There's the bottom. There's the top. It's obvious. We know the way. We don't need a guide.'

Disregarding the continued pleas for our custom, we started to scramble up the pyramid. Unfortunately, the Egyptian starting climbing up after us.

'Go away! We don't need you.' The man carried on climbing regardless.

'You're wasting your time. We're not going to pay you.' Still he climbed.

We put him out of our minds and concentrated on the ascent. The climb was hard work, and our thigh muscles soon ached with the effort. Before long we reached the summit and found a flattish area, as promised by Anton, easily large enough to accommodate three people. Except there was a fourth person, and he was being an exceedingly large pain in the opposite of 'top'.

It would have been pleasant at this point to relax and enjoy the panorama in the waning light – the immense outlines of the two larger pyramids, the impassive Sphinx and the broad expanse of the desert stretching away to the horizon to the west. Sadly, we didn't get the chance.

'Baksheesh. Payment. I have guided you up to the top of the pyramid.'

We could scarcely believe his audacity. 'Don't be silly, we're not paying you. We knew the way. Anyway, you were behind us for most of the time.'

The discussion continued in a similar vein for a few minutes, and eventually the three of us sat down and started talking among ourselves. We figured that if we ignored him for long enough, he would give in and go down. Not a bit of it. He changed tack.

'It is not allowed to be up here. You must go down now.'

'Where are you travelling next, Wayne?'

'You must go down. Not allowed. Very serious.'

'I'll head down to south Egypt. Ideally I'd like to cross into Sudan overland.'

'The police will arrest you if you don't come down with me.'

'I wouldn't mind doing that myself, but I've heard it's pretty much impossible to get a visa for Sudan at the moment.'

'I'll take you down now.' He grabbed Anton's shirt and started pulling.

'Ultimately, I want to hit Kenya. I've been told about this fantastic little island there called Lamu.'

'Down. Must go down.' Anton tried to push him away but he wouldn't let go of Anton's shirt.

'This is ridiculous!' Wayne jumped up, anger finally getting the better of him. 'Here's some money. Just go away and leave us in peace.'

But the Egyptian didn't even look at what was being offered. He kept pulling on Anton's shirt, trying to make him stand up. 'Money is not important. We must all go down. Very wrong being here.'

Strange as it was, the very man who insisted he had guided us up the pyramid in the first place was now telling us to go. Seemingly, he would not rest until he had ensured we had left the scene of the crime. It was a matter of wounded pride and civic duty. We were either going to have to throw him from the top or go down with him. Reluctantly, we all stood up and started to descend.

It was fully dark now, and we picked our way down the giant slabs, muttering choice insults at the 'guide' as we went. Inside, we were all fuming. Perhaps we were too annoyed at him and our thwarted adventure to take enough care in what we were doing.

What happened next happened in the merest instant, the blink of an eye.

Anton was a few steps in front of me. There was a slight scuffing sound and he lurched forwards, out into the dark, empty air. A puff of dust rising from the stone, a thin cry of 'Aiee', and he was gone. There was a muffled thump as he landed somewhere down in the blackness. Landed, but didn't stop. He must have bounced, because, sickeningly, another thump followed, and another. Each time quieter, sounding deceptively soft and gentle. We all froze on the pyramid, peering into the black void below.

At last, there was complete silence. An ominous stillness pervaded the desert air. We shouted down to him.

'Anton. Are you all right? Can you hear us?'

No answer, but it was such a long way down. Maybe we just couldn't hear his reply. Maybe he was simply stunned. Sure, it was a very long way down, but you could survive such a fall, couldn't you?

We hurried down the pyramid, too fast for safety in our shock and anxiety. I stumbled slightly myself, experienced a momentary, terrifying teetering, then fell back against the pyramid. I shivered at the realisation that I had so nearly made my own leap into the darkness. Wayne and I cautioned each other to take it slower after that.

Finally we were at the bottom. More shouting for Anton. Still no answer. We scrambled around the rocks at the foot of the pyramid, calling as we went.

It was Wayne who found him first. 'I don't think he's breathing,' he said, his voice drained of emotion. 'His skin feels a bit cool.'

I saw our would-be guide standing nearby, facing the pyramid. 'You stupid bastard,' I shouted at him. 'Look what you did.' He made no response at all, standing there, head bowed, hands clasped. His lips were moving silently and I realised he was praying. I instantly felt ashamed at my futile anger.

'I'll stay with Anton,' said Wayne. 'You go and find help.'

I stumbled off into the darkness, head spinning at the seriousness of it all. I had little idea of where I was going. Fortunately, I soon came across someone in a uniform and I breathlessly told the story to him. Then I was in the police station, explaining the same thing.

The officer chided me gently. 'That is why the pyramids are out of bounds,' he said softly. 'One or two tourists fall from the top every year.'

Then there were more questions, forms to fill out. Meantime they dispatched a vehicle to pick up Anton and Wayne. Before long Wayne walked wearily into the station, a sad nod confirming that Anton was indeed dead. A policeman carried in Anton's backpack, and the officers identified the contents, including the two battered apples.

At least the police will take care of everything now, I thought, but I was wrong.

Paperwork completed, the police officer turned to Wayne and me. 'Now you must tell the parents what has happened.'

Why us, I wanted to complain, we've been through enough already. But we agreed, expecting to be driven there in a police car. Wrong again.

'Walk to the right for five minutes. There you will find a bus to take you into Cairo.'

I couldn't believe it. There were two bereft Swiss parents somewhere within the crowded confines of Cairo, blissfully ignorant that their only son was dead, and we were being told to go by bus. It would take up to an hour or more to get into town and then we would have to transfer to another bus to Anton's parents' apartment. We took a taxi.

Anton's mother opened the door. One look at our faces and she knew that something was seriously wrong.

'We have some bad news,' said Wayne, 'I think you'd better sit down.' Such a cliché, but I'm glad he said it. Though no-one expected her to actually sit down, she had at least been given a couple of seconds to mentally get ready for what was coming.

'Anton's dead.'

'Aiee!' A sound very reminiscent of Anton's own cry on the pyramid, but this time much louder, much longer, filled with pure anguish. She rushed away down the hall, leaving us waiting bashfully on the doorstep. A few minutes later she returned, back in control and businesslike. Wayne was instructed to stay in the apartment, to baby-sit Anton's young sister. I had to accompany the parents back to the police station, then on to the morgue where Anton's body already lay.

The night seemed to last forever. At one point the mother asked me if I thought he had died instantly. I tried to work out which answer would cause her the least grief.

'I'm sure he did,' I said hesitantly.

'Good,' she said, and lapsed into silence. Right answer.

Back in the Swiss apartment, I fainted into unconsciousness rather than fell asleep. The next morning Wayne and I left as soon as politeness would allow, feeling uncomfortable amidst – and uneasily responsible for – the family's private grief.

That wasn't quite the end of the ordeal. Five days later came the funeral. Wayne and I stood awkwardly, in borrowed, baggy, dark suits as the memorial service was conducted. The whole time I was imagining the tacit blame that was surely being directed at us from the rows of newly arrived Swiss relatives. In their eyes, we were the older and theoretically wiser friends of their young protégé, so how had we allowed him to fall to his death? In the end, nobody did blame us, at least not verbally, but their faces were impenetrably expressionless whenever they looked our way.

Then it really was over. A few days later Wayne went off to wherever he went off to; I haven't seen or spoken to him since. I hung around in Egypt for a couple more weeks before I returned home to England. I've also never been in contact with Anton's family; I assume they've returned to Switzerland by now.

Coincidentally, I now write the Lonely Planet guidebook to Switzerland, and every time I return to the pyramid-shaped Alps I am reminded of that sad night in Egypt.

BEARANOIA

John Mock

John's first hike in California's Sierra Nevada was a 1974 trip to Desolation Wilderness near Lake Tahoe. In 1977 he set out to walk the John Muir Trail from Mount Whitney to Yosemite, but only made it half-way, interrupting the hike for several years of trekking in Pakistan, India and Nepal. He completed the Muir Trail in 1984, and has also walked from Tahoe to Yosemite. John studied at universities in India, Pakistan and Nepal, and holds a PhD in South and South-East Asian studies from University of California – Berkeley. He is one of a vanishing breed of itinerant scholars who believe that travel and experience teach lessons no classroom can ever impart, and he shared some of those experiences in *Lonely Planet Unpacked*. He lives with his wife and Lonely Planet co-author, Kimberley O'Neil, on the Pacific coast of northern California. Together, they have authored *Trekking in the Karakoram & Hindukush* and contributed to *Hiking in the USA* and *Pakistan*. They are currently working on *Hiking in the Sierra Nevada*.

THE JOHN MUIR TRAIL, PROVIDING PERHAPS THE BEST MOUNTAIN HIKING IN THE USA, RUNS FOR MORE THAN 350 KILOMETRES ALONG THE CREST OF CALIFORNIA'S SIERRA NEVADA RANGE. Named after the USA's most famous conservationist, it has everything you think a high mountain trail should have: ancient, bare granite peaks and deep river canyons; sparkling blue lakes and bright splashing cascades; flower-carpeted meadows and tall, old-growth forests, all in a continuous wilderness uncrossed by any road. The terrain is as rewarding as it is difficult, and the spirit of John Muir and America's pioneers lingers here, far from modern city life. Hiking this trail is a once-in-a-lifetime adventure, on which hikers can follow their dreams in solitude. Which is why I'm here, walking the upper half of the trail from Florence Lake north almost 180 kilometres to Yosemite Valley.

The official start of the trail is the summit of Mount Whitney, the highest peak in the USA outside Alaska. Years ago I'd walked the 175-kilometre-long southern section from the end of the road at Whitney Portal to the top of Mount Whitney and north through Sequoia and Kings Canyon national parks. Almost no-one hikes the entire trail in one go – the sheer weight of the food you need to carry makes that nearly impossible. Most hikers either leave the trail to resupply in towns along the way or, like me, do the trail in separate segments.

So I'm back at Florence Lake, having taken the midnight bus from Oakland to arrive in Fresno at dawn. Hitchhiking through Clovis and up Highway 168 past Shaver and Huntington lakes to the end of the road at Florence Lake took most of the day, but by nightfall I'm eleven kilometres up the trail, camping in late-June solitude under the open sky. In the interest of travelling light, I'm carrying just a nylon waterproof tarp in case it rains rather than a tent. It's early enough in the season that mosquitoes aren't a problem, and the Sierra's renowned good summer weather means the likelihood of a rainy night is almost zero.

I quickly fall into my familiar hiking routine. Up at dawn, I retrieve my two food bags that I leave suspended each night from a tree limb high enough off the ground to be out of reach of any scavengers. Black bears are my main concern, and they're smart enough to get my food if I don't hang the bags high enough or far enough out on the limb to be beyond the reach of a tree-climbing bear. But I long ago mastered the art of bear-bagging, as it's called, and using a long stick I can hook the spare rope I leave tucked into one of the bags and pull it down. I roll my sleeping pad and bag, have a quick breakfast of granola, then pick up my pack and head off.

The first days of summer are still too early for many other hikers. Lingering snow on the passes and high water in the creeks keeps them away. I have the trail pretty much to myself, except for a few fishermen lower down along the rivers.

As the sun warms the day, I stop for a midmorning dip in a clear blue lake. The water is shockingly cold, leaving me gasping for breath. But the coolness soothes my muscles and clears my head of random thought, focusing me intently on the moment.

Back on the trail, I climb in a steady rhythm past the timberline, and the view opens over the chain of high peaks that form the Silver Divide. Soon I'm standing on snow-covered Silver Pass, where the views are simply breathtaking. I look back to the south over deeply forested Mono and Bear creeks, at the Mono Divide and Seldon Pass, and ahead across Cascade Valley to the Mammoth Crest. A short glissade over the snowy crust is the easiest way down, and I stop for a long, cold drink from a pure stream.

My camp that night is along Fish Creek in the upper end of Cascade Valley. Tomorrow I'll climb along the creek out of the valley, but tonight I'm tired after the long descent from Silver

Pass. My small, single-burner camping stove makes a steady roar, drowning the rush of water in nearby Fish Creek. I turn the stove off and let my dinner, a mix of rice and split red lentils flavoured with a bouillon cube, quietly soak up the last bit of liquid.

It doesn't take long to finish my meal, and I set about locating a suitable tree far enough from my camp site to hang my food bags. Toothpaste, sun screen, soap – anything with any sort of scent goes into them. When I have both bags about the same weight, I tie a small rock to the end of my nylon cord and toss it over a branch that's about eight metres off the ground. I tie a bag to one end and hoist it up until it touches the branch. Then, standing on tiptoe, I tie the other bag as far up the opposite end of the cord as I can. I tuck the spare cord under the knot and give it a heave. One bag goes up and the other comes down until they are both hanging at the same level, about five metres above the ground. Satisfied that no bear will be able to get my food, I return to camp and lay out my sleeping bag.

The cliffs above are washed rose pink in the sunset glow, and I stroll up the trail towards the steel bridge over Fish Creek. Rounding a bend in the trail, I see a steel girder angled almost vertical. Moving closer, I find the bridge collapsed in the middle, its steel girders bent at an alarming right angle, as though a giant had stepped on the bridge and crushed it underfoot. Broken, it now rests on a boulder midstream. What to do? I put my foot on the end of a twisted girder and feel the whole thing vibrate from the pounding of the Fish Creek torrent. Is it crossable? Will the whole thing slide away if I put my weight on it? In the deepening twilight, I head back to camp and my warm sleeping bag. Overhead the stars shine with an intensity never seen in the city and I drift off to sleep.

I wake during the night. In starlight bright enough to cast shadows I see the dark outline of an almost fallen tree leaning against another, both alive and growing. The sight of the tree, broken but still solid, reassures me and I drift back to sleep.

In the morning the snowmelt flood of Fish Creek is lower, and the evening's pounding vibration has stopped. Gingerly, I climb down the wrecked girders and onto the sloping wooden planks that angle up towards the opposite bank. A few steps and I'm across, laughing and exhilarated at surmounting this unforeseen hazard.

Up I go, past blue Virginia Lake, blue-green Purple Lake, and on by the tiny aquamarine jewel of a tarn above. I cross the outlet of Duck Lake, then traverse the forested north side of Fish Creek Valley. With Double Peak and the Silver Divide soaring opposite me, I head on to camp and a peaceful sleep at Deer Creek. Sleep is the hidden motive for my trip. In the quiet solitude of the wilderness, soothed by the sighing murmur of wind and the water, I fall into a deep and profound relaxation until morning's glow brings a dawn chorus of birdsong.

Descending the next day between the two Red Cones – remnants of past volcanic activity – I leave the less-travelled expanse of John Muir Wilderness and enter the more heavily used Ansel Adams Wilderness. Ahead are Devil's Postpile National Monument, ski-lift-lined Mammoth Mountain and the popular crags of the Minarets, all easily accessed by roads. Yielding to temptation, I make a short detour to the Reds Meadow store and enjoy a grilled cheese and tomato sandwich for lunch.

Browsing through the books for sale at the store, I pick up Mike Crammond's *Of Bears and Man*, where these words of a black bear attack victim catch my eye: 'Park bears are more dangerous, because they're used to people . . . They aren't like the ones you see on TV, not like Smokey the Bear or Goldilocks' three bears. They are not only going to maul you; *they are going to eat you!'*

I put the book back down, deciding to avoid popular camp sites and stay in less obvious locations. Bears in this area, where there are lots of people, are bound to be more savvy and cunning. Creatures of habit, they return to places they know an easy meal awaits. Best to choose places where people don't camp. I'm not particularly worried about a bear attack, but would rather avoid any encounter with a hungry black bear. I pick up my pack and chug up the trail.

At Devil's Postpile, I climb to the top of the smooth, black, hexagonal columns, marvelling at another sight seen. That evening I stop and set up camp by hemlock-fringed Gladys Lake. Sunset draws colour across Mammoth Ridge while a chorus of frogs serenades me to sleep.

Next morning, heading up the trail past the craggy Minarets – by Garnet and Thousand Island lakes and beneath soaring Mount Ritter and Mount Banner – I meet more people than I've seen in the past week: several groups of hikers, a solo walker heading south, three German college students. Two young women from California, coming south from Yosemite, tell me they were the victims of bears in Lyell Canyon, just outside Tuolumne Meadows. They lost most of their food, but are undeterred and plan to resupply at Reds Meadow for the trip back. Brave souls.

The following morning, I cross snow-covered Donahue Pass, the highest point on my trip, and enter Yosemite National Park. It's a private achievement, my solo walk through wilderness: who else knows what I did; who cares that I hiked the high mountains camping and cooking alone? It's not easy – certainly not something anyone might do – but since I'm by myself, it's an unrecognised accomplishment.

I stop for lunch – corn-sunflower bread and a chunk of cheddar cheese – at the bridge over Lyell Fork of the Tuolumne River before heading down beautiful, forested Lyell Canyon. The Kuna Crest looms to the east and Amelia Earhart Peak and Potter Point soar along the west canyon wall.

At the junction with the trail leading to Ireland Lake I stop for the night at the large, well-used camp site. Park rangers have strung a steel cable high off the ground between two trees for hikers to use to hang their food. I've heard of the 'kamikaze bear' that visits this site. It climbs the tree until well above the cable, then launches itself out towards bags suspended from the cable, hoping to rake the bags with its claws as it falls past, risking injury for the reward of an easy meal. This is what happened to the young women I met the other day. Fortunately, the camp site is deserted and my two small bags, by now fairly empty, will hopefully not attract any nocturnal visitors. I move my sleeping bag far away from the wire, so that if the bear comes, I won't be in its path.

The night passes without incident, and in the morning I walk the few miles to Tuolumne Meadows and Highway 120. Now that I'm in the park, I decide I should get a wilderness permit in case a ranger asks me. They're free, anyway. Technically, I should have got one before I started, but there was nowhere along the way to pick one up.

The wilderness permit kiosk is in the hikers' car park across from Lembert Dome. I stand in the short line, listening to the ranger officiously instruct each applicant about rules and regulations for wilderness camping. On the bulletin board I see another bear warning prominently displayed: 'Bears are very clever, and are drawn to human food. Once they become conditioned to it, they seek it out, and become unnaturally aggressive and dangerous.' More good news from the National Park Service.

I hand my permit form to the ranger, and she hands me back my permit along with the list of rules and regulations. She goes over each and every point – how far to camp from streams, rules about fires (I never have one), being careful with drinking water, how to hang food so that bears don't get it – in a tone of voice that sounds like she thinks I know nothing. I'm sure she's just fed up with repeating the same information to the many hikers who stop for their permits, but does she have to treat each and every one of us like an incompetent halfwit? She really needs a new job.

At the Tuolumne Meadow Grill, with forty kilometres to Yosemite Valley, I stop for a turkey and cheese croissant and a bottle of Heineken beer. Tuolumne Meadows, beautiful as it is, is too crowded for my taste. I've camped alone in delightful solitude each night, so I figure I'll walk to Cathedral Lakes, renowned for good swimming and great views, and spend the night there. One more day will bring me to the official end of the John Muir Trail.

The late afternoon swimming at Lower Cathedral Lake is superb. After dinner, I carefully balance my two food bags on the high steel cable stretched between two trees. The wilderness camp site at Cathedral Lakes is glorious, with Echo Peaks, Cathedral Peak, the Unicorn and distant Half Dome washed in an orange alpen glow against a purpling sky. As twilight comes, I walk up onto the broad, polished granite backside of Medlicott Dome and watch the sky begin to sparkle with stars. A few dead trees stand in silhouette against the fading light, and two burly shadows lumber down the rock slab towards the camp site.

Damn. Those are bears. I had heard that Cathedral Lakes had problem bears who descend on the camp sites each evening, but I'm not really worried, as there's nothing in my camp to attract them.

What I'm forgetting, though, are the other campers at the lake, including the two latecomers who the bears surprise as they're cooking dinner. From their camp I hear a huge commotion, but somehow they manage to fend off the bears, get their food and unwashed dishes into bags, and toss them over the wire. Including mine, there are now four pairs of food bags, one of them dripping the remnants of a meal of baked beans, all hanging from the same wire and making irresistible bear bait. The sight and scent of all that food, and the tantalising drip of beans in tomato sauce drives the bears wild. They make the camp sites into a three-ring circus of chaos and cacophony going from camp site to camp site, back to the wire, then back to the camp sites.

My isolated camp, with no tent and far away by the shore of the lake, is quiet. I chose my site well, anticipating a bear visit. All my gear – cook pot, stove, pack – is on a large rock a hundred metres away with only my torch and boots near me. I listen as the other campers yell at the bears and bang pots together to scare them away. The beams of their torches wave wildly through the tree branches.

The bears grunt and lumber about. One of them climbs the tree with the wire and begins shaking the wire furiously! It must have learned that unequally balanced bags will slip down into easy reach. I'm sure my nearly empty bags are okay, but wonder about the other pairs. Anyway, there's nothing I can do now.

Too tired to listen to the nonstop commotion from the distant camp sites, I fall into sleep. Suddenly I'm awake. Hot breath hits my forehead and I open my eyes to the unmistakable shape of a large black bear looming hideously close to my shoulder.

The bear snuffles and grunts as my mind races desperately, thinking, *What do I do now?* Briefly I wish I had at least the thin nylon of a tent wall between me and the bear.

The bear grunts and raises its head. It's almost on top of me, but stops, seeming more curious than intent on attack. With grizzly bears, long exterminated from California, it's best to curl up and play dead. But with black bears, the expert advice is to yell and try to scare them off.

I sit straight up in my sleeping bag, fling my arms out to the side and make the loudest noise I can, hoping the experts are right. The startled bear stops, turns its head, lets out a woofing sound, then scrambles away.

Thinking that I'm obviously not far enough away from the other camps, I pick up my sleeping bag and foam pad, slip on my boots and move away from the bear-plagued site. It's a bad night for sleeping.

Park rangers say bears are a people problem and they're right. If not for those idiots who had shown up at dusk and started cooking, oblivious to the fact that they're camping at one of the most notorious bear spots in the park, we might have been spared this night of bearanoia.

Finally, about 4.30 am, the bears make their exit, leaving everyone terrorised but alive, and our food still hanging from the wire.

As soon as it's light enough to walk I retrieve my food bags and leave, disgusted and angry at a truly miserable night. The other camp sites are quiet – everyone no doubt exhausted after the sleepless night.

The morning, however, is fine, and as I cross Cathedral Pass, I can see all the way across the park to distant Matterhorn Peak in the north and Vogelsang Peak in the south. I'm still shaken from the bear incident, but am thankful that the bears were intent on eating our food rather than us. Park bears, I figure, are indeed more dangerous, but probably see people as a source of food rather than actually as food. It certainly made quite a spectacular end to an otherwise delightful walk. It's funny that all through the really remote wilderness I had no problems, but once I got near Yosemite things started getting weird. Too many people, too much impact, so that even the animals are affected.

Musing about all that happened, I come to the Merced Lake trail junction. This morning there's almost no-one on the trail, and the peacefulness of this part of the park restores my sense of well-being.

Suddenly I hear a sharp scream. I turn just in time to see a huge bird swooping down on me. Wham! Before I can even get a good look at it, it knocks me to the ground and flies off. In its talons it has my hat – a circular brown woolly cap from Pakistan. I reach up and there's blood on my forehead where the big hawk's talons raked the hat off my head.

Dumbfounded, I prop myself up on the ground and watch the hawk fly up into a big pine tree with my hat. It sits there and screams at me – a harsh, piercing shriek. I scream back, pick myself up and move under the tree. 'Let go of my hat you stupid bird!' But no, it won't drop it, even though it's not the meal the hawk must have mistaken it for. Instead, it just flies off, abandoning its inedible prey, which sits there twenty metres off the ground on a tree branch in Yosemite. Incredible. I shake my head in amazement and shouldering my almost empty pack, set out on the final stretch to the valley floor.

THE MOST BEAUTIFUL WOMAN IN THE WORLD

(OR I'M IN THE WRONG FILM)

Anthony Haywood

Anthony was born in Fremantle, Western Australia. He first pulled anchor at eighteen to spend two years travelling through Europe and the USA. He studied literature and Russian language at university and worked for various companies in Melbourne as a technical writer and trainer. In 1992, after sojourns in London and Moscow, he moved to Germany where he works as an author for Lonely Planet, online writer and editor, and translator.

He has co-authored a number of Lonely Planet guidebooks, including *Germany*, *Western Europe*, *Europe on a Shoestring*, and *Russia, Ukraine & Belarus*, as well as contributed to the *Out to Eat* series and the first *Lonely Planet Unpacked* collection. He is currently based in Frankfurt am Main.

Zagreb. Hot day. Our Man stands with backpack and unknown purpose on market square. Loud cries as crowds mill. Trams rattle busily down thoroughfare, disgorging passengers. Middle-aged women carrying shopping bags – fresh produce, bread – board trams. Rambunctious atmosphere. Our Man looks somewhat baffled. Wears sandals, old jeans. Close-up of face: Our Man is rather bedraggled, having slept rough for past months.

FLASHBACKS
Spain. In car with three petty thieves who are driving to Benidorm to 'hallucinate' at topless women bathers. Our Man thinks, *Topless women are not the only substance these men are on*, and opens knife cautiously inside pocket. 'You got money?' driver asks. Our Man thinks, *At least they ask*; but says, 'Fifty pesetas. Looked for work back in . . .' and mentions the name of last town he passed before getting into car. *Ah, camping ground! Get out here before things get out of hand. Get out slowly, no aggravation.* How to surprise a thief: 'Oh, nice camping ground. I'll stay'. Either they stop or they don't stop. They stop. Close, but not dangerous. Exhilaration. Man is born free but everywhere in cars full of thieves . . .

Things to Remember No 1: Never get so thirsty while waiting for a ride that it clouds your good judgement.

Barcelona, a staircase. Small, wiry guy pursues Our Man monkey-like up stairs on pretence of showing him a room. Halfway up, Monkey Man pats Our Man's arse and shrieks with delight. Our Man turns and beats a retreat.

Things to Remember No 2: Never let wily monkeys pat you on the arse on the promise of a cheap room. They bite.

Entrance to hotel off Barcelona's La Rambla. Smile at two women as they exit hotel. One purrs delight in rasping male voice.

Things to Remember No 3: Eighteen is probably a decent age to learn to tell the difference between a woman and a transvestite.

SCENE TWO

Market square. Voice behind Our Man. (But what was Things to Remember No 4 again?)

FRANJO: (heavy accent, educated appearance; holds large roll of paper that looks like poster) You want something?

OUR MAN: (surprised, turning) Uh?

FRANJO: Where you from?

Tram rattles past. Reply lost in din. Distant grotesque market cry.

Cut to leafy side street. Our Man walks along road with Franjo. Birdsong. Loud SNACK! nearby like gunshot. Football lands and bounces into frame. Child's shout. Child runs into frame. Retrieves ball.

OUR MAN: (out of shot) . . . so after waiting at the roadside in this heat and without water, I decided to walk back into town . . .

FRANJO: (casual, but penetrating) You can rest at my flat. But why do you hitchhike? Croatia has very good bus services.

OUR MAN: Nice way to meet people, and I don't like buses . . . hate buses . . . and I like *not* knowing what will happen next.

SCENE THREE

Staircase. Lots of wood. Our Man and Franjo ascend. Small metal nameplates on doors of flats. Residence for military brass. Our

Man's familiar sandalled feet patter up stairs. Taking 'Things to Remember No 2' to heart, Our Man is *behind* Franjo.

View through window in staircase. Crow consumes dead song-bird on street, watched by several curious children. One child holds football.

Franjo opens door of flat and both enter living room.

FRANJO: Put your pack down here. You want to shower?

OUR MAN: (indecisively) Alright.

Franjo opens sliding French window leading onto balcony. Outside, Franjo has unrolled 'poster', a large map of the USA. It is a computer print-out, and the map is created out of hundreds of numbers from zero to ten.

[Things to Remember No 3½: Never trust a man who prints such ridiculous maps.]

FRANJO: But first I want to show you this. I printed it at work. I work for the government.

OUR MAN: Army?

FRANJO: Yes, the army.

Bathroom. Our Man stands naked at wash basin and shaves. Showers. Later, Our Clean Man stands with Franjo again in living room.

FRANJO: I want you to meet my girlfriend.

OUR MAN: (incredulous) Now?

FRANJO: It's not far. She's in hospital.

OUR MAN: (lacking empathy) . . . um . . .

Two tattooed heavies (strapping thighs, rippling nose muscles) enter room. Franjo, now also lacking empathy, barks something at Heavy Number One. Heavies One and Two alter course and silently steer out of flat. Close-up of Our Man's face: perplexed. Our Man is looking a shade uncomfortable by now. He smells a rat.

SCENE FOUR

Scrub-tufted landscape in outlying suburb. Our Man and Franjo walk purposefully through wasteland and cross railway line. They stop at the gates of a hospital. Franjo fumbles for cigarette nervously.

FRANJO: (gives ID-like document to Our Man; insistent tone) Hold this, please!

Our Man holds the document. When Franjo doesn't ask for it back, Our Clever Man puts it in his shirt pocket. Triumphant expression on Our Man's face, for he thinks he now holds the trump card. Backpack back in flat, no key, no clear idea about location of flat: absolutely ridiculous. But the ID! Our Man thinks, *Ha! I've got that!*

FRANJO: My girlfriend is very beautiful. You're going to be surprised.

OUR MAN: (subdued, but pleased with himself) Oh, really? *(I like surprises.)*

FRANJO: The most beautiful woman in the world!

OUR MAN: Now you've really got my curiosity up.

They enter a hospital yard. Our Man is suddenly desolate. Sign indicates it's a psychiatric hospital.

OUR MAN: I'd rather not stay too long, you know. I'm still, um, tired from the morning.

FRANJO: (unreassuringly) Just a little while!

OUR MAN: I'd rather not, really. Not at all.

FRANJO: (close-up of Franjo's determined, angry expression) But we're here now!

OUR MAN: Look, this really isn't a good day for me. We should return to the flat.

FRANJO: I met my girlfriend here, in hospital. You'll see – The Most Beautiful Woman in the World!

Our Man thinks, *This better be good.*

They approach the main portal of a ward. All wards are free standing in pleasantly landscaped gardens. Our Man thinks, *Nice start, but this tranquillity is a tad menacing.*

OUR MAN: I'll stay out here in the fresh air.

FRANJO: But you *must* meet her.

OUR MAN: You go, I stay here.

Franjo approaches main portal. *Battleship Potemkin*-like matron bars door. She recognises Franjo and refuses him entry. Franjo begins to argue. Screaming crescendo. Franjo shouts something, matron falls silent, stunned. She stomps inside. Franjo, still determined, walks around side of ward to window. Shortly, woman appears at window. Most Beautiful Woman in the World. Dumpy. Dark rings around swollen eyes. Bags big enough to fill two left-luggage lockers. Depressed. Groggy. Tranquillised from top to toe. Looks forty-something.

Free-standing ward nearby. Our Disappointed Man has attracted the attention of disturbed children, who congregate on beds and peer at him through window. Most are four, five or six years old. Wretched gurgling sounds, grotesque expressions. Our Clever Man, thinking there must be a rule against this sort of thing, extracts ID and examines it thoroughly for the first time. Picture of Franjo. Name of hospital. Word 'Schizophrenia' decipherable in Croatian. Hospital admission ID. Pulled the Joker.

Franjo tenderly snogs craning neck of Most Beautiful Woman in the World at window, says something apparently flattering, takes her hand. Most Beautiful Woman in the World melts like the Snow Princess, loses herself in his eyes. Suddenly finding herself again, she looks over. Slow motion. Our Man waves quick motion to Franjo, indicating that they should leave. Both look over in loving unison. *Swan Lake* in a duck pond. She thinks Our Man is waving to her, waves back. Disturbed children nearby coo and gurgle more loudly. Tangle of heads and limbs at window.

Meanwhile, alarmed by gurgles, Matron smells altogether different psychotic rat and heaves herself around side of building. All take fright. Most Beautiful Woman in the World withdraws head. Franjo retreats in besotted daze. Our Man freezes. Matron gesticulates wildly, sweeps the entire scene with one angry glance, and stumbles backwards into ward in disbelief.

Franjo joins Our Man.

FRANJO: Very beautiful!

Our Man nods.

FRANJO: (angrily) You see the fat woman who wouldn't let me in?

OUR MAN: The matron?

FRANJO: The matron!

OUR MAN: Yes.

FRANJO: (angrier) Bitch!

Our Man frowns.

FRANJO: You see how she suddenly said nothing, went inside?

OUR MAN: Yes.

FRANJO: I told her I would kill her!

OUR MAN: Really?

FRANJO: (menacingly) I've got friends . . .

OUR MAN: Friends are good. I think I need to get back to your flat.

Cut to Franjo and Our Man walking across wasteland.

FRANJO: Have you ever heard of the Mafia?

OUR MAN: Yes.

FRANJO: I am Mafia. We steal cars, we break into shops and we sell what we steal.

OUR MAN: I thought you worked for the army.

FRANJO: During the day.

OUR MAN: Oh.

SCENE FIVE

Franjo and Our Man entering Franjo's flat. Familiar sound of sandals pattering up wooden stairs; Franjo *ahead* of Our Man.

OUR MAN: (unconvincingly) You know how I was trying to hitch to Belgrade? I've actually arranged to meet friends there . . . they're waiting for me and I'm already late.

FRANJO: (disappointed) But I thought you wanted to stay here for a few days. I can show you around, take you to discos. We can have fun together.

OUR MAN: (gathering backpack and belongings) I promised my friends . . .

FRANJO: Do you need a shirt?

OUR MAN: (perplexed) A shirt?

FRANJO: (opening door of cabinet; new shirts in original packing spill on to floor) Here, choose any shirt you like.

OUR MAN: (hesitantly) Are you sure you want to give me a shirt?

FRANJO: (holding up the least tasteful shirt) This one? (holding up another) Or this?

OUR MAN: (choosing unremarkable white shirt, not wanting to be seen in Zagreb wearing a rare shirt) This one is quite nice.

FRANJO: You can have it. (Reaches into cabinet again and this time key rings tumble in unseemly fashion onto floor) Would you like one of these, too?

Our Man selects a key ring with a plastic bear attached wearing a pullover. No keys though. Might be a car key-ring.

OUR MAN: Well, Franjo, my friends will be waiting . . .

FRANJO: But why do you want to go to Belgrade?

Our Man, who can think of several good reasons, heads towards door. Franjo follows and embraces him.

FRANJO: You see, I am too intelligent. Sometimes this causes me a problem.

Our Man thinks, *I'm all ears.*

FRANJO: She's very beautiful, isn't she?

OUR MAN: (nodding) Yes, very.

FRANJO: Goodbye! And good luck in Belgrade.

Door closes.

Our Man recalls Things to Remember No 4: Don't follow a certified psychopath into a lunatic asylum and hold his ID for him while he snogs beautiful women. Invest in a good water bottle instead.

LAST DAYS IN MEDAN

Emma Miller

A freelance journalist from Melbourne, Emma seems to be followed by disaster wherever she goes. A visit to Indonesia was plagued by political rioting, Hungary suffered floods and cyanide-poisoned rivers and England saw foot-and-mouth disease, fuel strikes and transport mayhem the year she moved there. At least she always gets away unscathed. A former tabloid news journalist, Emma most recently worked on Guardian Unlimited's travel website and the travel section of *The Times* in London. Before that she updated chapters of LP's *Indonesia*, *Eastern Europe*, *Central Europe* and *Europe on a Shoestring* guides. Pray she doesn't come to your neighbourhood.

I HAD BEEN BACK IN MEDAN ONLY A FEW HOURS WHEN I REALISED SOMETHING WAS WRONG. Stepping outside the air-conditioned comfort of the four-star Danau Toba Hotel – a steal at just US$10 a double, courtesy of 1998's anti-Suharto riots and the subsequent tourist slump – I was perspiring within minutes. Now don't get me wrong – Sumatra is hot, humid and generally unpleasant for those unused to the tropics. But I wasn't unused to the tropics. I had been travelling around the island for more than two months so my sweat glands had finally surrendered to the unfailing humidity and had ceased dripping. Completely comfortable in the heat, I now got goose bumps in an air-conditioned room. But, suddenly, my body was misbehaving again.

A twenty-minute walk to check out timetables at the western bus depot left my daypack so soggy it was glued to my back. By the time I arrived, I was so exhausted I could barely remember why I'd gone there in the first place. My customary patience with the gaggle of drivers and young conductors, who invariably gathered round when I started asking questions, had disappeared.

Trudging back, I surprised myself by hailing a cycle rickshaw, something I never did on principle unless I was dog-tired at the end of a day. Back in my ice-cold room I decided to take a breather, watch comforting cable television and go over my notes.

I had three days until I flew home, back to a world where I would no longer be the weird foreigner who travelled alone and ate by herself in roadside truck stops, the rash young woman who walked the streets unaccompanied at night when most local women were safe and sound in their homes. In three days I would cease to be ferociously independent, necessarily self-sufficient, happy in my own company, lonely on occasion and dressed in unspeakably unfashionable – but Islam-friendly – long, floppy clothes. In three days I would no longer be the Lonely Planet travel writer to my fellow travellers, viewed with a mixture of awe and suspicion, a participant but also an official observer of that strange pastime called backpacking. In three days, my research of Sumatra for the encyclopaedic *Indonesia* guidebook would be over.

True, there would be two more months writing up the chapter but it wouldn't be quite the same. I would be home in Melbourne. I would have Maria next door calling 'He-ll-oohh' as she pushed open the wire-screen door bearing a slice of chocolate cake, followed by Mary and Leo, her unruly cats. There would be trips down to St Kilda's Acland Street, just below my flat, where cafés, bookshops and record stores offered the perfect venue for a travel writer seeking comforting urban chic. There would be calls from my mother to see if I needed anything. There would be walks on the beach when I couldn't bear to write about another hotel. Friends would be available for dinner, an evening at the pub or a night in with a video. There would be food suitable for vegetarians – fresh vegetables, bread with grainy bits, tofu burgers, Vegemite on crackers, pasta, pizza, and cups of freshly-brewed coffee and Lady Grey tea.

In three days all this would be mine, but before that I had to tie up the loose ends of my research and make sure I wasn't missing vital information that would be impossible to track down once I was back in Australia.

I had already been to Medan, the capital of Sumatra, twice – once on arrival and again about one month into the trip en route across the country. I found it a huge, sprawling city, whose shops and offices all looked the same to my Western eye, and whose streets extended for miles, changing names along the way at illogical points. Few of the restaurants or shops seemed to have signage, or at least, no signage that made it clear that they were indeed the place you were looking for. The dust was so thick and the traffic so heavy that the whole place appeared coated in a hazy film.

As I lay on my bed in the hotel, I marked several locations on the 140-item Medan map that would need checking. I also needed to locate and review the many eateries and nightspots recommended by fellow travellers and locals throughout my journey. Lastly, I needed to pin down Merpati Airlines on their routes, schedules and prices as every office around the country had given me a different story. I made a to-do list, and mentally sectioned off parts of the city I needed to visit to complete my research. There would be no coming back if I missed something this time.

After a couple of hours I felt ready to face the maelstrom of the city again and headed out towards one of the huge, modern shopping complexes, where there were a travel agent and telephone exchange I needed to visit. But within minutes I was sweating heavily and finding it difficult to breathe. I dragged myself into the air-conditioned shopping mall and up the escalators to one of Medan's few modern supermarkets. Coasting around the aisles felt rather dreamlike, but it wasn't anything I could put my finger on.

I guzzled two bottles of water and a jackfruit juice then headed back onto the street, berating myself for being such a wimp. The travel agent was just around the corner and I checked their details quickly before lurching back into the traffic. A passing rickshaw driver called out to me with the usual 'Where you going, mister?' and before I knew it I had nodded and was in the back of the vehicle, weaving between belching trucks, ageing cars and screeching motorcycles. The driver took me to the telephone exchange, waited outside while I checked prices and opening hours, then whisked me back to the hotel.

Back in my room I collapsed in a heap. It started to dawn on me that perhaps I had worked myself into the ground. I felt like a mule ready for the glue factory. Having pushed my body to the limit for two months, taking only half a day off the entire time, it now seemed to be disintegrating.

And perhaps it should have been. I had made my way, in trembling buses seemingly held together with bits of string, from Medan, through the central highlands to Aceh, down the west coast, over to Palembang and Pekanbaru and down to the southernmost tip, Bandarlampung, the departure point for ferries to Java. I had done a gruelling jungle trek to see the famous orang-utans of Bukit

Lawang, had climbed Gunung Sinabung near Berastagi, had caught the boat to Pulau Weh off the Aceh north coast and taken a twelve-hour overnight boat trip in a most unseaworthy vessel to the surfers' haven of Pulau Nias. I had ridden on the back of countless motorbikes at high speed, had walked around the whole of Danau Toba's Tuk Tuk peninsula in a day, and had narrowly escaped plummeting into a ravine after a landslide caused part of the road to give way under a bus I was travelling on.

Now, it seemed, I was paying the penalty. My legs ached, my back felt creaky and stiff and my head throbbed as if I'd been drinking gallons of *arak*, the illicit home-brewed liquor sold by the roadside in old Coke bottles.

Overwhelmed by a sense of despair at having failed myself with just three days to go, I drew the blinds and tried to sleep. In the darkened room I twisted and turned but couldn't seem to lie still. My joints were aching. I sweated through the sheet. I shivered. Hugging my knees to my chest seemed to alleviate the pain in my legs, and eventually I drifted off. Some time later, the shrill, overlapping voices of Medan's muezzins, blaring from the loudspeakers of every mosque in the city, woke me up. I groaned and tried to smother the sound by holding a pillow over my head.

The calls of the muezzins across the city, and in every Sumatran city, had at first seemed exotic, but by the end of the trip the five daily calls to prayer made me feel as if I were trapped in an Islamic snow dome with a transparent, but impenetrable, glass roof. I could sense Islam everywhere and the muezzins' cries, omnipresent as they spread their blanket of sound across the landscape, had come to symbolise just how much I did not fit in. Although I had studied Bahasa Indonesia for four years at high school and had visited Bali and Java several times, nothing had prepared me for two months alone in Sumatra. Women were distinctly second-class citizens in this part of the world and no matter how demurely I dressed, how much I averted my eyes from men's stares or how well I spoke Indonesian, I was treated with a mixture of curiosity, suspicion and, on occasion, hatred. My work for Lonely Planet had taken me way off the beaten track: for the last month of my trip I hadn't seen another Western tourist and had barely spoken a word of English. In this often hostile environment my work was what had given me purpose and kept me going. Now it seemed my body was giving in to the elements too.

As, one by one, the loudspeakers ceased their sermons, I began to realise that beneath the din the phone was ringing. It was my boyfriend, Chris, calling from Australia. I wearily related my last few days of travel, then off-handedly told him I wasn't feeling well. He suggested I see a doctor but I scoffed. 'What for – exhaustion? Because I've worked ten hours a day for sixty days and now my body doesn't want to go any more? What are they going to do about *that*?' I told him I wasn't that bad and the most sensible thing I could do if I didn't improve was to stay in the hotel until I had to catch my flight home. Three days in bed, doing my final research by phone, with room service to feed me and a taxi to the airport – pretty simple really. We hung up.

Ten minutes later he called back.

'You have to go to the doctor,' he insisted. 'You don't sound normal. You sound delirious. You're speaking very strangely.'

'What?' I exclaimed. I was losing patience.

'I insist you go to the doctor. Really. I'm going to call back in one hour and you'd better not be in your hotel room when I call. Please! Go to the doctor!'

Hmmph. With every ounce of strength I could muster, I hauled my creaking body out of bed and got dressed. By chance, Medan's biggest, most modern hospital was just 500 metres from the hotel. Built by a Singaporean company, it glimmered with promise on the horizon. The distance had seemed minuscule when I arrived, but now it seemed infinite and plagued by insurmountable obstacles like side streets, cars, bicycles, raised footpaths and a man selling live bats, strung upside down on a pole. I pushed on, pausing to catch my breath every few metres, finally staggering through the front doors of the hospital and slumping over the reception desk.

Feeling dizzy and nauseous, I feebly announced to the two nurses on duty, *'Saya sakit,'* although I doubt they needed telling I was sick.

One of them smiled and told me to wait while the other nurse called the doctor. I leaned against the counter, overcome by a feeling of breathlessness. Suddenly the room was only half there and the faces of the women slipped out of focus. Then everything went black.

The next thing I knew I was being carried by several people down a corridor and my chin was throbbing. I was placed in a bed in a large ward and nurses started undressing me and wrapping me in a white hospital gown. Someone pulled up my sleeve and found a vein, piercing it with a needle attached to a drip. I lifted my hand to touch my chin and found it covered in blood. I had bashed my chin on the reception desk as I went down, one of the nurses informed me matter-of-factly.

Dr Supratman was a pleasant, round-faced man in his mid-thirties, who spoke English well. He told me he wanted to do some tests because it was a very serious matter that I had fainted – I might have malaria, typhoid or even cholera. He wanted to keep me under observation for at least a couple of days.

My mind was racing. 'But what about all my things at the hotel? All my notes and maps and precious rolls of film?' All the work I had slaved over for the past two months was spread across the room with no-one to look after it – but I felt so weak I knew it would be impossible to make it back there in one piece. I spent the night twisting and turning and sweating. At some time in the very early morning I dragged my drip-stand to the bathroom because I needed to go to the toilet. I don't know how long it was before the nurses found me passed out on the tile floor. They told me not to go to the bathroom alone again.

Three days later I was propped up in bed in a private room at the Mount Elizabeth Hospital in Singapore while Dr Ong showed me the jar of black urine that he keeps in his office. 'This is what happens to people who don't get to hospital in time,' he said sternly. The sample had apparently been produced by a hapless traveller struck down with a nasty strain of malaria. One of the world's leading specialists in tropical diseases, Dr Ong had taken one look at me when I was wheeled into his hospital and pronounced: 'You have dengue fever, I'm sure of it.' He turned out to be right. Despite wearing long, light-coloured clothes, using a mosquito net and insect repellent, I had been bitten by an infected insect and had contracted 'break-bone fever', as dengue was once known.

Lying prostrate in bed, with a drip hanging out of my arm and sweat dripping from my forehead, I nodded politely as Dr Ong regaled me with tales of the countless tourists who had been evacuated from all over Asia for expert treatment in Singapore's flashy, modern hospitals. Each day, when he came to check on my condition, Dr Ong reminded me that it was my duty to write about the dangers of South-East Asian illnesses, to warn other travellers what might befall them and, if it did, to get to a proper hospital as soon as possible.

To the doctor, I was more than just another traveller struck down in the tropics. Here was his chance to get his stories and warnings out to the general travelling public. Here was a writer from Lonely Planet. As for me, I just wanted to sleep.

THE LOST CURD

Larry Buttrose

Larry was born at the bottom of the world, in Adelaide, South Australia. He moved to the bright lights of Sydney as a singer in a cabaret group but these days earns his living as a poet, screenwriter, playwright and journalist. He is the author of two novels, *The Maze of the Muse* and *Sweet Sentence*, and two books of travel writing, one of which – *The Blue Man* – is published in Lonely Planet's travel literature series, Journeys.

THE SUN ROSE OVER THE SANDY FLATS ON THE FAR SIDE OF THE GANGES, BEAMS RIPPLING ACROSS THE SURFACE OF THE RIVER, ITS TURBID GREEN BLESSED BY MORNING WITH A PALE, CELESTIAL BLUE THAT STRETCHED UPWARDS INTO THE WINTER MIST. I walked down the steps of my hotel and turned right, passing Manikarnika Ghat, the main burning ghat and one of the most auspicious places where a Hindu can be cremated. I saw men bathing in the algae-green, stagnant water by the river's edge, using their lungis to clean themselves, then emerging from the water to dry and stretch their lungis out in the sun, the sheets of coloured fabric arrayed down the stone steps of the ghat. The men's bodies were nearly all slim and well-muscled, from a combination of adequate but not over-nourishment, and physical activity. So much is still done by hand in India that elsewhere is done by machines.

I passed a small temple just above the river's edge. A woman was dribbling water from the palm of her hand onto the forehead of a stone statue of Nandi, the bull vehicle of Shiva. Inside, I glimpsed other women working in wordless cooperation, with ancient, fluent movements of their hands, placing oils and garlands around the sacred Shiva lingam. A few metres further on I turned down some steps, passing the Eternal Flame from which the cremation pyres are lit. I stopped at a vantage point above the burning places, where the embers of the final cremations of the previous night still glowed. I watched men – it is only Untouchable men who perform the work – scraping a mixture of wood and human ash into large metal bowls, which they carried on their heads down the final steps of the ghat to the river and tipped into the water. The bones that sometimes survive the flames – pelvis for women, sternum for men – had been removed the night before and thrown into the Ganges.

They weren't the only large objects the holy river had to digest. Pregnant women, children, lepers and sadhus were not burnt at the pyres, being pure already, but were simply dropped into the river. But for the rest of humanity, for the soul to go 'straight to heaven', the path to purification was to be cremated in the ancient and holy city of Varanasi. Bodies were brought in cars and taxis, on trains, up on the luggage racks of buses, iced aboard aircraft from abroad. Upon arrival they were carried on bamboo stretchers down the narrow alleys of the old city by chanting bearers, the corpses stitched into muslin and covered with glittering gold fabric.

I watched as a man scoured a burning site back to the bare earth, ready for the next pyre to be constructed there, while beside him another man was well into building a new pyre, a raft of logs as a foundation, smaller pieces crosshatched above. Two old Indian men in dhotis, white shirts and shabby woollen Nehru jackets exchanged guttural greetings beside me, cleared their nostrils and spat. They pointed out a hospice, right above the ghat, from the windows of which the soon-to-depart could see the daily burnings, the fiery pyres to which their own bodies would soon be consigned, and feel comfort for the fate of their souls.

The pair drifted off, and I had just returned my attention to the tasks going on below, when a worker tossed a large bowlful of water onto a set of embers right beneath me. The steam and smoke billowed up in an enormous cloud, instantly enveloping me. As I stepped back from the railing, coughing and spluttering, I discovered that my face, hands and clothing were covered with a fine layer of white ash of mingled human and plant origin.

My first reaction was mild revulsion: I was covered with the earthly remains of a person I had never even laid eyes upon. But the feeling was followed quickly by one of calm. No, it was fine. It was in the nature of this place, right and fitting. Tourist and casual spectator, one of the daily influx of curious visitors who stood and watched the flames devour the marrow of the bones and lick the expressions from the faces of the dead, I had been briefly drawn into the reality of the crematory rites. As I walked away, my rationalism attempted to reassert itself: human ash or tree ash, ash is ash. But still I couldn't quite brush it off.

I entered a narrow, medieval alley above the ghat, one that led up through a tracery of similar alleys towards the main road and the new part of town, to distant banks and offices, railway station and airport. I passed the yards of wood merchants stacked high with logs to be carefully weighed on scales and sold piece by piece to the families of the deceased before being carried down by porters to the burning ghat. Wood was expensive, and a lot of it was required for complete consumption of a body by the flames. Poorer families could not always afford enough wood, and sometimes pieces of charred flesh remained as provender for dogs; even consumed, so I was told, by ganja-intoxicated sadhus for the power it imparted.

I passed tiny *chai* and *paan* stands, whose sellers sat cross-legged before fans of bright green leaves, steel pots of betel nut and sticky-sweet concoctions. They did a brisk trade with mourners who sat out on benches drinking their chai in earthenware cups and chewing betel. There were purveyors of flower garlands and sheets of golden fabric to be used to cover the corpses. Other stands were selling bags of powdered sandalwood to perfume the pyres. Further up the alleyways were the curd-makers, milk slowly bubbling in vats over the wood fires of their earthen *chullahs*; the well-fleshed vendors of Varanasi silk; the curio and trinket shops; and the tiny shopfronts, their keepers squatting on cushions in the entrance, selling bottled water, cigarettes and matches, toilet paper for the tourists and film for their cameras.

The alley narrowed as it began to climb away from the river, until it was just wide enough for a meandering cow and a bicycle to edge past each other. The flagstoned floor was coated with mud, cow dung and red, expectorated betel juice. The cold air, still heavy with mist, resounded to the slow thud of men driving iron stakes into the larger logs, breaking them up for burning. I heard temple bells, morning greetings and massed chanting drifting up from the ghats. A boy was milking a piebald goat as I squeezed past, while his little brother juggled its bleating black kid.

I climbed the alley as it steepened, looking for the turn-off to the Shanti Guest House, my favourite breakfast place, when at a crossroads between two alleys I happened upon a pathetic scene. A boy was crying, his mouth open wide in a wail. He clutched a small wooden spatula, and on the ground in front of him, smashed on the flagstones, was the clay cup of curd his mother had just bought him. The spilt curd had splashed into cow dung and betel, and there was no way anything could be retrieved. His mother was grabbing his hand and trying to hustle him on, but the child was standing his ground, staring down at the brilliant white of the curd on the floor of the alley.

My momentum carried me a little way beyond, but as I drew to a halt I was already unzipping my moneybelt. I felt the eyes of the mother, a poor woman with a sad face, light upon me instantly. She was dressed in the grubby red robes of a lower caste. On seeing me see her, she cast her eyes down. As I located a typically grimy two-rupee note and approached, she raised her eyes again and watched expectantly. The boy looked up, uncomprehending at first, his eyes still filled with tears for the lost curd. His mother gave me a shy smile and prompted him to take the money. Bewildered still, he did, and ran off up the alley, back to the curd stand. His mother smiled at me fleetingly, then turned her eyes downward again.

Walking on towards breakfast, I experienced the odd feeling of having 'done a good deed'. So tiny, yet it made me feel good. Perhaps it was seeing my own infant son as that boy, bawling helplessly on a street corner for something fallen and broken. Or perhaps it was more to do with the pale ash I discovered still adhered to my pullover, the flecked remains of some unknown, departed soul. Back in my room after breakfast, I meditatively washed out my socks.

FEAR & LOATHING IN FUERTEVENTURA

Damien Simonis

Back in the late 1980s, Damien had a hankering to go to Europe and live in France. Just how he thought he was going to achieve this by purchasing a one-way ticket to Cairo remains as much a mystery today as it was then. Since arriving in the Egyptian capital and steadfastly refusing to eat his first breakfast in any place suggested by a guidebook, he has spent many years contributing to precisely such publications. Led more by accident than intent, he has lived and worked in the Middle East, Sicily, London, Toledo, Madrid, Milan, Florence and Barcelona. France is still waiting (no doubt with bated breath). Journalist, linguist and photographer, Damien has managed, despite himself, to eke out a living by stumbling around the Mediterranean (mostly) and collecting information for various Lonely Planet guidebooks, Condensed guides and City Maps so that others might stumble after him with slightly more aplomb. When the hangovers clear, it all seems vaguely worthwhile.

I STRIPPED THE LIDS BACK FROM MY CRUSTILY BLOODSHOT EYES AND GLARED AT THE LITTLE TRAVEL CLOCK PERCHED IMPERTI-NENTLY BY THE BED HEAD. Jesus! One o'clock in the afternoon! I collapsed back into the pillow with one of those hung-over groans that come only on special occasions when you know the excesses of the night before are going to render the day after (or what's left of it) particularly painful.

A crumpled and self-pitying heap, I stared disconsolately at the ceiling. The facts. I was feeling remarkably ill and in dire need of hospitalisation and serious water transfusion. I was in a cheap and charmless hotel in Corralejos in the north of Fuerteventura, the Canary Islands. I was four hours' flying time from my squalid little London flat in stunning Stockwell and my charter flight was just about due to take off from the airport, thirty-five kilometres south down the coast.

My attempts now to string together one or two coherent thoughts were not unlike trying to start my car on certain cold, winter mornings. Bits and pieces came trickling back to me, attempting a break-and-enter into my dulled grey matter. The previous night had been my last in the Canaries. The job was in the bag, research and most of the writing done on a jolly new guidebook to the islands. A feeling of enormous relief, intense relaxation and even a little self-satisfaction at having churned out yet another 250 pages warmed my soul. My guard was down, I owed nothing to anyone. My time, just for a change, was my own. And so I proceeded, as usual, to break one the cardinal travel commandments: Thou Shalt Not Hit the Bottle the Night Before You Fly.

I'll spare you the tawdry details, if only because I can barely recall them myself. For weeks I had toured the islands, seeking out travel gems for those hoping to visit them independently and with sensitivity. How I had scoffed at the planeloads of lobster-red lager louts shovelled into the crass resorts that blight certain unfortunate corners of this Atlantic archipelago. With their real English break-fasts and wet T-shirt competitions, I had observed them slithering into raucous oblivion night after night. Now it was my turn.

There cannot have been a bar in Corralejos I did not grace with my increasingly insensate presence that night. By the wee hours I had long lost my very recently acquired Swiss friends, for whom earlier that day I had acted as interpreter with the Guardia Civil, the local constabulary. The young Swiss lads wanted to report a theft from their hire car but the sceptical men of the law weren't buying it. In the end they agreed to prepare a statement alleging the theft that, they hissed, would not be valid for insurance claims. Grateful for any result at all, the Swiss invited me to a large afternoon pint of ale, and another and, well, the rest is bet-ter left to the imagination.

I do recollect stumbling into an early-opening bar at dawn and stumbling back out again shortly afterwards following a brief and inconclusive interchange with a less than sympathetic bar fellow. Then, seized by one of those not-so-rare moments of alcohol-induced inspiration I blundered into my hotel room (I'm still not sure how I found it) in search of camera gear, determined to take Pulitzer prize–winning early morning shots. One was eventually published, showing just how divinely directed my judgement had been. A little later, back from my meaningful shutter-bugging mission, I showered, changed and laid myself out like a new suit on the unslept in bed. I'll just shut my eyes for ten minutes . . .

Judging by the movement of the ceiling one might have sur-mised I was pitching about on an inter-island ferry. No such luck. What was to be done? Action stations. Dammit, charter flights are always delayed, sometimes by hours. Encouraged by this com-forting self-delusion, I wrenched myself into a vaguely vertical pose, crammed goods and chattels into my bag and clambered downstairs to reception. Teetering on the verge of nervous col-lapse, I nevertheless raised a feeble smile for the surly reception-ist as I settled the bill. Sunglasses in place, I took what I hoped looked determined steps into the outside world. Wishing someone would turn down the sun, I hailed a taxi and set off on my quixotic quest. Without so much as a cup of coffee on board, I sank into a self-chastising reverie, grateful the taxi driver was the taciturn type.

Oh God, how many times do you have to do this? Grand travel writer you are! You've hitched across the sands of Syria and hiked through the mountains of Morocco but you can't even manage the simple operation of getting on a charter flight from the Canary Islands to London. Thousands of gormless package tour troops carry off this feat every day of the week, but not you.

Shelling out wads of pesetas on arrival, I remembered ruefully that I had planned a relaxing, cheap, morning bus ride to the airport. The taxi's meter might now be off but mine was barely beginning to tick away.

I still felt like something the cat wouldn't dream of dragging anywhere as I blundered my way around the small airport foyer until finally striking the charter flight desk. The sunglasses remained firmly in place. Gathering my shattered wits about me I inquired, feigning airy nonchalance, as to whether my flight was still hanging about.

''Fraid not sir. It left bang on time.' Bloody typical.

'And when might another be leaving for London?'

'Oh,' came the cheery response, 'in about an hour and a half.'

'May I purchase a place on it?'

'Absolutely. We have a block of empty seats on that flight. Come back in an hour.'

My spirits felt almost lifted: enough time to get comfort food, juice, coffee and a couple of litres of water. It would be stretching it to say I felt physically better but at least I didn't feel worse. The legs were holding up and I noticed that, in spite of everything, I was eliciting limited real-time responses from what I have on occasion been known to refer to as my mind.

Never count your chickens, or any other flying objects. My return to the charter flight desk proved a disappointment with a curious Kafkaesque twist.

'I'm sorry but we can't sell you a ticket on this flight.' And why, pray tell? 'Well, the empty seats were block-booked by a group that hasn't turned up. We haven't been able to contact them, so we can't sell their seats.'

That a charter flight with twenty empty seats was due to leave for London in half an hour and that I could not purchase a spot on board was a little more than this little black duck could bear. The flight left and I was still stuck at Fuerteventura airport. Further inquiries revealed that the next couple of flights to London were full. Only two others were scheduled for the day: a late-night London flight, on which they could not guarantee me a place, and another to Newcastle, on which they could. A one-way ticket would cost about a hundred quid. My heart sank. Well, I guess I could stay a night in the nearby town of Puerto del Rosario and leave tomorrow.

'Are there any seats available on flights tomorrow?'

'Er, no, because charters for the UK fly out of Fuerteventura only on Wednesdays and Saturdays.' You're kidding me.

'Right, I'll have to think about this then.' I sloped off. The word frustration doesn't quite do justice to my feelings at that moment. The only other open ticket counter was Iberia, Spain's national carrier.

'Good afternoon,' I smiled pastily. 'I was wondering if you might have any flights to London this evening.'

'Yes we do.' Good. 'The last flight today leaves at 7 pm and takes you to Madrid, where you have to change for the onward flight to London the following day.' Oh great, and all that for the mere bagatelle of four hundred quid.

I had by now become intimately acquainted with the remotest corners of Fuerteventura airport. In particular, I had patronised the coffee bar as often as would be necessary for one day. I couldn't stomach the thought of even resting my eyes on the newspaper I had picked up. The number of options available to me was dwindling. There was nothing for it. I shuffled back to the charter flight desk.

'Any news on the London flight?' No? Fine. 'In that case, perhaps I should take a ticket on the Newcastle one instead.' I handed over the money and a couple of hours later was winging my way to Newcastle, far in the north of England. The flight was reassuringly eventless and the pains in my head slowly receded to a more manageable, if constant, dull thudding.

I emerged from passport control at Newcastle airport and set to waiting for my bag. It was a long and fruitless wait. It is never pleasant being the last, sad, solitary figure hovering with ever-diminishing hopes by a luggage carousel that remains obstinately empty. It was an especially uncomfortable thought in my state of diminished physical and mental capacity. And it was made worse by the fact that my cotton shorts and T-shirt were rather inappropriate attire for the rigours of a northern winter. The headlines swam before my eyes – Travel Writer Dies of Frostbite in Newcastle After Marathon Canaries Piss-Up. It would be fair to say I was disgruntled as airport attendants ushered me about and took the details of my missing luggage. 'As soon as we have located the luggage it will be forwarded to you in London.' Oh great!

At Information I learned there were no further flights, trains or buses to London that evening. It was either a night at the airport or a hotel in tropical Newcastle. Not good. Upon taking stock, I realised that things could and had become worse. In my blurred packing frenzy earlier in the day, I had cleverly left my house keys and computer power cable in my now wandering luggage. The computer, whose battery had just died, carried locked in its bosom my address book, for which I happened not to have a print-out on my capable, travel-hardened person.

A call to my shared dive in London brought no result, so I called the only other number I could remember. My long-suffering friend in the Cotswolds responded immediately to my pitiful cry. 'Of course you can stay the night here – we'll leave the door open for you.'

And so to the car hire desk – I just wanted to get this nightmare over with. As I handed over my credit card for the car I wondered if toothpicks for keeping eyes open came with the keys. Suitably shivering and feeling a little silly I took charge of the shiny steed that would carry me back in the general direction of home. The night seemed endless and frostily menacing. I could have done with a drink but settled for a bag of crisps, a Coke and a full tank of super.

The following day, feeling a little steadier after a night's slumber in the Cotswolds, the time came to pursue the journey to its conclusion. Spare set of flat keys in hand and now dressed appropriately for the season, it was left only to drop the car off in central London. Sidling up to the kerb I managed to scrape the front wheel. Thinking nothing of it I left the keys in the hands of an employee and went inside to retrieve my deposit. No such luck. I was informed that, having grazed the hub cap and lightly punctured the tyre I would be charged £140, the amount held in deposit almost to the penny. I must have been looking green around the gills.

'Terribly sorry, sir.' The attendant looked awfully apologetic, almost pained. I looked back at her blankly.

'I am not having a very good day,' was all I could manage. I backed out into the cold night air and, shoving my hands deep into my coat pockets, did a few mental sums as I made for the Tube. Pushing the boat out in the Canary Islands had cost me almost £400 – the cost of about three return charter flights. My luggage returned a week later. Oddly, I haven't been to Fuerteventura since.

CHICKEN RUN

Reg

Reg was born into a banished sect of the Amish community entirely dependent on technology and quickly grew to become a circus's accountant. After extensive traversions of his backyard he moved into the Granny flat recently extended onto the back of the dog kennel.

Realising that this was a completely unrealistic way to live Reg moved to Queensland in the mid 1980s . . . Realising that this was a completely unrealistic way to live Reg moved back to Melbourne in the mid 90s.

Joining Lonely Planet in 1997 Reg began a meteorical climb to the position of GM until the now-whispered-about Smelly Gnaken debacle. Demoting himself directly to the warehouse, where he discovered there wasn't one, he has spent the last three years looking for the house and will continue to do so until it's found. This is Reg's first attempt at writing, before this he used rocks.

THE MOST DISASTROUS PART OF TRAVELLING HOME WAS THE DECISION TO GO THERE IN THE FIRST PLACE. Admittedly, things had gone a little haywire and Uncle Luck wasn't watching over me. He was actually down the pub shouting Comrade Sense beer. So, with just enough for the bus fare, I headed for my childhood home a mere 2000 kilometres away.

There are two good things about being completely broke during twenty-two hours of sleepless, cramped, bus dreariness down the inland wheat route from Brisbane to Melbourne. One is that at no stage was I able to purchase any of the 'food' on offer from the Bain-Maries of Death in exotic locations such as Boggabilla, Dubbo and Wangaratta. The other is that when I finally got off the wretched coach Mummy would be waiting with Sunday roast. Salivating as I disembarked McAfferty's Interstate Express, which, contrary to its name, did stop – in Boggabilla, Dubbo and Wangaratta – I caught sight of my mum with my stepfather. Things had never gone well between my mum and me when David was around and the sternness chiselled into their faces signalled that not much had changed since I had left three years before.

'David and I have spoken and decided it would be better if you didn't come home at this point in time. I don't think my health could stand it and you know how your brother has been. We're having such trouble with him you know.'

'Yes,' I thought, and I know the two reasons why. 'And what would you propose I do then, Mother dear?'

'Well we thought you could maybe find a spot in a hostel or some emergency shelter till you found something more permanent.'

Late Sunday afternoon and stone cold broke. Yeah that'll be easy. 'Are you serious? Did I mention I don't have two cents to rub together?'

She started to rummage through her purse. 'Well, here's some money for a public phone. We've got to go now; the chicken's in the oven.'

I watched them leave with some of my more cumbersome luggage, perused the $1.70-worth of options I had, remembered the reason I'd left Melbourne in the first place, crossed Elizabeth Street and started hitchhiking back to Brisbane.

Walking forlornly through the late Sunday afternoon city – carrying a blue suitcase and two pillows wrapped up in a doona and tied together with string – I thought this could be a rather long evening in town. As it turned out it was only a short wait before I got the first of the many lifts needed to reach my destination.

'Where's ya goin' bro'?' asked the facially tattooed driver of an ageing green Falcon.

'Brisbane.'

'I take ya far as Pentridge, hey? Gotta go see me bro'.'

'Cool mate.' The thought of being dropped off outside Melbourne's jail seemed odd, but at least it was out of the city centre.

'Whatcha going ta Brisbane for, bro'?' The conversation inevitably wound its way around to what would become my on-the-road, hard luck anthem.

'Shit bro'! That's just not choice.' His ponytail shook slowly as the driver seemed to lament my situation for a moment or two. Then he asked, 'You smoke bro'?'

'Yeah but I haven't got any. Sorry mate.'

'Naa. Have a look at that,' he said, pointing at the dash. 'I grew it meself. I'm gonna sneak it in for me bro'.' I admired his weed as we pulled up on Sydney Road, directly across from Pentridge. As this was the end of the ride I started getting out of the car. 'Here, bro'.' A heavily tattooed hand was thrust out of the passenger-side window. I took the piece of foil offered, thanked my now very good friend and decided it would be a good idea to continue my hitching a little bit further down the road. With half the bud I'd just seen tucked away snugly in my pocket I walked down Sydney Road, stuck my finger out and a small Mazda ute pulled up just in front of me and pipped its horn.

'Where you headed young fella?', a shroud of white hair asked.

'Brisbane.'

'I can take you as far as Seymour. Well, that's as far as I can get from the Missus before she sends out a search party. Brisbane, eh? Long way to hitchhike.' As we drove I told my story for the second time, putting my Samaritan driver into a sort of trance which made me think he looked like a cloud. 'Soooo,' the fluffy furrowed brow eventually supposed, 'it's been about three days since you last had a beer then?'

'Well, yeah, I suppose,' I conceded oh-so-ever reluctantly.

'Shit! That's bloody terrible!' And with that, two fuzzy, gnarled hands wrenched hard on the steering wheel at precisely the right moment to send the car straight into the drive-through bottle shop at the Kalkallo Hotel. 'Dozen cans of Melbourne Bitter, thanks mate,' The Cloud announced to the attendant. 'Ahh, we'll have a couple of these as we go, eh?' I didn't think it was a question.

'Sure.' It turned out having a few while driving up the road actually meant drive a bit, find a roadside parking area, stop the car, drink all the beer and then drive some more.

'Shid! Id's all gone,' exclaimed a now dripping cotton-ball beard. 'Ah well!' he exclaimed as the fuzzy fingers again wrenched the steering wheel. 'I could use a coupla more of dem eh?' Suddenly the car was heading back the way we'd come.

'Umm.'

'S'oright mate. Jez wanna grab coupla more.' For only the second and still the last time in my life I went to the Kalkallo Hotel and, as the sun set, I set off once more on my way up the Hume Highway.

Miraculously, I drank ten cans; even more miraculously I made it to the outskirts of Seymour alive. A now drooling and drunkenly depressed old man explained how he had to drive back to Kalkallo as that was where he lived. I wished him luck, watched him U-turn and, now in a extremely inebriated state, thought, 'Where can I get some cigarette papers?' Because it was quite obvious to me, as well as the service station attendants about a kilometre up the road, that the one thing I really needed at that point was a joint – although to this day I think they were being sarcastic. Drunkenly content with papers and a packet of cheese-and-onion chips I managed to make it about another fifty metres up the road, where I proceeded to roll a spliff, smoke it, attempt to start hitching again and, five minutes later, to fall fast asleep.

I awoke with what I thought was a semitrailer driving through my head. Unfortunately this was not a hangover. It was in fact an eighteen-wheel semitrailer roaring past my head and showering me with gravel. It was the positioning of my makeshift camp that was to blame. Unable to think logically I'd put the blue suitcase up as a windbreak, sleeping on one of the pillows and using the other pillow and the doona for their proper purposes. Comfortable enough, but potentially suicidal as I'd managed to do this on the hard shoulder on the inside of a blind bend. The gravel-showering truck that had woken me had passed no more than a metre from my head. I dragged myself off the road and behind a bush. Still amazed to be in the world of the living I ate some chips, sat on my blue suitcase and started hitching again.

I also had a wicked hangover.

A moustache-less beard with wispy comb-over hairstyle was the day's first ride – not a particularly memorable one since I fell asleep almost immediately. Nothing wrong with a nice sleep except that I missed the turn-off that led to the quicker inland route. Regaining in-car consciousness about thirty kilometres shy of Albury–Wodonga and communicating almost entirely in expletives I explained my dilemma to my bookish-looking driver. The hairy chin started moving and told me that there was a road I could use to cut back from the Hume Highway to the Newel Highway. Excellent! The family sedan stopped at an innocuous side road.

''Bout a mile up that way there's a road on the left. It goes all the way back to where you want,' said the librarian.

'Cheers mate.' And off I set up the road.

Finally coming across a dirt track I figured was the road, I once again sat on my blue suitcase and, when the odd car eventually came along, stuck my finger out.

'Jump in mate,' a blonde mullet said through a cloud of dust. 'Whadda ya doin' out 'ere?' came the logical next question. Metallica blaring, I yelled my story to my rev-head driver, punctuating sentences with frequent, sharp intakes of breath as Speed Racer hurled his shuddering Sigma at an ever increasing velocity around dusty corners.

'Like me car, mate?' asked the bad eighties haircut.

In the hope he'd think something was wrong with the car and slow down I said, 'Aww, sounds a bit rough to me.' It worked: suddenly we weren't going fast any more.

'What! That's me lumpy cam. Don't ya fuckin' know nuffin' 'bout cars? Get out!' And with that I was back on the road. Boy Racer sped off spinning the wheels and for the second time that day small parts of road were hitting me. The dust settled and I brushed myself off. There was a buttocks-sized indentation forming in my blue suitcase. I filled this hole with its creator and settled in, somewhere in the middle of nowhere. Nice: just quiet, with only the wind and birds in the trees.

My next lift was my first ride in a truck. A large, white flat-bed rig pulled up just in front of me. The cropped head of what would be jet-black hair already had the truck moving before I climbed all the way in.

'Where ya going?' an unmoving five o'clock shadow mumbled.

'Brisbane.'

'I'm not.' That was the last thing Prickly Head said. An interminable length of time later, the road became sealed again, the truck made a right-hand turn and I was back on the highway. The end of day two was drawing near when one of the greater public speakers of our time stopped the truck and, with no more than a grunt, indicated that my ride had come to an end. Over another handful of chips I assessed how things were going. So far I'd gotten drunk, stoned, nearly squashed, lost, abused and ignored. On the down side I was hungry, broke and had made it only as far as beautiful downtown Forbes, not far enough for a day and a half hitching. With that in mind I decided to hitch a bit longer and sat myself by a park so that if no lift came along I could find a safer place to sleep than the one I'd managed the previous night. This turned out to be an unnecessary precaution when two Akubras in a hotted-up Holden ute pulled up.

'G'day mate,' said a huge bushy beard.

'G'day mate,' said the beard next to him. 'How far ya goin'?'

'Yeah how far ya goin'?'

'Brisbane.'

'Ahhh . . . We can take ya as far as Parkes.'

'Cool.' Not far, but forward, I thought as I climbed between the two hairy hats.

'Wanna pie?'

'Yeah, wanna pie?'

Wow, stereo. 'Sure.'

'Help yerself.' Number One gestured towards the dash, which was stacked three high with Four'n'Twenty pies.

'Yeah, help yerself. We've just had our footy club end of season do and me an' me brother here stole a tray of pies.'

'Yeah a tray of pies an' a slab of beer.'

'Yeah, a slab of beer. Wanna beer?'

'Yeah, wanna beer?'

'Sure.' Forty minutes of beer and pies later we pulled into Parkes.

'We'll take ya through town to the truck stop.'

'Yeah, the truck stop. You should be able to ask one of the truckies to take ya all the way through.'

'Yeah, all the way through.' We pulled up at the Ampol road-house.

'Thanks guys.'

'See ya mate.'

'Yeah, see ya mate and good luck.'

'Yeah, good luck.' The tomato-sauce-encrusted beards waved a hand out of each window and drove off into the darkness. I was extremely pleased to have eaten something. I would have hated getting a nostril full of repugnant, stodgy servo food on an empty belly. Hopefully the cowboys would be right and a trucker would want some company on the drive up.

A truck pulled in and an incredibly large body with a tiny little head got out and headed towards Cholesterol Heaven. Bathed in the fluoro light his head shone in wavy furrows when I asked him if he was going to Brisbane and if he'd like a passenger for the trip.

'Nah, mate, sorry.' The doors opened automatically and the punching clown waddled in and had its dinner. About half an hour passed and the small head with a now slightly larger body waddled out again, rivets of sweat studding the furrows of the now shinier brow. A few dripped down on me.

'Can ya help me unload when we get there?' wobbled some grease-covered jowls.

'Sure.'

'Ya can't sleep in the truck.'

'Okay.' We climbed up into the truck and headed north in what I hoped would be my last lift of trip.

The next two days were pleasant enough. My small-headed friend was a decent fellow and bought road supplies for us both. We chatted and told jokes while I made us sandwiches. When we reached the outskirts of Brisbane we stopped to wash the truck and buff up the chrome. I helped Pin Head unload, as promised, and said my goodbyes. Filthy and exhausted I headed to the closest suburban railway station. People stared as I boarded the train with my birds nest hair, covered in road dust and dragging a dilapidated blue suitcase. I just wanted to get back to the house I had left a week earlier. A bumpy hour later I walked up the driveway and around to the back door, from which kitchen smells emanated and aroused my senses. I walked in to find my housemates sitting around the kitchen table looking well fed and content. A chicken carcass lay mutilated on a plate.

'Reg, mate. Where ya been? Ya just missed a wicked roast chook man.'

ROUGH JUSTICE

Deanna Swaney

The day after Deanna left university, she left on a grand tour around Europe and the Middle East, then came home to settle into a computer programming career in Anchorage, Alaska. But the travel imperative had taken root and, four years later, she seized an opportunity to write Lonely Planet's *Bolivia* guide. Abandoning all notions of a sane return to office work, she opted for a life on the road, and since then, has backpacked through more than eighty countries, written seven guidebooks to places as diverse as Tonga, Greenland, Norway and Namibia, and also updated existing LP guides, from Brazil to Madagascar. She currently divides her time between travelling, writing, photography, trekking, and finding time to build a cabin and work on other construction projects around her home base in Alaska's Susitna Valley.

Having finished my first Lonely Planet project – the first edition of *Bolivia* – within twenty-four hours of the deadline, I hopped on the first flight from Alaska to Melbourne to deliver it in person to the Lonely Planet office in the Melbourne suburb of Richmond. When I walked into the office, I was greeted with mild shock. 'We never had much faith that we'd ever see this manuscript.' [Author's note: This was a much earlier era at Lonely Planet.] After they'd had a good look at the results – which can't have been too bad since the book was published – Graham Imeson, at that time the head of the art department, ventured the following: 'By the way, your contract specified 150 publication-quality shots of Bolivia.'

'Er, I don't have any of my own photos,' I admitted, mentally reviewing the incidents that had befallen my photographic efforts over the past eight months: prized Nikon lost in Bogotá mugging; replacement Nikon sent from California to La Paz (incurring an additional 100% duty on its passage through Bolivian customs) dies in Arica, Chile; replacement Canon purchased in Arica; photos sent home from Paraguay (cheapest postage in Latin America) arrive yellow and useless; thirty rolls of exposed film tossed into the Amazon somewhere between Manaus and Fonte Boa, Brazil. They must have been drifting in the Atlantic by now, although I couldn't suppress visions of a great, ugly fish in the act of swallowing them.

In truth, I hadn't fulfilled my contract and Graham was rightfully unimpressed. 'So what happened to the photos?'

'Well . . .' I began.

It was a typically sultry June day along the Amazon waterfront in Manaus, and I was headed home to Alaska after eight months on the road. Along with my precious research materials, I had with me a backpack, a camera bag and a stash of South American souvenirs for family and friends back home. On the waterfront, Brazilian dock workers were busy loading cargo onto the river boat, *Almirante Monteiro*, which was to leave that evening for the scruffy Brazilian border town of Tabatinga, which fronted the upper Amazon opposite Leticia, Colombia.

Few people would consider Manaus a particularly salubrious metropolis, but all traffic between the Atlantic coastal city of Belém and the South American interior passed through this reeking, garbage-choked river port. Travellers seeking to penetrate the Amazonian interior were forced to block their noses while purchasing tickets before beginning their journeys upstream. The really keen – those who wanted a story to tell back home – might have shouldered a rack of bananas and joined the dock workers in negotiating the system of flimsy planks that connected the shore with the ship's hold. The rest would sit in the makeshift dockside bars and imbibe bottles of Brazil's refreshing Antártica and Brahma beers, tasty brews that give credence to Brazil's reputation as one of the world's most alcoholic nations. It was in one of these bars that I met another prospective passenger, François, from France, who was also headed upstream to Leticia, in hopes of catching a cargo flight to the Colombian capital, Bogotá.

On the *Almirante Monteiro*, the lowest-class travellers were relegated to hammocks on the upper deck, open to the tropical air and any other elements that might make their presence felt. For convenience, economy and security, François and I agreed to share a second-class cabin on the upper deck. It wasn't difficult to book a passage, and the eight-day upstream trip to Tabatinga cost us less than US$50 each, including (very) basic meals.

From the start, life on the river was divided into three segments: lounging, sleeping and eating. Food quickly became a focal point of our waking hours. After surprisingly palatable meals of *frango, arroz e feijão* (chicken, rice and beans), the three

Brazilian staples, diners were expected to *jeitar o lixo*, that is, clear their own tables directly into the river. In general, locals obliged while the few foreigners aboard fastidiously packed up their scraps and stored them away for disposal in bona fide bins further upstream – although no-one had any delusions about where they'd ultimately wind up.

The cabin occupied by François and myself wasn't especially spacious, but it somehow attracted a range of other, less fortunate passengers, who preferred to spend their shipboard time socialising with foreigners than sitting about on the open decks waiting for something to happen. Among the visitors to our cabin were the son of the ship's captain; a *garimpeiro* (prospector) named Paulo, who owned nothing but a T-shirt, a toothbrush and a straight razor; and a Peruvian witch, who was attempting to spread her pagan notions in wildest Brazil. What all these disparate folks had in common was a taste for *cachaça*, a Brazilian liquor of the most agonising sort. On reflection, it was undoubtedly partly because François and I had purchased a respectable quantity of *cachaça* prior to the voyage that our cabin became such a popular venue.

While the Amazon is much broader, busier and more industrialised than most travellers expect, it still provides a passage into and through the largest forested and oxygen-rich region on the planet. Because I'd been fortunate enough to learn a measure of Portuguese from a friend – a former missionary in Brazil – and during travels in several Lusophone countries, the upstream journey presented me with a joyful amount of human interaction. During the course of these conversations, it became apparent that most of our fellow passengers were entranced by their own personal aspirations and high on promises offered by the wild Amazonian frontier wilderness. Despite the region's increasing industrialisation, its vast forests continued to serve as the last frontier not only for foreign travellers, but also for South American dreamers.

On the second night of the journey, the usual crowd – the witch, the *garimpeiro* and several others – gathered in our cabin, drinking heartily, relaying tales and fears of the unspeakably raw horrors of life in that frontier region, as well as the goblins that inhabit the backwaters of the tropical forests. During our discussion, we were interrupted by the son of the boat captain, who barged into the room, only to apologise that he must have inadvertently got the wrong cabin. Paulo particularly captivated me with tales of the rough-and-tumble life in the gold mines of the Serra Pelada, and in my *cachaça*-inspired stupor, I found myself transported to a land of unimaginable conflicts between people whose very lives depended on physical strength and a ruthless mentality. The images Paulo's tales created obliterated my long-held assumptions about life in the pristine Amazonian rainforests. In all honesty, however, by midnight I was past caring. At this stage, everyone was sick on *cachaça*, and even the hardy locals had dragged themselves back to pass out in their hammocks. François and I – none too comfortable with the effects of the raw spirits – also retired to our respective bunks.

In the alcoholic haze of the wee hours, I awoke to the sound of the cabin door opening, but thought no more about it until morning when I awoke to discover that the bag containing thirty rolls of exposed film from my Bolivia research had gone missing. Distraught at the loss of the irreplaceable film, I immediately offered a reward of US$50, no questions asked, for anyone who could return it. Unfortunately, no-one came forth and I could only assume that the thief, in search of cash, had been disappointed to find only Fujichrome and had summarily tossed the worthless bag into the river.

On the same morning, however, a much more significant loss surfaced. A couple from São Paulo, Sergio and Cristina, who'd intended to restart their lives by setting up a restaurant in some remote river town in the Amazonian wilderness, had sewn their life savings of US$5000 in cash into the seams of their luggage. To save as much of this as possible, they'd opted for deck space and been relegated to the hammock deck. Unfortunately, their suitcase, which had been stowed beneath Sergio's hammock, had been sliced open in the middle of the night and the cash removed.

While the loss of my film was of interest to no-one but me, the news of this robbery excited everyone on board. It was a classic study in human nature. While some were indignant and concerned about the plight of Sergio and Cristina, others hoped they'd be the first to recover the stolen booty, perhaps to make off with it themselves. In the midst of the investigation, a search of passengers' luggage revealed that the *garimpeiro* Paulo, whose bag contained all his aforementioned earthly possessions, had stolen a T-shirt from a public laundry line. This clearly made him a thief and, by extrapolation, many passengers determined that he must be privy to the location of the stolen US$5000. At mid-morning, Paulo was dragged to the upper deck by emotion-charged passengers, who were determined to throw him into the river along with the rest of the ship's detritus.

At this point, my Western background interceded. While fifteen fellow passengers lifted Paulo off the ground and were counting *'um–dois–três'* in preparation to toss him into the alligator- and-piranha-infested river for his alleged crimes, I grabbed onto his foot and proclaimed that he wasn't guilty of the crime; that to throw him into the river was the equivalent of murder; and that murdering a poor *garimpeiro* would never recover the lost US$5000, especially if he were the only person who knew where it might be. Although I'd never been very successful in the arts of persuasion, the mob did reconsider, and left Paulo to return to his hammock, where he spent the rest of the day.

The next afternoon, the boat anchored at the lonely and sticky river port of Fonte Boa, which was home to an especially backwater post of Brazil's Polícia Federal. With the reports by our captain of shipboard robbery, the federal officers came aboard to search for evidence of the alleged crimes (including the loss of my film, surprisingly enough). All cabins were thoroughly searched – except those of the captain, his son, the crew and myself (because, they reasoned, I had been a victim of the crimes; on principle, I demanded they also search my cabin, but their efforts were half-hearted, at best). Not surprisingly, their search recovered nothing, least of all Sergio and Cristina's precious savings.

In a fit of outrage, I went ashore and attempted to speak with the police myself and make an official statement. Given the fact that the captain's son – who should probably have been familiar with the layout of the ship – had 'mistakenly' entered my cabin the previous evening, I was by now quite sure of what had happened to the US$5000. Unfortunately, no-one wanted to listen and my theories were summarily discounted. The police had already decided to blame the *garimpeiro* Paulo, despite the fact that they'd found no trace of the money in his possession. That left the real criminal free to share the booty with anyone in authority who could offer them a measure of protection.

As for Paulo, the police took him into custody as a thief and while he awaited interrogation, police underlings beat him to a pulp. When I saw him in the cell, they'd already blackened his eyes, knocked out his front teeth, broken his jaw and inflicted a number of bloody lacerations. 'It takes some pressure to get a confession from this sort,' an officer explained. As far as they were concerned, the crime was solved.

I'm still haunted by my last vision of Paulo, a broken man bleeding in an earthen cell, having confessed to a crime he never committed, and begging me to help him. A sense of injustice may be a bond, but in the end we both realised that even a foreigner was powerless to help in such a 'local' situation. With that realisation, I simply had to reboard the boat upstream to Tabatinga and Leticia, where I needed to find a cargo flight to Bogotá and, eventually, a passage back to Alaska. After all, I needed to get home to write up a book . . .

SURF OR BUST

Andrew Tudor

Although it's said that in homage to the surf god Huey, Andrew has been seen burning sacrificial surfboards, that he has taken flight without warning, surfboard (and not much else) tucked under arm, and that he is constantly day dreaming of a surf nirvana, it is his full-time job with Lonely Planet that pays the bills. His enthusiasm and respect for mother ocean has facilitated contributions to Lonely Planet surfing sections for the *Indonesia* and *Australia* guides. And though Lonely Planet continues to fuel his wanderlust, it is tempered by his dedication to his fiancée, daughter, Staffordshire pup, and their tree-top home on the outskirts of Melbourne.

AH, WHAT IT IS TO SURF! IT'S ONE OF THOSE THINGS THAT, WHEN DESCRIBED, ALWAYS SOUNDS GLORIFIED, AT LEAST WHEN ATTEMPTING TO ENLIGHTEN A NON-SURFER'S VISION OF THE SPORT. Of course, when surfer talks to surfer it's a different story. One knows where the other is coming from so there's no mystery, no expression of feeling required, just the facts: 'Slotted a hideous tube on the outer ledge today, mate' will convey not only the achievement at hand but also the associated emotional well-being.

If only I had known that explaining my way to the perfect wave wasn't the hard part.

After watching *Storm Riders*, the video that introduced the Indonesian island of Nias to the greater surfing community, my mate and I had decided, on the spot, that we too should seek out waves in exotic locations. We too could surf amidst the tropical palm-lined bays of Indonesia, camp out in tree huts close to the break, all with an added bonus: leaving the wetsuit at home.

Our minds made up, my next challenge was to convince Mum and Dad that their eighteen-year-old son could not only organise a trip overseas, but arrive back home safely and in one piece. Despite zealously poring over the natural high that is surfing, Mum had never placed so much as a big toe in the surf and remained sceptical. But Dad, an ex-Malibu rider with the Suicide Savages, understood the lure of the tube ride and this I would capitalise on. Before long, my teenage enthusiasm and sheer will to surf had twisted their collective arm, and I was off to Melbourne's Tullamarine Airport in search of waves that I had only ever dreamed of.

Touchdown in Medan, the capital of North Sumatra. To our surprise, the locals who had boarded in Yogyakarta gave a round of applause for our safe landing; unaware that this was customary, we pondered what they knew that we didn't.

Our meagre preparation consisted of obtaining a map that showed where our ultimate destination of Pulau Nias was in relation to the mainland and the discovery of a bottle shop attendant at one of the pubs near our local break who told us he had been to Nias, describing it in his best surf tongue –'Fuckin' epic, mate. Goes off. Sick rights' – and upon our insistence gave us, at best, sketchy directions.

So there we were in Medan (minus half our luggage), armed with our friendly bottle shop attendant's instructions: make your way to Sibolga on the Sumatran west coast, catch a ferry to Gunung Sitoli on Nias, catch a bus down to Lagundri in the south and you're there. It sounded easy enough. Not wanting to miss any chance of a surf and having only three weeks to do so, we decided not to wait an extra day and a half in Medan for our luggage. Our boards had made it, and that was all we'd need. Besides, a short walk around Medan revealed there was little on offer for the visitor. Its littered and heavily congested city streets, open sewers and stifling humidity were far from the *Storm Riders* dream.

Three days later we had come to understand the meaning of 'Rubber Time'. I had spent twelve hours squashed in a Datsun 200B between four surfboards, a driver and an unwashed mate; ten hours in a distinctly unseaworthy ferry that had been packed to the rafters with locals making the most of Ramadan; then twelve hours nursing a spewy local kid on a fluorescent bus that had windscreen wipers made of hand-picked palm leaves and elbow grease, during which we encountered a road-blocking mud slide. Rounding the last bend was a relief, to say the least: Lagundri Bay was in sight, we had finally made it.

The surf was about three feet and the outer reef wasn't working, as the swell wasn't big enough, but on the inside was a re-form that was surfable. We watched a few guys riding it as we jumped down from our final mode of transport, a six-metre flat-bed truck that usually carted rocks, but on this occasion surfers –

the bus hadn't been able to cross the mud slide. There were seven of us now. We had all met in Sibolga and found ourselves headed for the same place. After the journey we had just made and with a few hours of sun left, the smallish waves did the soul wonders.

The dawn came early, and so did breakfast. Waking to the sound of perfect six- to eight-foot surf wasn't something I had experienced before, let alone watching its majestic heaves and curves while eating a healthy porridge and fresh fruit breakfast, all from the upper level of a palm-thatched hut. And it was warm. Heaven. The family that owned our two-storey hut lived on the ground level. They cooked for us and washed our clothes (actually, beat them to a pulp), all for the princely sum of 3000 rupiahs per night.

The rigours of the past few days behind us and breakfast all but devoured, the upper level of our hut, named 'Gusties' after its owner, bustled with a feverish frenzy. Eager to be the first out and amongst it, boards were waxed and leg ropes affixed, while rash vests and board shorts coloured the worn wooden feel of the hut's upper level.

Down the bamboo stepladders to the ground floor, a quick skip to the beach, a walk up towards the point and a paddle out through the keyhole to the main break. Looking back towards the land from the water suddenly gave me shivers as the realisation struck of how far I had come to be here, in this spot, surfing these waves.

Lagundri's horseshoe bay is simply spectacular. The densely palmed shoreline would often release recently fallen coconuts out onto the reef with the outgoing tide, and the palm-thatched huts nestled along the bay bought the dream to life. Sitting on my board for a moment, quietly watching the shore, I couldn't believe the paradise that surrounded me.

A local man, silhouetted by the sun, his figure bent over, picked at the shellfish on the reef. I wondered how long he, and generations before him, had watched the surf at Lagundri roll in, pristine, unsurfed.

Startled by the hoots and hollers that signal an approaching set, I paddled towards the peak. Funnily enough I was having one of those days, finding myself in the right spot at the right time, and had caught several waves already. This set was bigger, but charged with adrenaline I launched into a wave and took off on a freight-train right, immediately looking for the tube. Deep inside the tube I realised that making this one would give me a bar-side story for years to come, but the wave shut down and I was pushed from my board and forced down towards the bottom. Fortunately it was deep and there wasn't a likelihood that I'd hit the coral bottom, but the water pressure was too much for my unusually narrow ear canals, and I felt the warm salty ocean water force itself into my inner ear. Not too troubled, I surfed a little more and broke for lunch.

After lunch I didn't feel so well. A vague sense of nausea and the beginnings of a prickly fever had begun to take hold. I figured it would pass so I surfed all afternoon.

The next morning I didn't wake as on the first. I lay half-covered by a sarong, conscious that I was awake but aware that something was wrong. I was sweating yet I was cold. The first attempt at movement sent me spiralling into a state of disorientation. I lay like this for the next two days and nights, shivering and shaking with fever. My mate, between surfing and eating, would poke his head in and inquire how I was doing. At one point he got me a drink, which I immediately threw up, which in turn prompted him to go for another surf.

Finally, on the sixth day of the trip and having surfed only one full day, it was time to get some help. The small town of Teluk Dalam, the nearest that boasted what might be called a surgery, lay about fourteen kilometres down the road.

When we had arrived at Gusties, we asked what everyone's names were. A small man wearing some Billabong board shorts and an old Crystal Cylinder T-shirt had smiled big and wide and said, 'You call me Fuck Off'. Certainly a legacy of previous surfers' visits, but, however ridiculous and unfitting it seemed to me, he seemed to like the label. Fuck Off was the one who took me to the doctor.

Still disoriented and feverish, I clung to Fuck Off's back as we rode on his motorcycle down to Teluk Dalam, where he dropped me in front of a ramshackle shop in the centre of town, which comprised a single unpaved street. 'You wait for doctor.' It began to rain. Soon it was pouring, monsoon-style, and the small bamboo shelter in front of the doctor's jerry-built surgery offered no protection. About an hour passed. Wet, cold and fever-ridden, I figured it was highly unlikely that I would make it home, which I was thinking fondly of by now.

The doctor turned up eventually and tried to tell me I had tonsillitis, even after I insisted he look in my ears. The only available remedy was penicillin, however, so it didn't really matter what I had: that would have to do. So down with the board shorts and, to the delight of the many smirking young faces looking around the privacy curtain, the doctor gave me the shot.

The next day I started feeling better and could even walk around and eat something, but the surf had gone flat. For the next four days we lazed in hammocks. No surf. The bay that had once shown me its potential seemed unwilling do so again.

Utterly pissed off that my time in Nias was up, and only having had one day's real surf, my only hope for salvation lay in our final destination: Bali. We packed up our gear and retraced our muddy tracks to Medan.

Arriving in Bali was a delight. Whilst knee-deep in Sumatran mud slides we had flirted with the idea of relaxing by a hotel pool, and here we were standing by the edge of the pool, ready to dive in. It wasn't a graceful dive but I didn't really care. I just wanted to cool off and chill out. I entered the water at a steep angle; as I headed for the bottom my ears popped with an excruciating intake of chlorinated water. My eyes closed, I surfaced slowly and took a breath, instantly feeling very ordinary all over again.

Not caring to endure the associated fever attacks again, I marched straight up to the receptionist's counter to make an appointment with the hotel doctor. In my haste I stubbed my big toe, splitting the toenail straight down the middle and gashing the fleshy part underneath. The doctor arrived and sorted out the ears – it turned out I had a nasty inner ear infection – and also tended to the toe. I went back to my room to rest, thinking that things had to change.

The surf had started coming up again but my time was running short. Eager to catch more waves before the trip's end, I hired a motorbike and set off for Canggu, a small village north of Kuta that has a fun right-hand reef break as well as its share of lefts. I was alone: my mate had met a girl and I wasn't to see him again until we were in the departure lounge in Denpasar.

Almost there, surfboard slung over my left shoulder, flailing in the wind as I sway with the turns on my DT100, as I approached the apex of a blind left-hand bend, an old man suddenly appeared in the middle of the already narrow road, frozen, clutching at his bicycle. I forced my motorbike to the right, missing him by a whisker, but the front tyre hit loose gravel on the road's shoulder and in a heartbeat I was bouncing and rolling across the gravel, tangled in a mess of surfboard cover.

I came to rest just shy of a sewer drain which ran along the side of the road. I checked my board – not too much damage – and then noticed my legs: lots of blood, skin chunks and studded with gravel. Of course it's mandatory to wear a helmet, but board shorts and thongs don't offer the best protection during a stoush with the road.

Gathering my thoughts I peered over my shoulder, through the settling dust towards where I thought the motorbike would be, but there was no DT100 in sight. I stood up and examined the area more closely. The bike's left-hand grip was protruding from the sewer.

Blinking in disbelief I was suddenly surrounded by locals. They retrieved the motorbike – its foot pegs bent, sopping wet and covered in black slime – and went to work on it. They also went to work on me, liberally dousing my wounds with a local remedy that stung like hell. The DT100 stank, but after a few noisy belts with a hammer it started. Hopping back on the bike, I cautiously made my way back to the hotel, having not surfed. Again.

Back at the hotel I was once again horizontal, my legs throbbing. With only two days to go things weren't looking good for some surf before I left.

On the second-last day of the trip the wounds of the previous day had caught up with me. I didn't dare venture beyond the hotel all day. On the last day I was much the same but I decided I was on a plane back home that night so why not try to get at least one surf in. Surely the worst was behind me.

A *bemo* ride in Bali is an experience in itself, but after the recent DT100 incident I thought a *bemo* was the safer option. Negotiating a fare wasn't big on my agenda at the time – I just wanted to surf – so I secured a *bemo* and driver for the day at a rather inflated price, but considered it a tip and good karma for my last day. I was wrong.

We were rounding blind corners at angel speed, making radical overtaking manoeuvres, and then it happened. We took a right-angled corner fairly quickly and, on the other side of the bend, was another older gent, but this time with a walking stick, moving very slowly and not as lucky. The *bemo*'s brakes did a remarkable job given the circumstances but we just had too much speed to wash off, and I watched from the front passenger seat as the old man braced himself for impact. For an instant that seemed like an eternity the old man – shoulder dipped, rugby tackle style – locked his eyes on mine. Then the *bemo* hit him; his face pressed against the windshield as we stopped. The old man lay on the ground, half under the *bemo* and just out of view.

I sat speechless, my mind racing, then the voice of the driver cut into the silence. 'Don't get out!' He was wired, intense, so I stayed seated.

Surely, I thought, the old man is dead. After a minute, though, he emerged and laboriously gathered himself. As he walked across the road, in traditional sarong, still not watching the traffic, he stared at the *bemo* driver with a look I had not seen on a man before. The *bemo* driver said again, 'Don't get out.' That was all he said. A small gathering tended the old man on the pavement on the other side of the road. His eyes were still intently locked on the *bemo* driver.

I wanted to get out and help, but kept hearing the *bemo* driver's chalky-mouthed, downright persuasive demand. What I had heard seemed to hold true: if you are involved in an accident, it's better to move on quickly and quietly, rather than deal with angry locals and police in person. Images of retribution and the Canggu prison flashed by, but I gathered the *bemo* driver was more concerned about this than me.

No-one approached the *bemo*, so once the old man had continued on his way, the driver turned the *bemo* around and headed back to the hotel. He dropped me off, not having spoken since the accident, and not choosing to speak then either; he just drove away.

Back home in Australia, my ears antibiotically fixed, my leg wounds drying out and my toenail showing signs of improvement, I reflected on my first independent overseas trip. It was only with hindsight that I realised surfing the world's perfect waves in remote countries would never be easy. One drama after another – and just one real surf.

PAKISTANI TAX REVOLT

REVOLT

Paul Harding

After several years in journalism in Australia and a period of aimless wandering with a backpack and a knack for losing things in Europe and Asia, Paul finally landed at Lonely Planet's Melbourne home for wayward travellers in 1996. For the past three years he has worked as a writer and researcher in India, Australia and other parts of the world.

Travelling from Kathmandu to Istanbul for Lonely Planet's new route guide, he faced armed *bandhs* (strikes) in Nepal, almost keeled over from heat exhaustion in India's Thar Desert, rode for twenty-four hours on the floor of a second-class train across Pakistan's Baluchistan Desert, and was mistaken for being Israeli (rather than Australian) by an Iranian soldier. All in all, it was great fun.

Paul has worked on Lonely Planet's *Istanbul to Kathmandu*, *South-East Asia on a Shoestring*, *India*, *South India*, *Australia*, *New South Wales* and *Read this First: Europe*.

THE GUIDE WHO WAS SHOWING ME AROUND PESHAWAR'S ANCIENT BAZAARS WAS DEEPLY PASSIONATE ABOUT HIS CITY'S HISTORY, BUT ALSO A LITTLE SAD THAT I SHOULD BE SEEING IT ON SUCH A DAY.

'There are no shops open today,' he said, reporting the obvious. 'They are all staying closed because of the strike.' I had arrived in Pakistan ten days earlier, just as a nationwide retail strike had virtually paralysed parts of the country. The strike was in protest at the general sales tax proposed by military leader, Chief Executive General Pervez Musharraf, who only six months earlier had ousted Prime Minister Nawaz Sharif and tossed him into jail. This was nothing new for Pakistan – in the fifty years since Partition the military had frequently decided the democratically elected government wasn't up to scratch.

What worried the traders now was not the concept of a new tax, but that they might actually have to pay it. Musharraf had ordered a tax survey in preparation for the new tax and had deployed tax inspectors to gather information. In the frontier town of Peshawar, where so much of the merchandise is smuggled across from Afghanistan (tax-free of course), such a survey would be disastrous. The result was a complete 'shutter down', referring to the roll-down shutters most traders use to lock up their shops. Occasionally, a shopkeeper would open up to do some clandestine business, but if word got out there was a tax inspector nearby, down the shutters would come.

Only a few days earlier I had been scouting around the cloth bazaars of Rawalpindi in search of a *shalwar qamiz*, Pakistan's utilitarian one-style-fits-all garment, so that I could make some concession to blending into this mono-fashion society. Most of the shops were closed, although vendors selling cheap watches, black market prize bonds, vegetables and umbrellas were arranged along the streets. I even found one enterprising young man selling incisors – *teeth* – on the street, but fortunately all mine were intact. No-one, however, appeared to be selling the national dress or even the material with which to have one made. After asking around, I was given some promising directions and soon found myself being dragged under a half-closed shutter into a shop full of designer pyjamas. It was a captive sale in the true sense of the word and the prices were high. After fifteen minutes of unsuccessful bargaining and a couple of escape attempts they released me, perhaps more in fear that other traders would get wind of their strike-breaking activities than of being accused of kidnapping.

I'm really not one for shopping, but the prolonged strike was hampering me almost as much as it was the general public. At the time I was on my way from Kathmandu to Istanbul for Lonely Planet's new *Istanbul to Kathmandu* guide (obviously I boarded the wrong plane), and the 'Shopping' section of the Pakistan chapter was clearly suffering.

Back in Peshawar, almost two weeks with hardly any business was beginning to take its toll on the traders – who were naturally pissed off at not being able to make a tax-free living – and street protests had begun to flare up. Rule number one on the subcontinent: avoid large gatherings of people with an axe to grind and too much time on their hands – it can get ugly. I'd never been sensible enough to remember rules and as small bands of chanting, drum-beating youths started appearing. I grew less interested in Peshawar's history as a trading town and more in its present as a non-trading town.

My guide – let's call him Iqbal – prodded me through the narrow, covered backstreets of the bazaar until we found a quiet tea stall. We arranged ourselves on a couple of ankle-high stools opposite a fat man who was presiding over an even fatter samovar – the huge copper urn used to boil water. Iqbal ordered a pot of green tea – the favoured brew of the Pashtuns, introduced from China – and began telling me about the locals' propensity to carry guns. Forty kilometres away, a tribal village called Darra Adam Khel was the North-West Frontier Province's very own arms factory. Teams of gunsmiths turned out more than 250 guns a day, mostly replicas of semiautomatic rifles, sawn-off shotguns and pistols, but also guns disguised as walking sticks and pen guns the size of a fat biro. Sometimes the pen really is mightier than the sword. In Peshawar it's illegal to own an unregistered gun but Iqbal explained that it was easy to have one gun registered, then have half a dozen replicas made at Darra with the same identification labels. Iqbal admitted that he owned three guns and often carried one – if he was carrying one now, it was well concealed.

We finished our tea and returned the tin cups to the *chai*-wallah, who casually wiped them clean with his shirt tail. Emerging from a narrow lane into the main bazaar, Qissa Khawani, we were confronted by a swelling crowd of demonstrators – many of them teenagers – marching around, banging drums, yelling and setting tyres alight. The burning tyres brought a new sense of tension; you could not only see but *smell* the potential danger. I could almost sense a CNN production unfolding before my eyes. At first, there seemed to be more of a carnival atmosphere than a threatening one, but I could tell that Iqbal anticipated all hell breaking loose any minute. 'We should leave this place,' he muttered, hustling me along the streets through an acrid cloud of black smoke.

Police began to appear, which suggested a confrontation. I scanned the crowd, half expecting to see an AK-47 materialise from the baggy folds of a *shalwar qamiz* but realised my imagination was way ahead of me: there was barely even a trace of anger, let alone fear, in the faces of these 'rioters'. Although a big part of me wanted to see what was going to happen next, Iqbal wisely suggested we continue our tour in the refuge of the serene Mahabat Khan Mosque. We ducked in, just as the narrow street outside began to fill with people. We could hear growing noise, though much of it was muffled by the thick marble walls of the mosque and eventually it fell silent. Around the central tank in the mosque Muslim men were going about their ablutions and prayers, oblivious to the outside world. Nothing looked out of the ordinary here. When we tried to leave the way we had entered, however, it was blocked. Iqbal had a hurried conversation in Pashto with a guard at the front, then explained that we would have to leave via the back exit.

All was quiet when stepped from the mosque. The streets were almost deserted until we threaded our way out of the old city and almost into the path of a bus reminiscent of a giant metallic cigar that had been dipped in glitter. We were back in the chaos of modern-day Peshawar. After unsuccessfully trying to gain entry to the military-controlled Balar Hisar Fort, Iqbal and I decided the tour was over and farewelled each other. He was no doubt relieved to be going home to polish his guns.

Needing to change money, I took an auto-rickshaw to Chowk Yadgar, where the street moneychangers have stalls. The main square of the old city was strangely deserted. When I got out and paid the driver, he sped away with unusual haste, not even bothering to feign disgust at my paying only the agreed fare and not a rupee more. As I wandered towards the street where less than an hour earlier I had been whisked into the mosque, I was hit by a sudden burning sensation. My eyes watered, my throat rasped, my nose felt like it was sucking in pepper. At first I could only think of the nearby spice market – a handful of paprika and chilli powder in the face wouldn't have felt much different. But realisation soon dawned. The police had used tear gas at this spot to disperse the crowd.

As I stood there, rubbing my eyes and trying not to breathe, a door opened slightly and a man waved me in. Once inside, away from the stinging residue of chemicals, he looked at me with sombre expectation and asked: 'You want change money?'

GOING NATIVE IN CUBA

Helen Fairbairn

A year spent teaching English on the French Caribbean island of Guadeloupe convinced Helen of the benefits of life in the sun, and she regularly escapes the dark winters of Ireland to rekindle her relationship with things more exotic. A mountain lover and a dedicated kayaker, she is particularly attracted by the wild areas of the world. She has written for several of Lonely Planet's walking guides, including *Walking in Britain*, *Walking in Italy* and *Hiking in the Rocky Mountains*.

That meal, eaten in the interrogation room of the police station, was excellent. Gerome liked it because it reminded him of his native Caribbean fare: rice and a red bean mush. Its appeal to me lay in the fact that it was the first thing I'd eaten for nearly twenty-four hours. The Cuban *policía* could be heard enjoying their meals on the other side of the crumbling stone compound. For the time being everyone was happy.

We had never really planned to visit Cuba, but Cubana de Aviacíon were offering the cheapest ticket from Peru to Europe, and who were we to turn down the opportunity of a stopover in a new country? The reason for their prices soon became clear, as our foldaway plane seats started doing just that with us still in them, but beggars can't be choosers and at least we got a good view of the Panama Canal.

First impressions of Havana were mixed. The crumbling, colonial architecture was reminiscent of the faded grandeur of Eastern Europe. In the streets classic 1960s American cars competed with smoke-spewing rickshaws, while tiny scooters sagged under the weight of entire families. An industrious bustle prevailed.

As for us, we were counting our pennies and looking for a final injection of Caribbean sun before being oppressed by the dubious climes of northern Europe. Wonderfully ignorant of everything about this new country, we began by mimicking the locals: we stuck out our thumbs and aimed for the closest place on the map that promised sand and seclusion.

Three hours later, still on the side of the road, it was beginning to dawn on us that things might not be what they seemed. Whole lines of locals were being whisked away while we received only long stares. Eventually an old man with a million wrinkles creasing his weather-beaten face stopped and told us why: it was illegal for Cubans to offer lifts to foreigners. A scribbled address pressed into our palms assured us of his sympathy as he nodded encouragingly. We watched as he was stopped 200 metres down the road to be questioned by the police. Before the old man had enlightened us, we had thought it was just by chance that they had chosen that spot to keep an eye on the traffic.

The receptionist of the five-star hotel, safe in the cavernous marble of her air-conditioned world, was distinctly unimpressed. If we couldn't afford one of the limousines that were lined up out front then we would have to head to the bus station. A wave of her hand and the mere suggestion of a direction were all she could muster for such a vulgarity.

We sweated across the dust of the city and squeezed our way through a hundred pairs of curious eyes onto a local bus . . . only to be evicted again triumphantly by a bullying official and taken to spend the afternoon in the station office. An employee's friend offered an alternate escape and took us on a taxi ride around the block in the name of extortion. Cuba was proving itself a place of character.

Another hotel receptionist, friendlier with her one-star expectations, told us the score. Cubans inhabit one world while tourists visit another. Currency exchange was discouraged but possible, for a specified amount of dollars per day, in one or two official outlets. Needless to say, the amount was well beyond our limited means. American dollars could be used, obviating the need to exchange money, but this meant frequenting different shops, using different transport and, in short, leading different lives. A black market existed, but interaction between the native population and tourists was otherwise strictly limited.

A tourist bus, whose fare was twenty times that of the local bus from which we had just been evicted, would accept our dollars if we were interested. So, with a serious depletion of our precious resources, we got to the town that we had in mind. But its hotels – the only official accommodation open to foreigners – were never an option for us. Exclusively package, strictly commercial, 100 percent artificial. We decided to check out the address that the old man had given us.

In the middle of a small row of concrete houses, chickens pecked at the dry ground of a wired-off garden. A mother was surprised to see us, but she recognised the old man's signature and offered us freshly squeezed mango juice to sip in the shade of her tree. Above us the sky did somersaults under the setting sun. A wonderful meal – largely of succulent pieces of the previously pecking chicken – was eaten in the presence of her muscle-bound, gold-chained son. When we were given the price of the woman's hospitality, payable in dollars, the gold chain connection became clear.

Explaining our currency predicament, we were kindly informed that a friend would be able to put us up for the night, if we would go the back way to avoid meeting the police. A very comfortable night preceded another harsh financial surrender. A lucrative thing for some, the black market. Trying to fight the system was proving almost as expensive as accepting it.

Hiding seemed the only option. We walked a few miles up the road and our luck changed; there we found a beach that seemed to fulfil our visions of paradise: fine grains of white sand, turquoise water calmer than a lake, palm leaves rustling in the breeze. At last the Caribbean that Cuban bureaucracy had been denying us.

We pitched our tent deep in undergrowth at the back of the beach and, our luck holding, located a fresh water tap not too far away. I danced at dawn in the lapping water, soaking up the beauty of nature. In the evening, we prised apart husks of dried coconut shells to feed the flames of our cooking fire.

The euphoria faded two days later, when the food ran out. We wandered up the beach in search of fruit or a miracle. The miracle manifested itself first, in the form of an all-expenses-paid holiday complex. Lunch – a plentiful selection of exquisite delicacies suitable for the most discerning of palates – was spread out beside the shimmering blues of the pool. Transported palms cast a perfectly mottled shade over the laden trestle tables, but the food itself lay untouched. The one or two guests around the pool had the uninterested expressions of those secure in their comfort. Even more lavish banquets of food would be laid out in state every night for the visitors, while ordinary Cubans couldn't get soap because it didn't appear on the country's ration cards. Well, rationalisation or no rationalisation, what would you have done?

As nonchalantly as we could, we availed ourselves of some sandwiches and made our way to the beach. But my travelling partner was a shiny black man, native of another island in the Caribbean, and this was our undoing. I have a fair skin and am easily recognisable as a possible hotel guest, but Gerome created confusion. Staff approached me and politely advised me not to feed the locals. Then they inquired after my room number for their records.

I uttered some nonsense . . . and we ran. Judging by the number of staff roused to give chase, it seemed like a serious offence. We hid deep in the bush and waited an hour for calm to prevail.

We returned to the tent hungry, but on entering we were dumbstruck. Then Gerome let out a savage roar, tears of rage springing to his eyes. The culmination of our struggles on the island was laid out before us with abrupt finality: the tent was empty. Everything had disappeared except the triangle of green canvas itself.

A search revealed a shoe and a notebook dropped in the undergrowth and a pair of knickers caught on a branch. Besides that, nothing. Our packs, our documents, our money, our clothes: all gone. More grist for the Cuban underground. We were incensed. Gerome's fury sent him chasing down the beach, dreadlocks flying, in search of blood and retribution. My English reserve had me sizing up the situation and sitting down on the sand to draw up a list of stolen articles for the insurance company.

When anger subsided to helplessness, we sought out the police officer who was sleeping in his car at the back of the beach. We knocked on the window and gave an emotional statement, then led him to the scene of the crime. We quietly packed the empty tent, fighting an instinct to abandon that traitor too, and climbed into the patrol car, me in swimsuit and sarong, Gerome more presentable in T-shirt, shorts and shoes. In the event I managed to scavenge a pair of flip-flops and a vile-coloured Hawaiian shirt from a hotel bin the following day. That was the sum total of our belongings.

The police car was old and dusty, and obviously had a few stories of its own to tell. The engine came to life after a push and we revved off to face the world once again . . . only to be brought to a sudden halt shortly later by a collision with a cattle truck. The slow speed of both vehicles prevented serious damage, but a large dent obstructing one of the car's rear wheels prevented further progress. Two scared cows backed out over the truck's tailgate, which had burst open on impact, and retreated to a safe distance.

The officer took the events in his stride, even looking mildly pleased at the prospect of an hour's alternative activity chasing cows. The farmer was already off in pursuit, waving his arms to try to persuade them out of a deep ditch. We were denied a similar pleasure and were bundled instead into a passing taxi, with instructions that we should be deposited at the police station without payment. Once there we were received with curiosity and kindness. As I've said, the meal that afternoon tasted as good as anything I've ever eaten.

Life is surprisingly simple when you have absolutely nothing to your name. You are at the mercy of the kindness of others and that's all there is to it. We spent an uncomfortable night on the tiled floor of the immigration office and received free passage back to Havana. Our respective embassies were businesslike, eager to get us on our way, contacting the airline and issuing emergency papers with a minimum of fuss. We were also offered enough cash in Cuban pesos to feed ourselves from street stalls and sleep at the airport while we awaited the departure of our plane.

In those final days, with all possessions gone, we were able to discover something of the real Cuba. The fried-food vendor offered us twenty-four omelettes for the amount he would charge for a single one in American dollars. We spent the days in the streets, observing the bustle of the city, waving at little children balancing on the back of scooters. I can't say we weren't relieved when our flight was finally called, but at least our misfortune had allowed us to slip outside the confines of being a foreigner and experience something of a native lifestyle.

It remained to be seen how we would be received during a Parisian winter with nothing but our beach wardrobe.

OFF THE ROAD IN ETHIOPIA

Tom Hall

Born and raised in north London, Tom was first drawn to the open road by the free rail pass he held throughout his youth thanks to his father's job. After finishing a history degree at Leeds University, a trip to the southern hemisphere ended with him flopping broke and ambitious into Lonely Planet's London office, where he now dispenses travel advice and pursues editors. He travelled to Ethiopia in March 2000 to visit the rock churches at Lalibela and would recommend the country to anyone in search of a great adventure. Tom combines a love of travel with a passion for Arsenal Football Club, Morrissey and ginger beer. This is his first published work for Lonely Planet.

I WAS ALARMED WHEN THE HOTEL MANAGER BURST INTO MY ROOM AT FIVE-THIRTY IN THE MORNING. A giant, overweight ghost dressed in a flowing white nightgown, sweating and waving his arms in panic, he was quite a sight. I quickly realised why he was so animated – I was supposed to have been on a bus out of town half an hour previously. Thanking him, I flung my alarm clock against the wall and charged out. I puffed through the pre-dawn gloom towards the bus station still putting on my clothes, a mess in contrast to the sleek, early morning joggers – all trying to be the next Haile Gebreselassie, Ethiopia's indomitable Olympic champion and national hero.

Harar had been a blast. I'd spent a couple of days spent wandering the alleyways and mosques of the walled city, imagining myself Arthur Rimbaud, the gifted and doomed French poet who set up as a merchant and gunrunner here in the 1880s. At the market I'd brought a bag of salt from Afar nomad traders that I didn't really want, but they waved their guns about a bit and their camels made some vomiting noises, so I thought it was the best way to get away. I'd managed to catch a look at the Hyena Man, a deranged lunatic who feeds raw meat to the wild doglike mammals that prowl the town using his hands, feet and other parts of his anatomy as cutlery. The climax of the show came when he had a mock fight with one beast for a piece of meat – they were both holding it with their teeth and growling.

I'd spent much of my last day trying to get my hands on a ticket out of there, in order to begin the two-day journey back to Addis Ababa and London. Harar was a deeply romantic and attractive place inside the city walls. The bus station – a sweaty, dirty, hot place – was outside them. It contained several ramshackle buildings, all of which threatened to sell tickets without ever actually doing so. Piles of burning rubbish sat next to stray dogs asleep in front of derelict vehicles. Intermittently a bus belching black smoke would come in and, without coming to a complete rest, take on an army of passengers, then wobble off again east towards the Somali border

While there, I encountered someone who called himself 'The Cuban', a scrawny, bearded chap who had arrived in Ethiopia by stowing away on a cargo ship. He grinned a mixture of gaps and gold when he spoke of home. Despite having no tickets to sell and no access to any he seemed determined to stop me from getting one. Over the three hours I spent queuing, he tried to stop me registering my name, told the ticket seller my passport was a fake, shoved me out of the line and, once I had the ticket, attempted to prise it from my hand in the crowd. He didn't take too kindly to my delight at retrieving a ticket from within the pandemonium of the queue and chased me out of the bus station. My ticket felt like gold dust and the thought of missing the bus quickened my step. I began to sprint up the hill.

Rounding the bend into the station, I was dazzled by the headlights on the bus. My bus. Fortunately, the Ethiopian bus boarding routine – which involves queuing for an eternity, being led twice around the bus by the conductor like schoolchildren, then breaking ranks and scrambling for the best seats – delayed departure sufficiently for me to hop on. I slumped down into a hard, rusty seat and, still breathing hard, reached up and pushed open a window. The woman next to me looked at me with a start.

'*Salam,*' I said, the greeting normally returned with a smile and laughter. She turned to face me fully and launched into a diatribe. '*Faranji,*' the Ethiopian word for white person that follows every visitor around the country, was followed by a ferocious and utterly incomprehensible lecture. From her hand signals I deduced the subject of her rant to be opening windows on buses. I did as I was told and closed the window. My neighbour settled down to sleep while I adjusted to the idea of twelve hours with no fresh air.

The bus quickly became a kind of rolling party. In fact, it was the end of a particularly good one: screeching local music on a twenty-minute loop, slumped bodies comatose over seats and a small gang of rogues chewing *chat* leaves conspiratorially at the front. I became better acquainted with my neighbour's chickens, which clucked proprietorially if I moved so much as a leg in her direction.

Charging over a particularly dramatic pass, there was a loud bang from behind me, followed by a skid, and the bus bumped to a halt. The problem was a burst tyre, which held us up for half an hour. As we gathered to watch the operation to change it, the *chat*-chewing lads took the opportunity to ask me how many donkeys I had. When I said none they found it very amusing and decided to discuss my poverty over a few more leaves of the local tipple. I wandered off for a piss over a lush green mountainside.

After lunch, somewhere in the middle of a very empty desert, we ground to a halt for no apparent reason. Everyone got off and began to unload their bags while I stood watching. Then, from nowhere, a troop of about fifteen youths – looking very much like the nomads I'd brought my salt from – appeared by the road and began loading anything of value onto the camels. Quite sanguine, I watched as one of the armed porters began to load my bag onto his camel. When I grabbed it back, he just looked disgusted and carried on his business. As they padded off into the desert, the woman who had berated me earlier explained in Amharic that they were smugglers who would carry your goods past the customs checkpoint. I think that's what she said, but no-one seemed very bothered about taxing my bag of salt when we reached the check.

So off we went again, rocking to the music whose words everyone knew by now, bouncing on the rough road. By nightfall we'd had another puncture and were still nowhere near our destination, Nazret. The driver, a *chat*-chewing dwarf impervious to tiredness or nerves, began to increase his speed, really gunning the engine. A couple of the women on the bus raised their voices in protest. One of them was on her feet shouting when a really loud BANG! sent the bus hurtling at top speed off the road. The woman went flying back and landed beside me. It was dark. We couldn't see a thing, but it felt like we were juddering across a field. I closed my eyes as we bounced around and waited – I didn't know for what, but I figured either the bus would stop or we would all die.

We didn't die. When I opened my eyes the woman who'd landed next to me was getting up and most people on the bus were praying. I helped her to her feet and staggered off the bus. We were in the middle of a hillside field and the bus had lost a tyre – the same one that had been replaced. Upon inspection, our vehicle had come to a halt twenty feet from a steeper slope. Had we not stopped the bus would surely have rolled over. It was a very narrow escape. The problem was, we were now stuck in a deeply ploughed field, in pitch darkness with a broken-down bus.

The lads, high on the energising effects of *chat*, decided to push the bus out onto the road where it could be repaired and beckoned me to help them. Images of Allan Quartermain heroically saving the day came to mind and, grinning, I strode over to help them shove the bus out of the dirt. I braced myself and shoved as the engine burped back into life and the bus began to move. Spinning wheels and dirt meant I got a circus-style covering in dust, and the bus charged away leaving me looking not unlike Al Jolson. For the second time, the boys (immaculate but for dirty shoes) laughed heartily at me, but we had given the bus enough of a push to get it back onto the road. I felt the journey was descending into the realms of fantasy as I brushed myself down and watched the driver and his equally small mate manoeuvre a tyre twice their size onto the rear axle. After a wait of around three hours for repairs and bit of first aid, the bus groaned into life.

Ten kilometres down the road we arrived in Nazret. The hub for transport to eastern Ethiopia from Addis Ababa had seemed nothing special on the way through but now it felt more like its namesake in biblical times – part of the Promised Land. Exhausted, filthy and slightly discomposed after the journey, I lurched into the shower. Although it was a cool night at altitude, I would gladly have stood under a bucket of anything liquid by that stage. Cold water would be fine. I turned on the tap and it squealed at me. What landed on my head was not the cool, if brackish water I was expecting, but three cockroaches, as long as my Swiss Army knife, who fell into the bath via my shoulder and scurried off down the plughole. I gave up and went to sleep, which is probably what I should have done at five-thirty that morning.

INTO THE
LION'S DEN

**Jean-Bernard Carillet
(translated by James Cannon)**

After earning a degree in translation and international relations from La Sorbonne Nouvelle in Paris, Jean-Bernard joined Lonely Planet's French office before becoming a full-time author. He has worked on a range of Lonely Planet titles, from *Diving and Snorkeling Tahiti & French Polynesia* and *Diving and Snorkeling Red Sea* to *Walking in France* to *Restoguide Paris* as well as numerous guidebooks, including *Marseilles*, *Corsica*, *South Pacific* and *Martinique, Dominique et Sainte-Lucie*. Diving instructor and incorrigible traveller, he will decamp at the slightest opportunity to travel, photograph and dive around the world. After several trips to Tahiti, he now considers French Polynesia a second home.

After completing an arts degree, James spent a year as an assistant English teacher in Bordeaux. Since returning to Australia he has worked as a freelance tutor and translator of French. He was recently one of the translators working on the *Paris* volume of Lonely Planet's *Out to Eat* series. In his spare time, James discusses and performs French popular songs in schools and cafés.

THIS WAS MY THIRD VISIT TO RANGIROA, OR 'BIG SKY', A PERFECT NAME FOR THE VAST CORAL RING EMERGING FROM THE LIQUID IMMENSITY OF THE PACIFIC OCEAN 275 KILOMETRES NORTH-EAST OF PAPEETE. Seventy-five kilometres long by thirty wide, Rangiroa is the second-largest atoll in the world, outranked only by Kwajalein, in Micronesia. There are barely 2000 inhabitants, who live in two villages, Tiputa and Avatoru, each built on the edge of a pass of the same name. Despite the idyllic, picture-postcard setting, living conditions are basic if not harsh. The houses are simple, traditional *fare* made of plywood, while the rhythm of life is governed by fishing and Sunday mass.

For the past fifteen years or so, tourism has been a godsend, enabling numerous guesthouses and a luxury hotel to flourish. Rangiroa is a mecca for divers, who come from all over the world to take on the two gigantic passes – teeming with fish – that link the ocean to the lagoon.

I was there to update the fifth edition of the *Tahiti & French Polynesia* guide and also to test various dives for a new Lonely Planet diving guide. The prospect of finding myself amongst a wall of sharks in a few hours was intensely exciting.

During my first visit, I'd stayed at a terrific guesthouse right next to the Tiputa Pass, along with my wife and daughter, who was barely a month old at the time. My second visit was spent updating the fourth edition of *Tahiti & French Polynesia* and had left me with the fondest of memories. Third time around, it felt like returning to the fold. I'd become familiar with the distinctive atmosphere of the Tuamotu Islands. I appreciated the unique environment of this silent, motionless, naked world, suspended like a raft between sea and sky on the threshold of infinity. I liked the people, huddled together in such a restricted space. Yet I still couldn't decide whether this was heaven or hell.

I stayed in Avatoru this time, at a guesthouse I didn't know, which was ideally situated near a dive centre. The owner showed me to a simple bungalow at the edge of the lagoon. After a short siesta, I set off in search of something to eat. Opposite the guest-house, I noticed a small, unpretentious, open-air snack bar-cum-restaurant. A few tables were set up on the sand, sheltered from the sun and rain by a roof of palm branches. 'This restaurant wasn't here three years ago,' I mused to myself. Guide in hand, I decided to begin my updating work without further ado.

I crossed the only street in the village and sat down at one of the tables. When the owner appeared, I recognised her immediately. It was Moana, Punua's wife. Punua was a well-known personality in Rangiroa, a militant independence activist and boat-builder descended from one of the Tuamotus' royal families. Moana and Punua had previously owned one of the atoll's cheapest guesthouses, at this same location. I'd even pointed out in the last edition of the guide that their guesthouse was instantly recognisable by the independence flag fluttering next to the house. In this one-street village, every house looked the same, and theirs had the advantage of being instantly identifiable thanks to Punua's overt political convictions. I was immediately curious. Why had the flag disappeared? Had Punua given up the fight? And what had become of the guesthouse? When Moana approached, happy to see the first customer for the day, I asked her straight out.

'Didn't there used to be an independence flag next to the house?'

Her face darkened immediately. She stared at me. Her black eyes seemed to convey a disturbing mixture of hatred and anger. What had I said to provoke this ravaged expression, these clenched fists? Had my attitude or words been disrespectful? Moana kept looking daggers at me, ready to explode. Never before had I encountered such hostility among the Polynesians. I became quite frightened.

'How do you know about the flag?' she burst out in a choked voice.

Instinctively, I knew my answer would be decisive. I stammered, pitifully, 'It's in the Lonely Planet guide.' This merely fanned the flames of Moana's suppressed rage. I felt the ground give way beneath my feet. I continued to flounder, adding 'And I was here three years ago, as a journalist.' I thought this detail might dissolve the tension, protect me, make it possible to regain an air of composure. Far from it.

'Journalist? Which journalist?' Moana raised her voice. 'For the guide,' I explained. Somehow I felt like I'd just committed the ultimate sin. Moana snatched the guide from my hands, opened it at the page entitled 'The Authors' and recognised my photo. She tore out the page and shouted, 'Punua, Punua!' in the direction of her husband, who was having a siesta in a hammock about twenty metres away.

I hadn't seen him. A sinister-looking giant weighing at least 130 kilograms, built like a market porter, bare-chested, arms tattooed with Polynesian motifs, Punua approached. 'That's him!' Moana screamed, pointing at me. My heart was pounding, disaster imminent. As soon as he saw me, Punua began to squeeze his hands as if preparing to strangle me. I felt like a chicken whose neck was about to be broken.

'Damn *popaa* [Westerner], you destroyed us!' he shouted in a rasping voice. 'Your book put us out of business! Because of the flag, our custom dried up!' he exploded, wild with rage. In a flash, I understood what he was saying. Obviously, the mention of the independence flag had frightened off potential customers, who'd fled in droves to rival guesthouses. Totally unaware of the situation, I'd delivered myself straight into the hands of my executioner, whose vengeful feelings had been smouldering for the past three years.

There was no chance of escape. I was cornered. I could run. But where? There was nothing but ocean on all sides. I could cry for help, alert the neighbours, ask for police assistance. But the area was hopelessly quiet and the rule of law seemed a derisory concept in this isolated, inward-looking land with its own codes and rites. The risk was too great.

'Why did you do it? Why did you do it?' Punua repeated the question compulsively, a crazed look in his eyes. I was scared stiff, but nonetheless managed to explain, in a sudden outburst which I attribute to my survival instinct, that it had all been a terrible misunderstanding. I tried to convey to Punua, in broken snatches, that to my way of thinking, his highly visible flag was a landmark and his political affiliations a 'plus', something positive I'd wanted to share with readers. In other words, they could expect an interesting discussion with someone who was committed to and proud of his beliefs.

The readers, it seemed, had interpreted my words quite differently. In their eyes, displaying pro-independence, anti-French convictions was incompatible with providing services to tourists who were, for the most part, French. The fact remained that I had intended no harm. As I stammered out my explanation, my genuine goodwill began to override my feelings of utter helplessness. Had Punua noticed? Because, instead of settling the score there and then, he grabbed me and sat me down in front of him. I'd been given a reprieve. He signalled to his wife. She brought back a piece of paper which Punua presented to me. It was a letter from a lawyer in Papeete advising Punua that he didn't have a case. This had increased Punua's desire for personal revenge tenfold. His only alternative was to take the law into his own hands and get even with this cynical journalist who had frightened off the customers.

He told me about the damage which the guide had apparently caused. In the space of a few weeks, there were no more customers. He'd been forced to close down the guesthouse and set up this little snack bar in its place. As he listed his grievances, he stared hard at me, waiting for my expression to falter, searching for the smallest trace of a lie to justify his rage. For my part, I spoke to Punua from the heart, with complete frankness. As the minutes ticked by, I felt that I was beginning to correspond less to the image of the perverse, heartless journalist he'd imagined. He began to see the possibility of there having been a misunderstanding, a misinterpretation, an unfortunate error, a clumsy, spontaneous gesture on my part. My presence here was proof in itself. Would I have been so senseless as to walk straight into the lion's den?

Punua gradually calmed down. Suddenly, his tone changed. 'What'll it be?' I didn't understand at first. 'Come and have a meal. What'll it be, tuna or *mahi mahi* [dolphin fish]?' I breathed a sigh of relief. Three years of suppressed rancour and violence had just broken against the wall of my good faith and naivety. Punua made it clear we were quits and we shook hands as a sign of friendship.

Moana served the meal. Too traumatised to really savour the delicious *mahi mahi*, I shared their food then said goodbye. I returned to my bungalow and, totally wiped out by the confrontation, collapsed on my bed, abandoning all thoughts of going for a dive.

After gathering my wits the following day, I attempted to find out more about Punua's circumstances. I spoke to various *popaa* and Polynesian acquaintances. As it turned out, Punua's business had been floundering well before the guide was published. There was stiff competition from other guesthouse owners, who discouraged tourists from going to Punua's, pointing out that he was pro-independence and claiming that he despised tourists. With words as weapons, they used dirty tactics to bring down a competitor whose personality they disliked. Punua's pride was hurt, and I seemed to be the catalyst for his misfortune.

This incident left me chastened. My job has hidden risks: the slightest word, however well founded or apparently innocuous, has the potential to upset the fragile balance of a confined, isolated community such as this.

In any case, Punua well and truly bounced back. His little restaurant, listed in the new edition of the guide, became a huge hit with the tourists.

ICE COLD IN NIKKO

Simon Richmond

One thing that Simon knew instinctively while growing up in the British seaside resort of Blackpool was that it would NEVER be the location for one of his favourite Bond movies. Perhaps it was this early diet of testosterone tourism and exotic escapism that led him to a career as a travel writer, via stints in the more workaday byways of journalism. For Lonely Planet, among other things, he has fearlessly ventured around Kazakstan (where a policeman aimed a pistol at his car), braved belligerent moneychangers, religious fanatics and carpet salesmen along the Istanbul to Kathmandu overland trail for a route guide and put his stomach on the line in the restaurants of London and Sydney for the *Out to Eat* series.

USING YOUR FIRST LONELY PLANET GUIDEBOOK IS LIKE LOSING YOUR VIRGINITY. IT'S EXCITING, EVEN THRILLING, BUT COMES WITH A WHOLE HEAP OF UNREALISTIC EXPECTATIONS AND NAIVETY, WHICH, INEVITABLY, MEANS JUST ONE THING: AT SOME POINT YOU'RE GOING TO GET SCREWED.

The fact is I should have known better. It wasn't as if I lacked experience as a traveller. I'd backpacked around chunks of Europe and bused across the USA – twice! But this was my first trip to Asia and, what's more, to the most Oriental part of the Orient: Japan. So I turned to what I considered an infallible source of guidance. And therein lay my downfall.

I had arrived in Japan barely four months earlier. My plan, not dissimilar from that of thousands of other *nama-gaijin* (raw foreigners, newbies to Nippon), was to work as an English teacher for, say, six months, then party around Asia on the proceeds. That was the plan. But, it has to be said, there were problems from the start.

First, although it took a while for the country to own up officially, the economic bubble – when Japanese real estate values went through the roof, the stock market soared and people ate gold-leaf-wrapped sushi for breakfast – had well and truly popped by the time I stepped off the plane in 1991. I had prudently lined up a job before leaving the UK, but the days of sky-high salaries were history. Instead, I considered myself fortunate to have secured a place in the production line of a multi-branch *Eikaiwa* (English conversation) school, not to mention a half-share in a pricey six-tatami rabbit hutch home.

Second, I had fallen madly in love with this city. In comparison to London, struggling to throw off the last shackles of

Thatcherism, Tokyo blazed with activity and promise. Its fashion, technology, bars and clubs were the last word in cool. On a minimalist salary my lifestyle was practically Zen-like, but still I was inspired. The idea of chucking it all in after a few months was unthinkable and I began searching around for better prospects (not to mention roomier accommodation). Fortunately, with a background in journalism and a burning determination, I didn't have to look far.

Within a few days of arrival I'd bagged myself a part-time job on the English-language listings magazine, *Tokyo Journal*. Two months later, I was hired as an editor by a major Japanese newspaper group. At the same time, I was offered a room in the very salubrious house of an expat I'd met on the plane on the way to Japan. Alexandra – mother Italian, father German, studied Japanese at the Sorbonne – was one of those people whose accomplishments and self-possession leave lesser mortals jibbering. Need I also mention she was a babe? Amazingly, though, there was no boyfriend in the picture. Life was looking good.

In celebration, I immediately chucked the teaching gig, much to the chagrin of the school, which refused to pay my last month's wages. Despite this sudden cash flow-problem I decided to take a few days' break from the city before commencing my new job. I turned to my, so far, trusty guidebook and decided on Nikko. My fate was sealed.

Nikko, 128 kilometres north of Tokyo in the mountains of Tochigi-ken, is one of the 'must-sees' of Japan. Here, amid a forest of towering cypress pines lies the dazzlingly decorative shrine complex Toshogu, the last resting place of the first Tokugawa shogun, Ieyasu, and his grandson, Iemitsu. Millions of tourists tramp through the shrine grounds every year, many uttering the ambiguous Japanese phrase 'don't say *kekko*, until you've seen Nikko'. It's meaning is ambiguous because *kekko* can be translated as 'magnificent', but it can also stand for 'enough', as in

'I've had enough'. And I had already had more than enough of James chirping, 'don't say *kekko* . . . ' on the train from Tokyo.

James was a fellow Brit to whom I'd been introduced soon after arriving in Tokyo. With a few days off work, he'd decided to joined me for the trip. It wasn't just nationality and being new to the country that James and I shared; we were both Jewish, which gave us a kind of neurotic Woody Allen–style outlook on the many quirks of life in Japan.

When I look back at the photographs taken on our first day in Nikko – of the visit to Toshogu, miraculously free from its usual hoards of visitors on this midweek late-February day, of us skating at the outdoor rink in the hills above the town – I can clearly see the snow. Lots of snow. Still, what I remember most about that visit is how spring-like the weather was, with clear blue skies and sunshine warming skin long huddled beneath layers of winter clothing. So it was only natural, on day two – another perfect one – that we should plan a hiking trip at Lake Chuzenji, a famous scenic spot in the mountains above Nikko.

A twisting, one-way road leads up to Chuzenji, each of the bends labelled with a *hiragana* character (one of the two phonetic syllabaries the Japanese use in their writing system). Just before reaching the lake, the bus passes the Akechi-daira cable car. The guidebook waxed lyrical about a trail from the top of this cable car to another directly above the lake – a walk of no more than thirty minutes, it promised. On such a clement day this seemed an ideal plan, so we hopped off the bus and climbed aboard.

Cable cars in Japan generally have a jauntily dressed female conductor in the cabin parroting off the facts and figures of the ride: how long, how high, what you can see, please don't forget your belongings. You get the picture. Incessant noise is like a security blanket that Japanese seem to crave wherever they are. Even when there's not an actual person – as was the case on our ride – a recorded voice is sure to hang over the proceedings.

So, on our arrival at the top of the cable car, there was no-one around to warn us against the lunacy of our hiking plan. Nor were we deterred by the thin coating of snow that lay on the ground.

After all, we could see fresh tracks heading off up the mountain, so knew that at least one other had very recently gone before us. We took off at a brisk pace.

An hour later we were still slogging our way up the mountain through snow that now clung to our shins at every step. We really should have turned back then, but our faith in the guidebook was so absolute that we continued. Since it clearly said the walk to the other cable car would take only 'thirty minutes', surely it must be just over the next hill?

We were still following the tracks left by the earlier walker, but the footprints now appeared much larger, as if we were on the trail of Bigfoot. That would be something: to encounter the Japanese yeti! Instead, I recall James quipping something droll about our mothers reading in the *Jewish Chronicle* about how their hapless sons, inappropriately dressed in jeans and sneakers, had been found frozen on the snowy slopes of Nikko. We were slipping into Woody Allen territory.

Eventually we reached what appeared to be the Chanoki-no-daira plateau. At least, it was flat. Which meant the snow was now twice as deep. I became so desperate to move forward at speed that I took to crawling on all fours, like a baby – the greater surface area stopping me sinking so quickly into the snow. It was official: our expedition had descended to the level of farce.

All around was white, the icy surface and clods on the trees glinting in the sunlight. It was a truly sublime scene, beautiful and horrific at the same time. And over it all was laid the faint, mocking soundtrack of the recorded message blaring back down the mountain from the cable car. If either of us had known more than a smattering of Japanese, I'm certain we would have understood: 'Honourable customers, please take care not to leave anything behind and please do NOT climb the mountain if it's covered in snow.'

Others might say I should never have been on the mountain in the first place. Not with all that snow. Not when it was so obviously dangerous. As for me, I was so exhausted by now I could hardly speak. The same could not be said of James, who had taken to blaming me exclusively for our predicament. I held my tongue as each accusation was hurled. Wasn't it my idea to make this hike between the cable cars? (Hadn't James been equally enthusiastic about the plan?) Wasn't it me who had urged us to go on instead of turning back? (Actually it was James who had the led the way from the start.) Wasn't it my stupid guidebook? Well, that I couldn't argue with.

Then, suddenly, the recriminations stopped. Coming towards us was Bigfoot. Surely delirium had set in? But, no, advancing from the trees was a hiker, kitted out – as any self-respecting Japanese in these wintry conditions would be – in full Alpine gear, including snowshoes and ice pick. It speaks volumes about the mutual perceptions of *gaijin* and Japanese that neither of us found anything extraordinary in what we saw. If we thought it perfectly acceptable that this man would be so overly equipped on such a perfectly clear late-winter's day, he, in turn, didn't bat an eyelid at our hopelessly under-prepared state – at least as far as I could tell beneath his anti-fog goggles and fur-lined parka hood.

As he approached us we babbled out what little Japanese we had between us, filling in the gaps with English and sign language. We were in search of the cable car down to Lake Chuzenji, we said. Was it, perchance, in the direction from which he had come? In similar semaphore manner, Bigfoot confirmed that the cable car did exist and that it was a mere 200 metres ahead through the trees. At least that's what we thought he'd said. Thanking him profusely, we continued with renewed vigour towards our elusive goal.

Some 200 metres further, Bigfoot's tracks stopped dead and our inflamed spirits were instantly doused. Now we were both blaming Bigfoot rather than the guidebook or each other. Surely he'd misled us? There was no cable car after all! Getting a grip, we rescanned the forest and thought we could make out the shape of a building through the trees.

The way there was treacherous. With no tracks to follow we had no idea how deep the snow was. I literally hit rock-bottom when I stepped into a hollow and sank up to my chest in snow.

Flailing there for a few moments I thought this was how swimmers drowned: they just went out too far and lacked the strength to get home. James' quip about the *Jewish Chronicle* was seeming less funny by the second.

After a few moments of struggle I somehow managed to crawl out of my snowy grave and make it to sturdier ground. At last we were making progress, approaching what could only be the cable car station. Concrete structures were now clear in the woods ahead and I remember we both let out ecstatic whoops of joy, the end of our ordeal in sight. On reaching them, though, we discovered we'd whooped too soon.

The station was shut and the cable car was resting off its cable. There was not a soul in sight, although the lake and the town were in clear view below. We started shouting down the mountain, but this far up no-one could hear our screams. We were trapped. Why on earth, I fumed, had the guidebook not said this cable car was shut in winter?

Slumped in exhaustion we considered our options. Returning the way we had come was instantly ruled out. Heading on foot down the mountain from here was risky, too: there was no trail and what if we became stuck? We screamed for help pointlessly a few more times. Then we caught sight of the spade.

Beside the cable car station was a cafeteria. There had to be a telephone inside from which we could call for help. If not, we would have shelter should we be forced to spend the night on the mountain, as seemed depressingly likely. The cafeteria's plate glass door was locked; the only way in would be to smash it with the spade.

James and I pondered this course of action for a while, knowing we would do it and already guilty for the damage that would be caused. I confess: it was I who – in a moment of utter desperation – smashed the glass door of the cafeteria beside the cable car station in Nikko. Eventually, I picked up the spade and committed my first (and last) act of vandalism in Japan. We were in, but our grim comedy of errors had yet to reach its conclusion.

The phone didn't work. What's more, the body warmth generated by our seemingly epic struggle through the snow was beginning to wear off. We were hungry (of course we were hungry, we were Jewish!) and our clothes were soaked from the snow. The afternoon was drawing in. When the sun set the temperature would plummet, freezing us along with everything around us. We had to get off the mountain.

Taking another look at the map in the guidebook I noticed there was a walking route down from this cable car to Chuzenji. It was worth a shot. If the way became too difficult, we could always return here and camp out. There were some blue plastic bin liners in the cafeteria, from which we fashioned crude gaiters. Like vagrant versions of Antarctic explorers we bravely set off again into the trees.

I wish, with hindsight of course, I could write of another titanic struggle against the elements, but the truth is that, compared to the two-and-a-half hour slog up the mountain and across the plateau, the yomp down to the lake was a breeze. Within no time we'd hit the main road and were hastily ripping off the bin liners and burying them in the snow, lest anyone spot us for the vandals and thieves that we were.

At Chuzenji, falling into the first restaurant we came across, we celebrated our escape on a feast of *kare raisu*, the gloopy brown comfort food that is the closest Japanese cuisine comes to grandma's chicken soup with dumplings. All the mountain-top recriminations were forgotten in our euphoria at having avoided becoming human Popsicles. Well almost. That guidebook in my backpack was still dangerously close to being considered excess baggage.

'I could write a better guidebook than this!' I confidently told James, little thinking that eventually I would. Not only that, but I would also work for Lonely Planet. To be honest, though, at the time all I cared about was getting back to Tokyo for a date with the gorgeous Alexandra.

Outside the cinema I breathlessly rattled off the details of my trip, which had in the retelling assumed the status of a brush-with-death experience. Alexandra flashed her dazzling smile, tossed her flaxen hair and chipped in with some news of her own. Her parents were coming to visit. I had a month to move out. And, by the way, she'd finally got it together with a guy at work. Yes, indeed, life was looking good.

In a heartbeat I was homeless, loveless and practically yen-less in Tokyo. Sometimes there are worse things than guidebooks that leave you ice cold in Nikko.

DOING BRAVE

Melita Granger

Before working for Lonely Planet, Melita worked as a project officer in a rural health organisation, was a researcher for a politician, DJ'd at weddings, twenty-first birthdays and football parties, was fired from McDonald's, and was Assistant Editor of the short-lived *Hemp Times* magazine (banned by the Film & Literature Classification Board after one issue). Melita studied Hindi at a university in Lucknow (India) and German in Melbourne, but unfortunately doesn't get much chance to practise either. Her travels (so far) have included Hong Kong, New Zealand, Singapore, Indonesia, Australia – and India. She is currently unwinding by writing cult-crime novelist Kinky Friedman's authorised biography.

MEN WATCH ME STRUGGLE WITH FOUR BAGS AT COLLECTION POINT. Three get too close. Go away. Man, I'm freaked. I've never been out of Australia before. In fact, I've never been out of Melbourne without my parents and two younger sisters. I know I'm whingeing and not being the model, hardened traveller I had envisioned. It's just that I'm finding it hard to walk with my heavy load. Give me some space, people. Jeez. Occasionally I can discern the odd inch of floor visible beneath the swirling heaps of humanity. Oops, sorry. Well don't lie there then!

What am I doing, apart from standing on the masses? I need a goal. I just wish my head wasn't so cloudy with sleep. A pull. What? I contort my sore body to see my left-hand bag being pulled by a dirty man. 'Hey!'.

'I take,' he says.

'No!' My voice sounds louder and more panicky than I wanted. How embarrassing.

I continue my baby steps with the load on my back, front and sides, making my way towards . . . I'm not sure what, but away from the dirty man. I need to reach the YMCA Tourist Hotel in central Delhi. Do they have taxis in India? They must! Okay, so find a taxi rank.

Two men launch themselves at me and try to separate my limbs. One manages to yank my shoulder bag off its rightful place. I want to be a whirling dervish and spin around with my bags flying in their faces, partly to get some breathing space and partly, I admit, to hurt them in the process.

I can't deal with being in India yet. I'm not ready. I've had no sleep. I'll be a brave adventurous traveller in a threatening developing country after a night's sleep and breakfast with Bronya.

'Ma'am . . . ma'am . . . I have a taxi for you, ma'am.' Voices everywhere. I'd zoned out for a minute or two. Stay on the ball,

Melita. Come on. Pull yourself together, for God's sake. Because one man is giving me some personal space I acknowledge him favourably.

Oh no! A fifth worry gets added to my list of sleep deprivation and dislike of crowds, heat and heavy bags. All I have are travellers cheques in US$100 denominations. I need a bank.

'I have no Indian money,' I tell him in faltering Hindi.

'Which money do you have?' he asks me in Hindi. I show him a handful of Australian coins and also some coins from my stopover in Hong Kong.

'*Tik he.*'

'Tik he?'

'Please come with me, ma'am.'

I start walking after him. 'I'm going to the YMCA.'

He waggles his head. Does that mean yes?

'The money is okay? . . . Really?' I ask in English. There's probably about A$25 there. More than enough. In fact I'm getting ripped off in a big way, but that's cool. I'd do anything to get to bed right now. He can exchange it at the bank tomorrow.

'Very good, very good. Come.'

It seems as if all the children in Delhi are awake on the streets at three in the morning. 'No, no money,' I mutter as I walk through them. 'Sorry. No. No, I have no *paisa.* No. *Nahi!*' A girl grabs my arm. It hurts. '*BHAG JAO!*' cries the taxi driver to the little beggar and she runs away.

The taxi has no sides so I hold all my bags tightly in the back. We are on the road for less than five minutes when the man turns off the meter.

I look up meter in my dictionary. 'Why is the meter not on?'

'Broken,' says he in English.

'Press that switch,' I order.

'Broken.'

'I only have the money I showed you earlier,' I reinforce.

Once again he waggles his head from side to side. 'This your first time in India?'

Oh no you don't. There's no way that you're going to take me for a sucker.

'No. I come here every year with my family. I have relatives here.'

We sit for a while in silence – apart from the grating of machinery and the roar of traffic. Suddenly another man hops in the front passenger seat and begins speaking Hindi at such a fast pace that I can pick up only a couple of words. I know they are talking about me as words filter through: foreigner . . . girl . . . hotel . . . baksheesh . . . clouds; no, not clouds . . . cheques? I give up.

'*Namaste.*' The guy who hopped in is being friendly. 'We're brothers,' he explains as the golden gates of Delhi whiz by.

'Hey! Delhi!' I say, pointing.

'You can't get into Delhi tonight,' says the taxi driver in English.

'Go there anyway,' I say adopting a hard tone.

'Delhi's barricaded because of the terrible floods,' says the brother.

'Haven't you read about the floods? It's been in the paper for months,' states my driver.

'Well, you can let me out here. I'll catch another taxi, one that doesn't mind going into the floods.'

Laughter sounds the same in every country.

A sign. Whatever it says, it isn't Delhi. We are out of the city now. It's so dark. I can see some curled up bodies on the sidewalk; a white, bony thing; a cow. There are no children, no traffic, no shops open, no phone booths, no banks, no houses, no hotels.

I am in the country.

Taking a pen from a bag to use as a dagger, I use my dictionary to explain to the men that my friend is expecting me at the YMCA tonight and will call the police immediately if I'm not there by 3.15 am (I wonder if Bronya is worried?) and that I start studying Hindi at Mrs Sharma's school, Lucknow, on Monday. I'm babbling, trying to be pleasant, so they will think of me as a vulnerable person with a soul, not a piece of meat. The men find this humorous too.

The brother says in Hindi that all first-timers to India are 'fuck-ing stupid'. After scrambling through more pages in my dictio-nary I tell them again, 'I come to India every year.' I transfer the pen to my left palm; the right one has become too sweaty.

'Take me to a phone.'

They ignore me, talking in Hindi that is hard to follow.

'Let me out!'

Finally the driver speaks in English: 'If I let you out here you will be raped and killed in minutes. You want that? You want to be raped? You want to be killed? I guarantee. Get out means raped and killed. I take you to friend's hotel. Or raped and killed? I drive you to nice hotel.'

'You are horrible men,' I begin in Hindi, but I don't finish what I intend to say. What's the point? If the men want to look at me closely they would see tears.

My watch reads 4.45 am. 'How much longer?' I ask in Hindi. The men don't answer. I don't want to press for fear of angering them.

Twenty minutes later we stop. The wooden building is in the middle of a bare dirt field. The brother nudges my back until I enter the building. There is a foyer of sorts. There are no women or children here, which disturbs me. If I could see just one I would be okay. Instead, there are ten grown men lazing around the front desk drinking from a whisky flask. Hindi flies to and fro. I don't even try to separate words. I let it all wash over me like the tears in my eyes that I am trying desperately to curtail.

I look outside. I know it's stupid to sleep on abandoned coun-try streets . . . but maybe I could hide somewhere under a tree or something?

'How many nights?' some joker asks me.

'None,' I say. 'I just came here for the phone.' I point to the phone.

'Broken,' says my taxi driver. 'Look *ji*, this is a hotel.'

Ten men are looking at me quietly. I remember vividly Richard, my tutor, lecturing on the caste system. '*Ji* is a term of utmost respect you give to those older or of a higher caste than you,' he had said. My driver was turning it around, using it as a term of utmost sarcasm and scorn.

'One night, *ji*,' I say to no-one in particular, wondering what I am doing.

'Three hundred American dollars,' the mustachioed man at the desk says in English.

'Three hundred rupees?' I say in Hindi.

'Three hundred dollars,' he repeats in Hindi. He writes the figure on a scrap of yellowing paper near the phone.

'Three hundred dollars!' I'm incredulous.

Brother punches a few numbers into the phone and two minutes later two more mustachioed men walk in for the kill.

'Dollars,' he says, satisfied.

'I don't have any money . . . I haven't been to the bank yet.'

'You just got off the plane. You have travellers cheques.'

It wasn't a question but I decided to take it as one. 'No.'

'*Bhag jao.*'

'*Kya*?'

'Get out. Go away.'

'Okay . . . I have travellers cheques.'

I get out three of the six American travellers cheques that were meant to last me for six months and slap them on the desk.

'Sign here, ma'am,' he says enjoying himself.

He scrutinises my signature. 'How can I verify this?' he asks. 'I don't know.'

He is taken aback at the fury behind the monotone.

Another man comes over for the fun and says something, perhaps a question. '*Ling*?' he repeats. I don't know the word and don't want to know. Firmly resisting the pull on my arm I say, 'I want a single room. I paid my money.'

The *ling*-man leers. 'No single rooms.' I look in the dictionary. *Ling* means penis.

'No "*ling*". Take me to a room with a woman then.'

I follow the *ling*-man upstairs with my bags into a small single room with a single wooden bed. The sheets have dried blood on them, obvious from the doorway. He stands in the middle of the room watching me expectantly. Stripping the sheets and turning the mattress over because of the urine stain, I unfold my sleeping bag on the wooden slats. I lie in foetal position, hugging my rucksack and still clenching the pen. Straight in his eyeballs, I muse. I notice wryly that the part of the rucksack I'm hugging has the Australian flag on it. The *ling*-man unbuttons his green trousers in the doorway. With his eyes on me all the while, he strokes his erect penis.

He makes no noise and takes an eternity to ejaculate. I lie waiting, eyes open. As soon as he comes, he turns and leaves. To wash his hands? Will he be back? I rush up and lock the door, realising despondently that they would have a master key. I push the bed over the door so I'll wake up if anybody tries to enter.

I thought I wouldn't sleep but I was wrong.

I wake up around 7 am and pick up my stuff. I am prepared to walk to Delhi if needs be! Soon there is a knock on the door. '*Chai?*' It's the brother.

I take it, wondering about poison, but perhaps the sugar rush will restore my will and courage. I close the door on him as he doesn't appear to be going anywhere. 'I can do brave,' I mutter to myself in English. Past the four men now in the foyer I run into the outside world, where it is raining, my thoughts racing and my heart beating. Okay, Melita, calm down. I start my trek into the city, with my bags, $300 in travellers cheques and the remnants of whatever optimism was rationed to me in this crazy world.

COVERT LONE RENEGADE MERCENARY RECONNAISSANCE AGENT

**Rowan
McKinnon**

Rowan might have been a career criminal and libertine had he not been caught shoplifting a *Playboy* magazine at the age of thirteen. Instead he fumbled through a university degree studying philosophy, and for ten years almost made a living out of being a bass player in an arty rock band called Not Drowning Waving. After much pleading from his mother he eventually got a 'real' job with Lonely Planet as an editor. Rowan has part-authored Lonely Planet's *Papua New Guinea*, *South Pacific* and *Eastern Caribbean* guidebooks. He has three children, lives in Melbourne and these days plays his guitars in the garage (coming full circle).

NO-ONE GOES TO PAPUA NEW GUINEA (PNG). The last traveller had left three years ago, and that was me. And I suspect that the only people who use Lonely Planet's *Papua New Guinea* guidebook are those of us who are involved in its update every three or four years. We've got a little cottage industry.

People say that PNG is dangerous. Certainly, it's fierce, raw, intense, incredibly varied and not at all set up for tourism. I was beguiled by PNG the first time I went there in 1988, and I keep going back. It's a heady and compelling mix of cultures and land-scapes, confounding contradictions and unique experiences. There's nothing contrived about PNG – every experience is authentic. I might have been imagining a guidebook introduction line just like this when I boarded the flight from Rabaul via Hoskins to Bougainville. This was March 1997, and although the Bougainville War was relatively quiet, it was still a war.

When I booked my Air Niugini tickets a month earlier I'd inquired whether it was possible to fly to Buka. 'Yes,' I was told. Buka is a small island separated from its big sister (the 'mainland' in local parlance), Bougainville Island, by the stunning Buka Passage. The war was confined to the distant south end of the big island. If the airport is open and the domestic carrier is landing three times a week, then it must be safe – or so I figured. In the naive belief that it would be an adventure to go to a war zone, I added, 'Let's take in Bougainville too.'

It was only as I was about to board the tiny de Havilland Dash-8 at the Kokopo airstrip that I began to feel nervous, but the infec-tious excitement among my fellow passengers – kissing friends and family, laughing and wishing well – soon fortified me.

Of course, almost everyone got off at Hoskins, the one touch-down between Rabaul and Buka/Bougainville. I remained in my seat gulping air, wondering whether I should join them and abandon Bougainville altogether. Perhaps simply because I couldn't make my mind up in time, I didn't. I sat tight in the nearly empty plane looking around at the quiet faces of the Bougainvilleans flying back to their troubled province. The co-pilot closed the door, the propellers sucked air as the engines revved, and we were off again. Well, there was no turning back now.

The secessionist war had waged since 1987, when soldiers from the Bougainville Revolutionary Army (BRA) began raiding and sabotaging operations at the copper- and gold-rich Panguna mine, soon forcing its closure. In one fell swoop, they denied PNG of 40 percent of its export income. Bougainvilleans have been seeking independence from PNG ever since. The people from Bougainville (the darkest-skinned people in the world) are much closer racially, culturally and geographically to Western Province Solomon Islanders than to any Papua New Guinean. That Buka and Bougainville are part of PNG at all is a mere quirk of colonialism. They were originally considered part of the Solomons, a British territory, but were traded to Germany in 1898 in exchange for British ascendancy over the rest of the Solomon Islands and Vavau in Tonga. Australia seized the German New Guinea territories at the outset of World War I; the Japanese invaded in World War II. For their part, the Bougainvilleans do not regard themselves as Papua New Guinean at all and this has fuelled their secessionist desires.

I stepped off the little plane at Buka airstrip into a sea of Papua New Guinea Defence Force (PNGDF) soldiers. Buka township is the PNGDF-controlled capital of PNG's North Solomons Province, which includes Buka and Bougainville islands as well as a handful of tiny, scantly inhabited, far-flung atolls and island groups. My baggage was opened and searched, and I was made to spread-eagle as a soldier gave me a thorough rub down. This happened to all the passengers. I was meeting Martin, a guesthouse manager. He had no trouble finding me – the one six-foot-two-inch white fella looking lost and bewildered. We left in Martin's van and went to the central military checkpoint, the cumber-somely named Movement Office Forward Base HQ, so that I could be registered and thus able to move about Buka township without being arrested. At the time, this should have been a simple rubber-stamping procedure. In this instance, we'd been too quick and the Movement Office soldiers were still busy at the airstrip checking baggage and frisking people. We waited a while, but nobody came. Martin reckoned it would be fine to come back in the morning.

We drove his van through the township. Although it appeared busy, even prosperous, there were soldiers and shabby resistance fighters (disaffected Bougainvilleans fighting alongside the BRA) with M-16s everywhere. When I looked closer, the faces of people walking the street wore haggard and weary expressions. Suddenly, this did not feel like an adventure at all – it was at once sad and deadly serious. We reached Martin's boat which was perched upon the edge of stunning Buka Passage. This image – the most beautiful body of water I've ever seen – lives with me still.

Martin's guesthouse was on tiny Soharno Island, a steep-sided fleck in the middle of the deep tidal passage that runs between Buka and Bougainville, just a kilometre long and three hundred metres wide. When tides are strong the passage runs like a river, its surface undulating wildly as the currents and whirlpools boil below from the sheer volume of water passing rapidly through the channel. To cross this violent current, as I was about to do in Martin's four-metre, fifty-horsepower, fibreglass dinghy, meant aggressively pitching the boat into the current at forty-five degrees, and surfing the weird rise and fall. The experience was not unlike crossing a moving mogul field on snow skis. The passage was abuzz with the sound of these little boats, all flying white flags to proclaim their neutrality in the conflict. 'Water taxis,' said Martin. 'They ferry people between Buka [safe] and Bougainville [dangerous].' We made a brief stop on Bougainville so that someone else aboard could be dropped off. You must pass military checkpoints to go past the landing area (the military monitors the movement of all people in the province), but for a few minutes I got the chance to wander around this tiny cluster of trade stores and tread the troubled earth of the island that I'd read so much about. And then it was time to go, and we surfed the passage again, across to tiny Soharno where I was lodging for the night at the guesthouse of the laconic Martin.

My room was quite comfortable, with a little balcony overlooking the passage to Bougainville, seemingly a stone's throw away. Alexander Downer, the Australian foreign minister involved in the machinations of negotiating a long-talked-about cease-fire, had slept in the master suite next to mine (the *really* nice one) just the week before. I slung my backpack down and slumped for a moment on the bed, exhausted from travel, nervous anxiety and the breathtaking midday heat.

Soharno Island must have been much larger aeons ago, but the volume of water that passes around it has eroded it to a tiny knob. The little craggy island that remains pokes out into the passage like the blunt end of a pencil. It had once been the colonial provincial capital and retained a very gentrified atmosphere – lots of old colonial buildings, well-manicured lawns and gardens, and an old hospital. Best of all was a cliff-top lookout over the whole of Buka Passage, the islands of Buka and Bougainville lying to the left and right. This is the site of a Japanese monument to the dead from its World War II Solomons campaign – Bougainville fell to the Japanese in early 1942, and by the time of their surrender 57,000 Japanese soldiers had either been killed in action or died in the jungle from disease or starvation.

Having recovered from my momentary fatigue, I scurried down the lawns and descended some steep steps that led down to the miniature reef-sand beach where the boats tie up. Timid crabs as big as your face scurried down their fat holes in fear as I rounded a little point. I sat for a while on a rock at water level transfixed by the motion of the water through the passage. Suddenly, on some impossible primeval cue, a thousand tiny flying fish launched themselves in perfect formation and glided above the water for a hundred metres before disappearing again below the surface. Some time later my blissful torpor was broken by the thud thud thud of helicopters passing overhead, carrying troops and equipment from the south of Bougainville – Arawa, Kieta and Buin – where the fighting was taking place. I felt like I was in an Oliver Stone film.

I went back to the room to 'freshen up' before dinner. I turned on the (satellite) television and it was then that I learned two things: first, Chinese president Deng Xiaoping had died; second, mercenaries had landed in PNG to retake Bougainville from the BRA.

I should explain . . . when I landed in PNG a story was breaking in the Australian media about the PNG prime minister, Sir Julius Chan, and a government cabal hatching a secret plan to deploy private military personnel and equipment on Bougainville. Chan continued to deny it, but Australian intelligence had the media abuzz with a story about mercenaries having already landed in PNG's capital, Port Moresby. This had made my flight from Rabaul to Bougainville all the more harrowing. As I watched, in my room at the Buka Soho Luman Lodge, Chan finally admitted that there were foreign soldiers – employees of a British-based company – in PNG to assist in the 'training' of PNGDF soldiers who served in Bougainville. All sorts of rumours had preceded this public admission, but this was confirmation that I was in the thick of it. I reflected on the grim harried faces of the people in the streets, most carrying heavy weapons; the soldiers in Rambo garb who frisked me at the airport; the thick humid tropical air cut by the sudden presence of choppers; and now the news that hi-tech mercenaries were here to help deal with the BRA. The seriousness of the situation I was in began to dawn on me.

I dined in the common room on fish, rice and vegetables with three Papua New Guineans: a lawyer and two politicians. They were important and interesting people, but the conversation was awkward and I got the feeling that they didn't want to be here. Nobody came to Bougainville unless they had to here; nobody except me. Perhaps it was the lack of alcohol (prohibited in PNGDF-controlled Bougainville), but we were all a little uptight, and soon found reason to excuse ourselves from the dining table.

In the heavy tropical darkness I visited the cliff-top lookout and, standing beneath the monument to the Japanese dead, I gazed over the lights of Buka township from my vantage point. The six o'clock curfew meant the township was deathly quiet.

The morning was bright and hot. Martin took me in his boat to register with the PNGDF in Buka township at the Movement Office Forward Base HQ. There were no soldiers there this time either, so I was still an illegal with no official status. However, fired with early-morning guidebook-writer verve, I told Martin I had no time to waste and that I was off to do some work.

I began at the Department of Lands, housed at a desk in the ramshackle government building. There are no commercially available maps of Buka Passage and I needed one for my guide-book, so I was there to photocopy town-planning sheets, aerial photographs and anything else I could convince the clerk to let me see. Then I trod the town from one end to the other with a com-pass around my neck, marking the post office, bank and airport on my 'map'. I took photographs and scribbled notes in a journal, ignoring quizzical onlookers. After a while I was arrested.

An army vehicle locked up its wheels on the gravel road as four soldiers leapt out and surrounded me. There were no uni-forms and no way to distinguish rank, just jungle-greens, bandan-nas, boots and torn, tough-guy T-shirts – an image born in *Rambo* movies and spawned by the video-rental phenomenon. I knew immediately what was happening, but I don't remember anyone saying anything – I just got in the vehicle and got out again when it stopped. I found myself in a M*A*S*H-style village of army-green tents, encircled by yet more extras from a post-Rambo war movie.

The experience was surreal. I was ushered to an upturned tree stump where I sat waiting for something to happen. As I waited in silence the soldiers chewed betel nut – lips and teeth vivid red, boiling eyes, nothing to say – and cleaned their fingernails with oversized hunting knives in a scene from *Crocodile Dundee*. Nobody would meet my gaze. I didn't really feel frightened – I knew that my death and dismemberment (even my death by dismemberment) would cause a major diplomatic furore between Australia and PNG, and these guys were government soldiers after all. This did not stop me from imagining what these same soldiers might have been capable of in the deep south of Bougainville, where awful atrocities had been committed by both sides. Yet I hadn't done anything wrong.

A humourless man approached, dressed in more conventional military gear and flanked by a couple of tough guys. 'I am Eagle, head of military intelligence,' he announced. I wanted to giggle. (Just 'Eagle'? Not 'Commander Eagle' or 'Extraspecial Superintendentguy Eagle' or something more pretentious?) Eagle reminded me that I was in a lot of trouble. There'd been rumours about mercenaries and spies coming into the province, he said. 'The newspapers and television have made people very nervous lately'. I tried to explain who I was, what I was doing, why I had a compass and why I was taking photographs.

'What's in your bag,' he asked, and so I arrayed its contents on the ground – notebook, town-planning photocopies, camera, compass, water bottle and teddy. I proffered my Lonely Planet business card on which he read 'Rowan McKinnon, Travel Writer/Editor' and passed him the previous edition of the *PNG* guidebook I was updating. These did little to convince him that I wasn't a covert lone renegade mercenary reconnaissance agent. 'Why weren't we advised that you were coming?' Protocol, it seems, demands that one makes application through diplomatic channels to visit a war zone – if only I'd known.

It wasn't until I could produce a letter of introduction from my commissioning editor that Eagle was satisfied that I was who I said I was. (In fact, the letter was back in my hotel room on Soharno, and I was taken by military boat to collect it.) Eagle was much more relaxed when he read my letter of introduction, and the tense atmosphere eased palpably. At my feet I had seen a bullet on the ground, unspent but damaged, dysfunctional and trodden-upon. I picked it up and asked Eagle if I could keep it as a souvenir – he nodded and I slipped it into my pocket.

I was released and told not to photograph ANYTHING, and to make sure that I boarded my plane the following morning after checking out at Movement Office Forward Base HQ. I spent another hour in town under the ever-watchful eye of two PNGDF soldiers in the distance. Then I took a water taxi back to my guest-house on Soharno Island to write up my notes and rest from a rather stressful day. The following morning I boarded my flight to Kavieng.

The three elite members of the Chan government – Sir Julius Chan himself, deputy Chris Haiveta and defence minister Mathia Ijape – had secretly negotiated a deal worth US$35 million with a British-based company, Sandline International, to supply soldiers (South Africans mostly) and military hardware, subcontracted from Executive Outcomes, to end the ten-year Bougainville secessionist war. The plan was to return Chan as prime minister on a wave of public support in the forthcoming elections. This would become known as the Sandline Affair, and was the greatest crisis the country had ever faced.

When the military commander, Brigadier General Jerry Singirok, heard about this covert operation he refused to support it. He was duly sacked, but the military remained loyal to the deposed Singirok, insisting that the mercenaries be expelled from PNG and that Sir Julius Chan step down as prime minister. For a while it looked as if a *coup d'état* was imminent. For ten days Port Moresby was rocked by rioters and looters calling for Chan's resignation. Anarchy reigned. There was a tense stand-off between the police, loyal to Chan, and the military, loyal to Singirok. Chan held on for as long as he could, but under enormous pressure he eventually acquiesced on 26 March 1997. The Sandline mercenaries were deported and I returned home to Melbourne, Australia.

On my mantelpiece at home in Melbourne's southern suburbs, in amongst my collection of tin toys and Melanesian statuettes, sits a single dysfunctional bullet from an M-16.

A LESSON IN MARTIAL ARTS

OR

THE WAY OF THE CHICKEN

Patrick Witton

Patrick's interest in Indonesia was born out of necessity, when he found himself lost in a market on Java at the age of twelve. He has since studied Indonesian (and martial arts) both in Melbourne and in Bandung, under the Darmasiswa scholarship scheme. More of his short stories can be found in the *Daytripper* anthologies (Vandal Press). He works as an editor and author of Lonely Planet's *World Food* series.

PENCAK *SILAT* **(LITERALLY, THE BEAUTY OF FIGHTING) IS THE MARTIAL ART OF INDONESIA.** It can be practised as a sport or performed to music. Performances can incorporate weaponry or ornamental fans. In some regions, *pencak silat* competitions and performances are carried out at weddings, harvest festivals and circumcision ceremonies.

In this martial arts lesson, you learn what fear is. You have come to Mr Uho's for your twice-weekly lesson in *pencak*, the traditional Indonesian martial art of which Mr Uho is a master. Sixty-year-old Mr Uho teaches by example, his body flowing across the white-tiled practice room that takes up the first floor of his house. He enacts moves with the agility of a gazelle, moves with such names as Striking Viper and Tiger Claw. Mr Uho is a true martial arts master.

Sick of travel with no itinerary, you've committed yourself to becoming Mr Uho's student. Consequently, every Monday and Wednesday you head for his home in the depths of Leuwi Panjang.

There are two ways to get to Mr Uho's. You can take the city bus for 300 rupiahs, but there are drawbacks: the trip takes at least an hour due to gridlocked traffic, you get no seat and you're subject to adept pickpockets. The other option is to take a Kelapa-bound minibus then change to one heading for Kalang Setra. The cost is 800 rupiahs, but the size of the bus enables it to weave through the mess of Bandung traffic and you're guaranteed a seat (although you may well be sat upon).

You arrive at Mr Uho's exhausted. At this point you wonder whether you'd be better off crawling back home to a soft bed and cup of sweet tea. Inevitably, Mr Uho is absent when you arrive. Mrs Uho, however, is home and ready to shuffle your travel-weary body into the sitting room, place a viscous coffee on the table and leave you to await the return of the Master.

While sitting silently, you peruse the many ornaments that clutter the room, including a stuffed leopard with an expression of immense anger on its face and a line of stitching reaching up to its anus. There are ornamental knives, oversized fans and trophies, many trophies. When your wait reaches the point at which you are contemplating swigging the sweet mud at the bottom of the coffee cup, Mrs Uho re-enters the room, drops two hefty photo albums onto the table and closes the door behind her. Inside these leather volumes is a short history of the martial arts Master, Mr Uho.

From looking at the photos it's clear that Mr Uho is a well-travelled man. In one picture he stands on a sunny beach; the sign behind him directs the needy public to the *Toiletten*. There's a shot of Mr Uho bracing himself against the northern winds that race through Amsterdam's Schiphol airport. Another shows him lost in a swarm of the fearless grey pigeons that reside in every European *platz*. There's photographic proof of Mr Uho's visit to Miniature World, in which the spire of Köln Dom barely reaches Mr Uho's midriff. Yet another has a very handsome Mr Uho striding the streets of Chicago, dressed in a plush sheepskin jacket and sporting sunglasses that can only be described as groovy.

By the time Mr Uho finally arrives you've almost fallen asleep on his velvet couch, your finger probing a hole left by a cigarette burn. Mr Uho smokes clove cigarettes; you smell him before he enters the room. He pokes his head through the doorway and flashes you a grin.

Your heartbeat is comatose, yet you know you'll soon be needing boundless energy. Luckily, Mrs Uho, who for some reason is dressed impeccably, serves you a bowl of banana and jackfruit swimming in coconut milk and palm sugar. The effect of this dish is not dissimilar from that of speed and you're soon practising martial arts moves, agitatedly, around the coffee table.

But something is up. Mr Uho tells you that a small martial arts get-together has been arranged in his home town of Soreang. And it is for this reason that Mr Uho looks excited, different. He's wearing a nifty black suit and a Javanese *peci* on his head. He looks regal. Initially, you're impressed by his attire but then you start thinking that tonight will not be the 'small martial arts get-together' he has described.

Mr Uho is motioning everyone out of the house for the trip to Soreang. You are introduced to Mr Uho's son, Eri, who is to join you on the journey. You greet Eri with enthusiasm, which is returned with indifference. It seems that Eri is not at all into this martial arts caper. He's probably had enough of it, growing up with his father's trophies littering the living room and a continuous stream of strangers entering the house and making grunting sounds for hours on end in the white-tiled room above the kitchen. He ventures you a look that says, 'It's not your fault'.

You all venture out onto the main road and flag down a minibus with the words SOREANG and BAD BOY plastered over the windscreen. The driver bends low over the steering wheel so as to see beyond the advertised destination. You try to strike up a conversation with Eri, asking if many other foreigners have taken up Indonesian martial arts. 'Heaps,' he replies while he takes hold of a pair of ornamental martial arts swords, passed through the minibus window by Mr Uho, who climbs into the front.

'These are for you,' says Eri, passing over the pair of ornamental swords.

'Oh! Actually, I have these,' you say, holding up your ornamental fans. Mr Uho had given you the choice of learning martial arts with swords or fans, and you had chosen the latter since your health insurance probably didn't cover martial arts sword mishaps. Eri stares at your fans and, slowly, smiles for the first time.

'For girls,' he says.

'For girls?'

And he lifts the swords up from between his legs.

'These, these are for boys.'

The minibus moves away from the kerb and melds into the river of traffic. Mr Uho directs orders at the driver. Outside, night-time scenes on the main road to Soreang flash past: a continuous trail of fried catfish outlets, beggars and cassette stores blasting out Indonesian disco pop . Trying to forget about the fan issue, you ask Eri if he likes disco music. He hates it.

You arrive in Soreang and climb out of the minibus at the city park, a square of mud and overgrown grass. You follow Eri and Mr Uho down one of the many dark alleys between the surrounding houses. Eri tells you that this was where he grew up, but he doesn't seem nostalgic; his tone is more like that of a checkout attendant telling you that your transaction has been declined.

Most of the people you pass in the alley seem to know Eri, greeting him with default civilities. As they pass Mr Uho, however, they prostrate themselves at his feet, basking in the presence of a martial arts master.

As you approach the end of the alley, your deepest fears turn into reality. A large stage of wood and tarpaulin has been erected directly in front of the town's mosque. In the shadow of this onion-domed construction are 200 seats of varying styles: wooden chairs borrowed from the local school and ornate red velvet couches lifted straight from the living rooms of surrounding houses. All seats are occupied. A screaming, entertainment-hungry crowd awaits. As you approach the performance area the crowd collectively senses your presence and simultaneously turns to take a long, hard look. The person on stage pauses from his speech on the benefits of education to join the inspection, and Mr Uho quietly ushers you onto the side of the stage.

A man with horn-rimmed glasses informs the audience that there will be a small interval before the martial arts commences. He promises the crowd 'a solo performance by our foreign friend' and waves his hand in your direction, offering a wide, yellow smile. During the interval, the bulky lectern is moved to the side of the stage. While the audience mumbles, a group of teenagers pile gongs, drums and horns onto the stage. Once the musicians are settled, they break into a completely erratic melody, the horn player wailing like a snake-charmer. The crowd goes mad. Mr Uho leads you to the front of the stage, then walks away.

You have been learning martial arts from Mr Uho for three weeks, during a long stay-over in Bandung. In these three weeks you have learned the Striking Viper and the Tiger Claw. Your interpretation of these moves, however, is more akin to the Inebriated Kitten and the Pigeon On Heat. Now you find yourself in the middle of a stage wearing polyester pyjamas and holding two oversized tasselled fans that you now realise are, to say the least, effeminate.

The band starts its elaborate rhythm. It sounds like what you have been practising to but they're adding extra clunks on every off beat. It is said that Indonesian rhythms are some of the most complicated in existence; this information doesn't help you feel any better about the situation. You're opening your fans with as much vigour and machismo possible, but it is no use. As Eri pointed out: fan dance equals girly dance. The teenagers sitting at the front of the crowd are roaring with laughter. The master of ceremonies is shouting over the top of the music; from your limited Indonesian you can make out only 'boy with fan' and 'very funny indeed'. The finale of this sequence, now known as the Pouncing Chicken Dance, comprises three thrusts of the sword or, in this instance, three thrusts of the fan. On the third thrust the fan slips out of your sweaty hand and falls off the stage. At this point you notice Mr Uho is capturing the whole traumatic experience on video. You imagine copies of this video being sold throughout the Indonesian archipelago. White bloke does fan dance: a comic genius.

The music stops. The crowd roars. Your dream of becoming the next Jean-Claude Van Damme has been well and truly snuffed out.

LONELY PLANET JOURNEYS

JOURNEYS is a unique collection of travel writing – published by the company that understands travel better than anyone else.

It is a series for anyone who has ever experienced – or dreamed of – the magical moment when they encountered a strange culture or saw a place for the first time. They are tales to read while you're planning a trip, while you're on the road or while you're in an armchair, in front of a fire.

These outstanding titles explore our planet through the eyes of a diverse group of international writers. JOURNEYS books catch the spirit of a place, illuminate a culture, recount an adventure, or introduce a fascinating way of life. They always entertain, and always enrich the experience of travel.

'Lively, intelligent and varied . . . an important contribution to travel literature' – *Age (Melbourne)*

LONELY PLANET UNPACKED
Travel Disaster Stories
By Tony Wheeler and other Lonely Planet Writers

Every traveller has a horror story to tell: lost luggage, bad weather, illness or worse. In this lively collection of travel disaster tales, Lonely Planet writers share their worst moments of life on the road.

From Kenya to Sri Lanka, from Brazil to Finland, from the Australian outback to India, these travellers encounter hurricanes, road accidents, secret police and nasty parasites. Reading these funny and frightening stories from the dark side of the road will make you think ·twice about a career as a travel writer!

'Lonely Planet celebrates its road-stained wretches in . . . a collection of tales of delightful disaster' – *Don George, Travel Editor, salon.com*

THE LONELY PLANET STORY

Lonely Planet published its first book in 1973 in response to the numerous 'How did you do it?' questions Maureen and Tony Wheeler were asked after driving, busing, hitching, sailing and railing their way from England to Australia. Written at a kitchen table and hand collated, trimmed and stapled, *Across Asia on the Cheap* became an instant local bestseller, inspiring thoughts of another book.

Eighteen months in South-East Asia resulted in their second guide, *South-East Asia on a shoestring*, which they put together in a backstreet Chinese hotel in Singapore in 1975. The 'yellow bible', as it quickly became known to backpackers around the world, soon became *the* guide to the region. It has sold well over half a million copies and is now in its 9th edition, still retaining its familiar yellow cover.

From our original Shoestrings we've expanded to produce 22 series. Our list of titles has more than doubled over the last five years to 650 individual publications. Series include travel guides and phrasebooks, atlases, maps and travel-related books on topics including food, cycling, walking, diving and wildlife and, of course, travel literature. We also produce CitySync, Lonely Planet's digital city guides for Palm Pilots and other handheld devices. Lonely Planet is the largest independent travel publisher in the world. Although Lonely Planet initially specialised in guides to Asia, today there are few corners of the globe that have not been covered.

The emphasis continues to be on travel for independent travellers. Tony and Maureen still travel for several months of each year and play an active part in the writing, updating and quality control of Lonely Planet's guides.

They have been joined by over 80 authors and over 500 staff at our offices in Melbourne (Australia), Oakland (USA), London (UK) and Paris (France). Travellers themselves also make a valuable contribution to the guides through the feedback we receive in thousands of letters each year and on our web site.

The people at Lonely Planet strongly believe that travellers can make a positive contribution to the countries they visit, both through their appreciation of the countries' culture, wildlife and natural features, and through the money they spend. In addition, the company makes a direct contribution to the countries and regions it covers. Since 1986 a percentage of the income from each book has been donated to ventures such as famine relief in Africa; aid projects in India; agricultural projects in Central America; Greenpeace's efforts to halt French nuclear testing in the Pacific; and Amnesty International.

'I hope we send people out with the right attitude about travel. You realise when you travel that there are so many different perspectives about the world, so we hope these books will make people more interested in what they see.'

– Tony Wheeler